LEARNING LIFE'S LESSONS
Inspirational Tips for Creating Peace in Troubled Times

William M. Timpson, Ph.D.

Peace Knowledge Press

Learning Life's Lessons:
Inspirational Tips for Creating Peace in Troubled Times
William M. Timpson, Ph.D.

First edition

Published by: Peace Knowledge Press
www.peaceknowledgepress.com
Tucson, AZ

ISBN: 978-1-7329622-0-0 (print edition)
ISBN: 978-1-7329622-1-7 (ebook)

Proofreading by: Kathryn A. Wright
Project management, layout, & cover design: Tony Jenkins

Peace Knowledge Press is an imprint of the International Institute on Peace
Education (IIPE) in partnership with the Global Campaign for Peace Education
(GCPE). All net proceeds benefit these two global peace education initiatives.

Special thanks to all our contributors and collaborators over these past two decades, all those who share our dream--and the reality--that if we study and practice the skills of building peace we can lessen the violence that too often erupts when values, beliefs, and basic needs collide with the desire, by some, for power and control.

Special thanks also go to our copy editor, Kat Wright, for her careful attention to this manuscript as it developed.

FOREWORD
Tony Jenkins

"The very ability to imagine something different and better than what currently exists is critical for the possibility of social change... People can't work for what they can't imagine." - Elise Boulding (2000)

Time can feel a bit like quicksand. The more obsessed we are with escaping the present the more we seem to get trapped by it. With each bodily flail of frustration, the sands of the present find a way to fill in every empty space, slowly squeezing out hope through shallower and shallower breaths. The only escape from quicksand, and the presumed linearity of time, is counterintuitive. Remain calm. Don't struggle. Move slowly and with purpose. This is the opposite of everything our instincts seem to tell us to do. And it works. In moments when we are engulfed by the pessimism evoked by the dark shadows of violence, oppression, political turmoil, and ecological insecurity, our minds can lose the ability to hold onto hope. With hope gone, so is the possibility of a more preferred future. We can't work toward peace without hope.

Hope comes from many places: from faith, from community, from witnessing change past and present. Peace researcher and sociologist Elise Boulding (2000) reminded us that hope is dependent on our ability to see the future we desire, to be able to image the preferred future. The metaphor of quicksand illustrates how our thinking about the future has a direct relationship to the action we take in the present. Many see the future as a linear path. The destructive path humanity, and the planet, are currently on leads us to projecting an image of a dystopian probable future – an image that is shaped more by cynicism than hope. Releasing our minds from this pessimism requires an unleashing of the imagination. Positive action in the present is shaped by positive images of the future.

With *Learning Life's Lessons*, Bill Timpson has collected 147 stories of hope that should inspire the most pessimistic amongst us toward transcending a diversity of present-day crises. These stories are complemented by "tips" for applying lessons learned from historical examples to present circumstances. These tips will aid the reader in reflecting on reality and taking small actions that lead to hopeful future change. The tips are an invitation to release the imagination and foster inspiration. They support the development of inner moral strength and cooperative capacities that are essential to engaging in much needed political action for positive social and ecological change.

In serving as the Managing Director of the International Institute on Peace Education since 2001, I've coordinated and/or participated in peace education initiatives in more than 20 countries. Whether it's grappling with the possibilities for reconciliation in divided societies such as Korea and Israel, overcoming historical trauma and memories in the Basque country in Spain, or seeking peace after 50 years of violent conflict in Colombia, I've found that fostering hope is the essential building block to sustainable political change. In all of the difficult circumstances in which I've worked with formal and non-formal educators, I've discovered that resilience can be fostered through reflecting on the small successes that go unnoticed in the rhythm of daily life. While one's worldview may be veiled in a history of violence, the quotidian reality of life is comprised of peaceful and cooperative experiences. Developing this awareness is key to developing hope. I've also observed a similar trend in teaching peace studies to undergraduate university students. When exposed to the breadth of cultural and structural violence students generally feel overwhelmed. *There's no way to change something so complex – I'm just one person.* However, positive change is always happening. We've seen dramatic changes in the past century– things that changed that we never thought would: the abolition of legalized slavery; women's suffrage; the 2017 Treaty on the Prohibition of Nuclear Weapons (an effort led by civil society!). Hope comes from challenging the presumptions of our constraining worldview.

Peace educators and peacebuilders will find this book a valuable addition to their toolkits. The practical tips are rooted in well-researched pedagogical methods, providing queries to support cognitive and critical awareness of issues of justice: inquiries to support moral and ethical reflection; experiential activities designed to nurture and embody hope; and contemplative and imaginative exercises to foster positive thinking about the future.

Any concerned citizen will find these lessons valuable. In our post truth era shaped by political polarity, we've seemingly lost the capacity for meaningful dialogue. We fear family gatherings because of the inevitable verbal conflicts we anticipate based on observed patterns of social media posts carefully constructed by machine algorithms. *Learning Life's Lessons* provides stories of hope that can foster constructive and meaningful dialogue to bridge the political abyss. Timpson's tips light the path for how we might move past political impasses. Constructing our preferred future is something we must do together, regardless of political beliefs, and a common vision of hope can be found when we share the journey together.

Learning Life's Lessons is the first publication of Peace Knowledge Press, a new publishing imprint dedicated to advancing the holistic fields of peace knowledge: peace research, peace studies, peace education, and peace action. What better publication to begin with than a guidebook dedicated to hope and change? Peace Knowledge Press is a project of the International Institute on Peace Education and Global Campaign for Peace Education. All net revenues of Peace Knowledge Press book sales support these global peace education initiatives. So by buying this book today you've already made a difference –you've helped spread hope to peace educators around the world.

Sitting and contemplating this foreword, I've been reflecting upon the call for creating utopian visions of peace educator Betty Reardon, whose life work was the inspiration for launching Peace Knowledge Press. Utopias are misrepresented as unattainable perfection. In reality and practicality, utopias are a way of describing an imagined, highly desirable social order, one that is designed to effectively meet the needs of its citizens. All societies are rooted in the pursuit of utopian visions – capitalist, consumerist, socialist, communist, the culture of peace. Often, as these orders take tangible political shapes, the initial utopian vision is lost. The state of affairs becomes normalized, accepted as inevitable, and the initial utopian vision is no longer reflected upon. When that happens the vision becomes stagnant and ceases to inspire. It is my hope that *Learning Life's Lessons* will encourage revitalized reflection on old utopias and kindle new utopian visions and movements that might propel us on more desirable paths. I close with this passage from Betty Reardon on the practical imperative of striving for utopias. I hope you will find as much meaning in this, and the stories of hope found in this volume, as I have.

> *"Utopia is a pregnant idea, formed in the mind as a possibility toward*
> *which we might strive and in the striving learn how to realize the con-*

cept, to make it real. Without conception, new life, in human society as in human beings, cannot become reality. Utopia is a concept, the germinal idea from which new life in a new social order can germinate into a viable political goal, born into a process of politics and learning that could mature into a transformed social order; perhaps what we have come to call a culture of peace, a new world reality. Absent the germinal concept, there is little chance for a better world to evolve from a possibility to a reality." - Betty Reardon (2009)

INTRODUCTION
William M. Timpson

Inspiration is often credited for great achievements but is so very elusive to define, create and use. It's much more than a passionate call to action. Inspiration must go deep and call forth conviction and commitment. Of course, the real test for inspiration is during troubled times—personal, family or friends, work or career, community, nation or world. This book is dedicated to every teacher and instructor, every presenter and leader, every student and community leader, who needs to be reminded of some light even in the darkest hours, practical ideas that are grounded in solid research but that can be taken into any classroom or group to light a fire for others.

My own first teaching experiences were a baptism of fire in junior and senior high schools of inner city Cleveland just after the rioting, conflict, confrontations and tensions that followed the assassinations of Martin Luther King Jr. and Bobby Kennedy. In graduate school at the University of Wisconsin-Madison I deepened my understanding of teaching and learning across the divides of social class and culture, ethnicity, gender and ability. In my work at Colorado State University I have followed a similar path and added work on sustainability, peace and reconciliation. During this period of time I also had extended interactions with Native American communities wanting to improve their schools as well as those in migrant communities wanting some share of the American dream.

Throughout the decades I have also worked with Aboriginal people in Australia to understand those deep cultural differences and what educators and community leaders need to know. I have collaborated with peacebuilders in Northern Ireland, working to rethink hundreds of years of conflict between Catholic and Protestant paramilitaries and what could—and should—be changed in schools. I have taught a course on peacemaking at the Graduate Institute of Peace Studies in Seoul, South Korea just below the DMZ; a few of my students were active duty South Korean military officers eager to know more about peacemaking. For many years I have worked with colleagues on sustainable peace and development in Burundi, East

Africa, a country emerging from colonization and civil war while dealing with the ongoing pressures of extreme poverty—a challenge for every teacher in every discipline.

Extended international experiences in other parts of the world have also helped to broaden and deepen my study of these issues, from looking into literacy enhancement in Nicaragua, Cuba and Brazil to educational challenges in China, to the school-industry interface in Japan, and the tensions between indigenous Taiwanese and their domination by Chinese after the Maoist takeover of the mainland. I have looked into the genocide of Cambodia and the work of the Rotary International Center for Peace and Conflict Studies in Thailand. In Europe I followed the tragic trail of the Holocaust through Lithuania, Poland, Germany and Hungary. Before it imploded, I was able to visit both the USSR and the Ukraine. Support from a Kellogg Fellowship, several Fulbright Scholar/Specialist awards, along with Global Grants form Rotary International, have made this work possible.

Throughout this extended initiation into teaching and learning in diverse environments in the U.S. and overseas, across languages and cultures, I would have loved to have had a resource like the one we offer you here. I did not need the typical theoretical analyses from academics who had spent little if any time in the challenging places where I was working. I wanted and needed a very practical set of core concepts that had a solid line of research underneath them but were also grounded in the kinds of complex and too often troubled contexts that I was facing. Most importantly, I wanted and needed a set of core ideas to inspire me, to keep up my hopes in the face of problems, both in class and in the greater society.

Many people report being inspired by certain people or events. Some will point to people who got them excited about a certain career path—a mentor, friend, family member, someone in the news. Others will refer to specific teachers, leaders or friends who inspired them to persist through all manner of problems, setbacks and difficulties. Whatever the source or the manner of expression, we know that people can "feel those vibes" and respond.

For example, in early 2018 I heard from atmospheric scientist Scott Denning who sees a "bright future" from our human history of resilience and innovation, despite the constant clamor of doomsday thinking about the onrush of climate change or the parallel challenges from those who are in denial about its impact and sure that the real agenda is a left-wing, academic and big government austerity program to "take away our cars."

I understand that fear itself can also be inspiring. But once the adrenalin fades, can we persist "for the long haul?" For Tibetan Buddhists, the words of Pema Chödron challenge us to "smile at the fear" that may be blocking our forward movement. The Buddhist dharma or teachings also challenge us to go past "hope" and become "fearless' in our push for engagement in what could be possible.

Who can forget the shock of the 1999 shooting at Columbine High School in Colorado where 12 were killed and 21 injured or the shooting rampage at Virginia Tech in 2007 when 33 were gunned down and 23 more wounded? Then we were horrified by the 2012 shooting at Sandy Hook Elementary School when 20 six and seven year-olds along with 7 school staff were gunned down? And then came the school shooting in Parkland, Florida where 17 were killed and 14 wounded. While previous shootings had sparked nationwide calls for gun control measures what was different in 2018 was the involvement of students in demonstrations. Inspired activism can spring from the most troubled of times.

My work overseas has provided so many lessons and just as many examples of inspired change. For example, facing angry mobs as they hurled threats, rocks and bottles, Mairead Maguire and her fellow peace activists chose umbrellas for defense amidst the "Troubles" in Northern Ireland in the 1970's and helped spark a revolution in thinking about guns, security, fear, peace and prosperity. Mired in polarized positions following British colonization and the wounds of three hundred plus years of fighting between independent minded Catholics and Protestant loyalists to the United Kingdom, people needed new thinking.

Like the students who protested the gun violence in 2018, these activists in Northern Ireland did not choose to be "soft targets" as the advocates for arming school staff argue. Instead they chose to become peaceful warriors in the face of fear mongers who insisted on guns and bombs as the ways to fight for a better life. Eventually the Good Friday Peace Accord was signed in 1998. For her courage and leadership, Maguire was a co-recipient of the Nobel Peace Prize in 1977. Visiting with Maguire in 2002 as I worked on my book, *Teaching and Learning Peace*, I remember her insisting that arming themselves would have only deepened the fear, the bloodshed and the wounds.

In the light of the Florida school shootings we must remember how the decommissioning of weapons in Northern Ireland has been critical for reducing the violence there. It is also important to know that funding from American supporters of the IRA largely shifted from weapons to economic development.

Following their own experience with a mass shooting in 1996, Australians rallied for a saner gun policy and quickly voted to ban citizen access to assault weapons. Unlike hard-core American defendants of the second amendment who will not tolerate any perceived threat to their interpretation of what the framers of the U.S. Constitution intended by granting the citizens the right to form regulated militias in the face of tyrannical threats, Australians have not had a mass shooting since 1996 and live in a safer democracy than do the citizens of the U.S.

The challenge for those of us who teach and lead, who study and get involved as activists, is to share our own inspirations and look for ways to ignite those same fires in our students and other audiences. Clearly this is both art and science. We can never know exactly what in our lives, beliefs and exhortations will register with others. However, we can share honestly what has moved us and why. That would be the "art" side of the "art and science" equation for effective teaching.

The "science" side of the equation challenges us to look for those many ways where ideas, activities, explanation and study combine to light that fire. Using the principles of mastery learning, for example, can provide the small steps and successes needed to build a strong base of understanding for moving forward. Cooperative learning can provide the interactions with others that help spark engagement and excitement for a subject and project. Peer tutoring can provide that close personal connection, support and assistance for opening the doorway to a field of study. Discovery learning can offer those "Aha" moments that light a fire. Simulations let students and others see the connections between the foundational knowledge that they have been studying and the "real world" of applications and meaning. Understanding the stages of development allows us to see the changes in thinking that will be possible and to guide our plans accordingly.

Beyond the classroom, however, and the inspiration that an individual teacher or instructor can bring, is the spark that a program or curriculum can bring, for example, in the face of longstanding problems with poor performance in low income schools. Or in reaction to policies of social promotion that moved students into higher grade levels despite their low performance, thus ensuring that these students would be trapped into a cycle of failure. An emphasis on mastery learning can help break a curriculum down into small steps and ensure success before moving on. Dramatic successes in particular inner city schools seemed to offer a way forward that inspired similar programs nationwide. However, the hope that mastery learning would be a cure-all did not—and could not—solve educational problems that were deeply rooted in poverty, residential segregation and unequal funding of schools.

After the success of the Soviet Union in being the first nation to put a satellite into orbit in 1959, many were energized into funding new curricula that wanted to inspire more young people to think like scientists and thus the emergence of "discovery" or "inquiry." The focus for teaching shifted to engaging students with hands-on activities. When this approach did not prove to be a cure-all, the national tide eventually shifted to tested knowledge and more approaches that often undermined teacher creativity and initiative.

Internationally, one of the greatest educational initiatives that served to inspire millions were the literacy campaigns that grew out of Paulo Freire's (1970) work in the *Pedagogy of the Oppressed*. Challenged to develop a program that would motivate the illiterate peasants of Brazil to want to read and help the nation develop, Freire's idea turned traditional schooling on its head by using small study groups in the field and a curriculum often led by advanced students that focused on what was very practical, i.e., what was needed to improve lives.

These ideas eventually proved very threatening to the ruling military junta that rested comfortably atop a hierarchical system that was built on a "banking theory of education" where the emphasis was on knowledge transfer and the selection of the "best" students for further opportunities, leaving the poor and supposedly "unmotivated" to endure generations of indictment as school failures not worth the investment of educational resources, i.e., Brazilian authorities were comfortable in "blaming the victims" of exclusionary policies that kept the poor "poor" and used school results to explain—and justify—the disparities. Freire's literacy campaign was so successful that he was exiled from Brazil. Similar campaigns were adopted with great success in post-revolutionary Cuba and Nicaragua.

Measures of literacy grew dramatically, especially in Brazil and Cuba, setting the stage for rapid development in various segments of the economy. In my own work overseas, I have had opportunities to spend time in Brazil, Nicaragua and Cuba looking at these literacy efforts up close. I talked to teachers who had to bury their books in between lessons so that they would not be targeted by the U.S. supported contra rebels after the Sandinistas took power.

And of course there is the value of mindfulness, of awareness to your own inspiration as well as what it happening to those around you. Add to this the central role of meaning to our lives and what is inspiring and you have the elements you need in front of you. We can only do this, however, if we are willing to take up the challenge and break out of the routines and comfort zones that at times serve to immobilize so many talented people, what Buddhists refer to as the "cocoon" that restricts our thinking and our creative possibilities. Can attention to what inspires us help fortify us with the fearlessness we need to take on great challenges and by so doing inspire others?

Even in those dark hours when you cannot see the lights in the eyes of those who have gathered before you, know that at a very bare minimum, your energy and enthusiasm for what may be possible, even the smallest steps, can spark that fire. Conditions can improve. Life can get better. We then extend that expectation into concrete classroom actions.

With all this in mind, our book of "inspirational tips," concepts and ideas connects the problems, challenges and breakthroughs of the past to what we can do in the present. Our examples come through history, my major as an undergraduate. In these examples, people saw a need and stepped up to do something. Our own books in this series of "tips" addresses the challenges of climate change and human diversity, of conflict and peacebuilding, and the alternative approaches beyond the classroom that can open us up—teachers, students, community and business leaders—to new insights and new inspiration.

Every incident highlighted here has its own story of inspiration. Of the 147 "tips" or core concepts we offer here, we know that you will find many that touch your heart and soul, energizing you to move forward and inspire others. It cannot be formulaic, however. You must decide which ideas work best for your content, students, place and community, what ideas magnify your own talents.

For me, much credit goes to students in the Honors Program at Colorado State University (CSU) who have enrolled in my seminars on peacemaking and sustainability. These young people have helped me refine these ideas as they took up the challenges of studying the complex and compelling topics of peace, reconciliation, diversity and sustainability. In a similar way, graduate students in the School of Education at CSU helped to explore ways in which these issues could best be analyzed and taught, understood and learned. Internationally, students and colleagues in Northern Ireland, South Korea and Burundi also offered input.

So pick this book up at least once a week and read through three to four ideas for that month. Remembering those past challenges, and what others have done, think through what might work for you and your situation. Try something new; that alone can help provide some needed new inspiration.

As I searched for that inspiration when writing my earlier book, *Teaching and Learning Peace*, I found this jewel from Martin Luther King, Jr. who was looking back over the first half of the twentieth century and could have been despondent. He could have interpreted the wars and conflicts, the barriers, injustice and resistance as clear evidence of an oppressive system unwilling to bend. Instead, he chose to frame the historical record from a different perspective, one of hopefulness. Now that we are in the twenty-first century, do we see King's assessment as unrealistically naïve, a tangible sign of his insightful genius, or a choice we can make in framing our own thoughts, feelings and commitments? How do we stay grounded in realistic possibility, articulating an achievable though distant goal and inspiring others through difficult times? In *My Pilgrimage to Nonviolence*, King had written in the late 1950's, sentiments that could apply today:

> "We who live in the twentieth century are privileged to live in one of the most momentous periods of human history. It is an exciting age, filled with hope. It is an age in which a new social order is being born. We stand today between two worlds — the dying old and the emerging new. Now I am aware of the fact that there are those who would contend that we live in the most ghastly period of human history... They would argue that we are retrogressing instead of progressing. But far from representing retrogression and tragic meaninglessness, the present tensions represent the necessary pains that accompany the birth of anything new."
> (King, 2000, p. 178)

This book is for anyone needing to be inspired in these troubled, contentious and polarized times, anyone wanting to play an active role in creating peace. Know that other times have been darker and somehow, someway, people found ways to pull through. Based on those historical examples as well as a few from recent events, "tips" of core concepts for teaching others can help rekindle hope and possibility. For teachers at all levels and across all disciplines, for instructors in colleges and universities, for students of all ages, for leaders in business and organizations, in churches and communities—even for individuals wanting to see some promising possibilities for themselves—here are ideas for inspiring others—neighbors and friends, family members here and afar, co-workers, professional contacts, government employees, elected officials as well as those who aspire to elected office.

The ideas here are drawn from four published books of proven ideas for teaching peace and reconciliation, sustainability, and diversity as well as ideas for experiential learning. The short entries draw on specific "tips" and build on a solid research base. We stay with the number 147, the total number of "tips" in each of these four books, by offering twelve of these core concepts per month (n = 144) plus three more. Twelve events from each month are linked to a particular "tip" from one of the four books. These book are:

- Timpson, W., Yang, R., Borrayo, E., Canetto, S., Gonzalez-Voller, J., and Scott, M. (2019). *147 practical tips for teaching diversity*. 2nd ed. Madison, WI: Atwood Publishing.
- Timpson, W., Dunbar, B., Kimmel, G., Bruyere, B., Newman, P., Mizia, H., Birmingham, D., & Harmon, R. (2017). *147 practical tips for teaching sustainability: Connecting the environment, the economy and society* (2nd ed.). Madison, WI: Atwood Publishing.
- Timpson, W., Foley, J., Kees, N., & Waite, A. (2013). *147 practical tips for using experiential learning*. Madison, WI: Atwood Publishing.
- Timpson, W., Brantmeier, E., Kees, N., Cavanagh, T., McGlynn, C., & Ndura-Ouédraogo, E. (2009). *147 practical tips for teaching peace and reconciliation*. Madison, WI: Atwood Publishing.

Teachers, in particular, must bring an upbeat attitude to their work if they hope to motivate students. Research has taught us a great deal about the importance of energy and enthusiasm in the promotion of learning. Inspiration can be infectious. If events that we all experience prove disheartening, those who rely on our energies may also become disheartened. Finding those ideas that have helped others get through difficult and dangerous challenges and then contribute to creating peace can help us navigate our own troubled times.

So enjoy what we offer here and pay forward those lessons you find most inspirational in creating peace for yourself, others and the planet.

JANUARY
Tips #1-12

In the northern hemisphere, the cold of winter and the dawning of a new year can—and should—inspire new thinking and initiatives once the basics are understood. As we prepare for classes or presentations we can read through what history can teach us about the challenges of the past, just where there are significant points of light to remember, and how the ideas that emerge can help us connect to what we can do in the classroom or with other audiences. So reflect on those tough issues you face and consider new possibilities that would energize you and carry over to others.

For example, on January first of 1863, in the midst of a divisive, bloody and exhausting U.S. civil war, we saw a courageous President Abraham Lincoln issue a proclamation that freed slaves in the rebellious Southern states and inspire deep change. In January of 1925 in that traditional bastion of rugged male cowboy mentality, Wyoming inaugurated the first female governor in the U.S. Less than forty years later, Senator John Kennedy announced his intention to run for president on January 2nd, 1960 and bring his youthful energy to that office. After many years of a tense and seemingly intractable stand-off during the Cold War when many feared a holocaust should a conflict escalate between the U.S. and the U.S.S.R., these superpowers announced a treaty in January of 1993 eliminating about two-thirds of each country's long-range nuclear weapons.

#1. Embrace complexity while connecting systems, values and sustainability

Thinking about sustainability means embracing complexity and drawing on inspiration from various sources for ways forward. In January 1964, the U.S. Surgeon General released a report indicating that smoking was a definite health hazard. Over many years it eventually became public how aggressive the tobacco industry had been in attempting to conceal this connection and refute the medical evidence, efforts that included the hiring of social scientists to either refute those arguments or conduct "research" that might raise doubts.. A commitment to sustainability means asking hard questions and interrogating the responses that we get, including questions about the systems that operate our economies, our societies and our politics and that inspire our values. The following "tip" is adapted from #16 in *147 Practical Tips for Teaching Sustainability*.

> Examine how capitalist and democratic ideals and sustainable practices interact with each other. Richard Fox, then with the non-profit organization, Trees, Water, and People, reminds us that democracy is not something we made *once*. He insists that it is an ongoing evolving experiment in working collectively and that *we* are the ones on the cutting edge of that powerful force.
>
> As an example, Fox points to the fundamental question of water and asks if clean and sufficient water is a human right that government should provide or a commodity that can be sold to the highest bidder? In the U.S., Fox insists that we face our own version of water privatization but that it comes in the form of bottled water. He notes that if you look at any convenience store, you will see that we have somehow accepted the marketed premise that we should pay more for a gallon of water than we do for gasoline. Think about that!
>
> Worse yet, as people turn to bottled water as the solution for a perceived failure of our public water systems, we have less money to improve those very public water systems under question. Instead, we are now faced with a huge new form of trash (i.e., mountains of plastic bottles). The truth is that we don't adequately fund our water systems." Just think about the tragic events in Flint Michigan in 2015 when dangerously high levels of lead surfaced when the city's source for water was changed.
>
> However, the real irony is that many tests are showing that some of the bottled water is no better than the water we get from the tap or, in some cases, it is tap water but sold with a fancy label." For insight into the international debate, read *Blue Gold: The Fight to Stop Corporate Theft of the World's Water* by Maude Barlow and Tony Clarke, or view the film "Thirst."

Ask yourself and your students or audience members: In what other ways do the current economic and political systems undermine sustainability? What would be inspiring?

#2. Begin with the fundamentals and recognize achievements

In January 1946, the first meeting of the United Nations General Assembly took place in London with delegates from 51 countries. When disasters strike, especially in the developing world, most of us now look to the U.N. for inspiration and a response. Since its inception, the U.N. has played an important role world-wide in leading and coordinating efforts to improve the interconnected health of the environment, society and the economy. Despite the recurring criticisms of what the U.N. does not do or the scandals that occasionally rock its organization, the role of the U.N. in charting a collaborative and diplomatic way forward will only become more salient as the world becomes increasingly interdependent and the presence of nuclear and other weapons remains a threat. The following "tip" is adapted from #4 in *147 Practical Tips for Teaching Sustainability.*

> Every instructor can teach something about basic ecological, social and economic concepts—for example, analyzing case studies or assigning projects—that provide a foundation for understanding sustainability so that we are then able to discuss more complex topics in every discipline. This will become all the more important when disasters strike and we look to organizations like the United Nations to take action and help coordinate efforts for new policies and practices.

> In his chapter "What is Education For?" David Orr (1994, *Earth in Mind*) identifies ten concepts that he argues all college graduates should understand: (1) the laws of thermodynamics, (2) basic principles of ecology, (3) carrying capacity, (4) energetics, (5) least-cost and end-use analysis, (6) limits of technology, (7) appropriate scale, (8) sustainable agriculture and forestry, (9) steady-state economics, and (10) environmental ethics.

Assign students or others to research one of these concepts within a particular case or project. Argue for other perspectives and ask for brief presentations. You can also ask people to make applications of these concepts for their own lives and identify what is inspirational.

#3. See the damage and listen to the elders

In January 1848 the California Gold Rush began with an accidental discovery near the construction of Sutter's sawmill. The frenzied response that erupted drama-tized both the promise and the perils of perceived "get rich quick" opportunities as pristine environments were quickly invaded and native peoples overwhelmed. The inspiration for so many to rush for their chance at riches was mixed with failure, sadness, and tragedies for the land and those already living there. The following "tip" is adapted from #5 in *147 Practical Tips for Teaching Sustainability*.

> Oren Lyons, (1996) Faithkeeper of the Turtle Clan, Onondaga Council of Chiefs of the Hau de no sau nee, gave an address to World Bank, October 3, 1995, entitled, "Ethics and Spiritual Val-ues and the Promotion of Environmentally Sustainable Develop-ment" (*Akwesasne Notes New Series*, Winter, January/February/March, 2(1): "The democratic laws of most indigenous peoples arise from their understanding of the natural law and the regen-erative powers that sustain life. Therefore, 'sustainable' in our terms means working with these laws that could be termed spir-itual. We were instructed to make all of our laws in concert with these principles thus insuring life in endless cycles. To challenge these cycles and the interdependent processes of life that sustain us will insure our defeat and demise on this Earth" (pp. 88-93).

Dig into the literature and journals of people "on the margins" and from indigenous cul-tures to discover the wisdom of their respected elders. Imagine an inspirational dialogue with that person about the future of human society.

#4. Pause for reflection

In January 2009, Barack Obama was inaugurated as the 44th President of the United States of America, inspiring millions world-wide as he became the United States' first African-American president. While he proved to be enormously popular, his legacy was challenged when Donald Trump won the electoral vote in 2016 despite losing the popular vote. Pausing for reflection can create some space for deeper exploration, listening and processing. The following "tip" is adapted from #11 in

147 Practical Tips for Teaching Diversity.

Young people often are overwhelmed with the amount of information that comes at them in class, from friends and certainly through various news outlets and social media. Discussions can also be problematic when opinions range widely and many are unsure where or how to focus, what to put into their notes let alone what to think in a day of "fake news," both real and imagined. The "addictions" that many people have to their smart phones and internet connections can be barriers to deeper reflections.

In *It's Up To You*, Dzigar Kongtrül (2006), a Tibetan lama who has taught at the Buddhist inspired Naropa University in Boulder, Colorado, and now heads up retreat centers in Colorado and Vermont, describes the various ways in which meditation and self-reflection can add clarity and inspiration to our experiences in life. He writes: "The point of the practice of self-reflection is to experience things clearly, without muddying the water by trying to change or control them" (p. 13). It is this kind of clarity that becomes so important when complex aspects of diversity surface.

Find ways of pausing so that you and others can reflect. Try counting silently to yourself to provide a little more "wait time" to help some individuals come up with thoughtful responses to complex questions. Pause and review periodically to help underscore key points and reinforce a conceptual framework that helps to keep everything connected. You can also use a brief in-class free write to accomplish some of this. Remember that "less (coverage) can mean more (and deeper learning)."

Finally, as the instructor or presenter, you too should pause to reflect. When problems surface in class or in the community, when things don't go as well as planned, when your confidence is shaken, take some time to yourself to reflect honestly on events and your own reactions. You might find the inspiration for a new and creative insight during the time that these conflicts incubate in your mind and heart.

#5. Study diversity

In January of 1863, Abraham Lincoln signed the Emancipation Proclamation ending slavery and one of the darkest stains on American history, stains that reverberate today. With the Civil War raging, the body count growing and no end in sight, this was an inspired move by Lincoln to shore up Union support and allow for the recruitment of former slaves within Union forces. In our own times, huge social forces can ripple through society and leave much that challenges instructors at every level and across all disciplines. The widespread concern about diversity and the need for institutions, schools, colleges, universities, the curricula and communities everywhere to reflect a commitment to inclusion are only the most recent and recurring challenges we face. The following "tip" is adapted from #4 in *147 Practical Tips for Teaching Diversity.*

> Know that you can also enlist students or audience members in reporting on cases, problems or projects that incorporate aspects of diversity. For example, in her chapter "Multicultural Education in South Korea," teacher Jungsook Shim (2014, in W. Timpson and D. Holman (Eds.), *Controversial case studies for teaching on sustainability, conflict, and diversity*), wants to explore the needs of refugees from North Korea as they attempt to assimilate in the South and get past historic prejudices. She asks, "How can Korean schools adapt and develop multicultural education in the midst of such dramatic change" (p. 37)?

As instructors, students or leaders, any of us can work toward understanding the contributions of diverse individuals to our own disciplines and areas of influence. As such, we can profit from varied readings, from reports and biographies including the mass of primary sources yet to be uncovered. Make a plan to research areas of diversity for your own classes.

#6. Welcome contradictions and get people to think on the edge of their comfort zones

In January of 1977, the Alex Haley book "Roots" became a TV mini-series and inspired huge audiences as stories of Black people in the U.S emerged from African backgrounds and focused on their struggles with slavery. The social-emotional aspects of the resulting discussions and reflections challenged everyone to get beyond the "facts" and look at what was in the background and what lay underneath that needed to be spotlighted and unearthed. The following idea is adapted from "tip" #7 in *147 Practical Tips for Teaching Diversity.*

> A book of ideas for teaching diversity might be misleading if instructors believe that handling the inherent mix of intellectual and emotional factors is a simple matter. In fact, one of our most important tips is to expect a challenge. Nina Roberts (2003) contends that instructors should both encourage and challenge students, getting them to express themselves fully and, then, validate (acknowledge, accept) these feelings and beliefs. Instructors can spark open, even heated, discussions—"I ... feel the need to respond in a way that broadens their thinking and puts them on the edge of their comfort zone" (p. 233) —but require respectful dialogue from everyone.

Tell audiences that you will be deliberately provocative at times, that you will "play the devil's advocate" and pose alternative ideas in order to inspire reflection and deeper analyses.

#7. Rethink the war and dominance paradigms

In January 1973, U. S. President Richard Nixon announced that a peace accord has been reached in Vietnam. After so many years of bloodshed and protests, it may be difficult to see the inspiration here but those of us who teach or present can consciously walk that "road less travelled" as poet Robert Frost remembers and look more deeply into the lessons of peace building here. In truth, Vietnam and the U.S. currently have an active, promising and peaceful trading relationship with each other. The following concept is adapted from "tip" #1 in *147 Practical Tips for Teaching Peace and Reconciliation.*

> The telling of history from limited, violence-based perspectives constructs social memory in ways that help to perpetuate violence

as inherent, natural, and a human absolute—in short, 'just the way things are.' The telling of violent histories saturates collective memory with violent images and struggles of the past; these violent narratives can serve to inspire the power of present transformative action toward actualizing nonviolent futures.

In *Cultures of Peace: The Hidden Side of History*, Elise Boulding (2000) writes of the war-steeped telling of history as related to western civilization, that history is often written as stories about the rise and fall of empires, a description of the rulers, their armies, navies and air power, their wars and battles, i.e., the history of power—who controls whom. In this provocative book, Boulding critiques the telling of history from violent, power-dominated, and patriarchal viewpoints. She furthers her argument by providing historical examples of groups and societies who lived relatively peaceful and harmonious lives, solving conflict in nonviolent ways.

Brainstorm a list of examples of peaceful responses out of conflicts, either big or small. Who were the key players, leaders, and 'behind the scenes' people and groups involved in these conflicts? What methods, besides violence, were used to actualize change? Reflect on how peaceful, nonviolent, and cooperative paradigms can inspire a transformation of present community, societal, national, and global conflicts into mutually beneficial outcomes that can benefit everyone.

#8. Create concentric circles for positive peace

In January of 1892 Ellis Island opened to immigration providing a gateway that inspired millions of immigrants to leave their ancestral homelands, emigrate to the U.S. and escape from oppressive conditions in the hope of starting a new life. While life was often very difficult, new opportunities awaited these immigrants. Yet we must also recognize that too many of the Native Peoples who inhabited the Americas were killed, pushed aside, devastated by diseases for which they had no immune protections, or restricted to reservations while prime land was given to homesteaders from Europe. The following idea is adapted from "tip" #2 in *147 Practical Tips for Teaching Peace and Reconciliation.*

Johan Galtung (1969, Violence, peace and peace research, *Journal of Peace Research, 3*; and 1988, *Peace and social structure: Essays in peace Research*) infused peace theory, or a set of principles that guide peace thinking and peace education practices, with the concepts of negative peace and positive peace. Negative peace can be understood as the absence of direct physical violence—war, domestic violence, etc. Positive peace can be understood as conditions without indirect violence—both a lack of trust, intimidation, the presence of fear, bullying, and conditions without structural violence. Educative efforts toward positive peace seek to build new macro-structural alignments that promote capacity, prosperity and happiness for all, as well as trust in peace, trust in relationships, hope, and reflection on positive conditions that create peace.

The activity that follows provides an opportunity for people to reflect on past, present, and future conditions of peace, thus generating positive memories, present mindfulness, and future possibilities. Outside or in a large room, ask a group to form two circles with even numbers—one inner circle, one outer circle. People should stand face to face. Ask them to introduce themselves to their partner.

Use the following series of questions and time each question (about 3 minutes each) and then rotate. "Describe a peaceful time in your life." After 3 minutes of back and forth discussion, ask the inner or outer circle to move one, two, or three people to the left or to the right; this promotes interaction with multiple members of the circle.

Then ask: "Describe a time when there was peace in your community, your nation, or the world?" Then ask them to fill in the blank: "I currently find peace when ____; my community finds peace when____; the nation ____; the world ____." Finally, ask them to fill in the blanks: "I will find peace when____; my community will find peace when _____; the nation____; the world____." Debrief by identifying the conditions for peace from the personal to the global level; write them on a chart.

#9. Enhance holistic thinking about peace

In January 1990, Lithuania declared its independence from the Soviet Union after Mikhail Gorbachev had inspired many under Russian control in the era of *glasnost* (openness) and *perestroika* (restructuring). Much of the world held its collective breath, wondering if the Soviet army would march in to crush the revolt as they did in 1956 in Hungary. But no, that did not happen and we should understand why. The following concept is adapted from "tip" #3 in *147 Practical Tips for Teaching Peace and Reconciliation*.

> Linda Groff (2002, A holistic view of peace education, *Social Alternatives*, 21(1)) positions the need for "peace thinking" on multiple, interdependent levels in order to actualize a peaceful world. The benefit of using Groff's conceptual model for thinking about peace is that it adds the more complex "integrated peace" dimension and it includes vital foci on feminist, intercultural, planetary, and inner peace. This model delineates seven central concepts in peace thinking:
>
> 1. War Prevention (Negative Peace)
>   a. Peace as Absence of War
>   b. Peace as Balance of Forces in the International System
>
> 2. Structural Conditions for Peace (Positive Peace)
>   a. Peace as no war and no structural violence on macro levels
>   b. Peace as no war and no structural violence on micro levels (Community, Family, Feminist Peace)
>
> 3. Peace Thinking that Stresses Holistic, Complex Systems (Integrated Peace)
>   a. Intercultural Peace (peace among cultural groups)
>   b. Holistic Gaia Peace (Peace within the human world and with the environment).
>   c. Holistic Inner and Outer Peace (Includes all 6 types of peace and adds inner peace as essential condition) (pp. 7-8).

Facilitate a group brainstorm about specific actions that could inspire peace at each level of Groff's model. Guide a conversation about how these various levels of peace thinking are interconnected and also unique. Then have a conversation about how one can work to promote peace on various levels.

#10. Explore difficult issues

New 55 mph speed limits were introduced in late 1973 in the U.S. and made official by Congress the following January, inspiring important but difficult conversations, debates and arguments about potential limits on American "freedoms." Big engines and fast speeds had become synonymous with the "American dream." However, alternative vehicles from foreign competitors were waiting in the wings with inexpensive, smaller and more efficient engines. Apart from the advertisements for big, flashy cars, what was the experience of Americans with alternatives? Or in long lines at gas stations during periodic "oil shocks" when supplies were curtailed? The following idea is adapted from #2 in *147 Practical Tips for Using Experiential Learning*.

> One arena where experiential learning has critical value is in exploring difficult issues. Too often we are locked into particular positions or blinded to our own prejudices and assumptions. An extended focus on direct experience can unlock new insights. For example, Timpson, Canetto, Borayo and Yang (2003, 2019) pushed beyond the usual campus celebrations of different cultures to review the published research on handling diversity in the classroom and then drew on their own experiences as well as what others contributed to offer a new synthesis.
>
> Following a similar path, Timpson, Dunbar, Kimmel, Bruyere, Newman, and Mizia (2017) wanted to bring new thinking to the issue of teaching sustainability, a very complex and contentious concept that is inherently interdisciplinary, even trans-disciplinary. Similarly, Timpson, Brantmeier, Cavanagh, McGlynn and Ndura-Ouédraogo (2009), representing different disciplines and cultures, also came together to share their experiences and exper-

tise in order to create a new synthesis about teaching peace and
reconciliation.

*Reflect on instances when you were stuck in old, dysfunctional thinking and new experi-
ences allowed you to get to different insights and to inspire new possibilities. Brainstorm
activities that would help others explore new thinking about a difficult issue.*

#11. Immerse yourself in new possibilities

Apple Computer was incorporated in January, 1977. Who could have seen the inspiration back then of this dynamic new company so tuned into the needs of the
future? Confronting new technologies and new products, people world-wide were
suddenly immersed in new possibilities where their creative initiatives continued
to open up new possibilities. The following "tip" is adapted from #3 in *147 Practical Tips for Using Experiential Learning.*

> One powerful aspect of experiential learning is gaining new ad-
> vocates as more and more students find ways to serve or study
> abroad. Whether it is a church group taking teenagers to Central
> America to help build homes, day care centers or health clinics,
> or college students wanting an alternative experience over one of
> their breaks or to study abroad for an entire semester, experiences
> in another culture can be challenging, difficult, and life changing,
> far beyond what academic studies alone can provide. The U. S.
> Peace Corps prides itself on offering the "toughest job you'll ever
> love." Note how they describe what they offer in the way of ex-
> perience.
>
> "The Peace Corps traces its roots and mission to 1960, when then
> Senator John F. Kennedy challenged students at the University
> of Michigan to serve their country in the cause of peace by living
> and working in developing countries. From that inspiration grew
> an agency of the federal government devoted to world peace and
> friendship. Since that time, 200,000+ Peace Corps Volunteers have
> served in 139 host countries to work on issues ranging from AIDS

education to information technology and environmental preservation. Today's Peace Corps is more vital than ever, working in emerging and essential areas such as information technology and business development, and contributing to the President's Emergency Plan for AIDS Relief. Peace Corps Volunteers continue to help countless individuals who want to build a better life for themselves, their children, and their communities."

Reflect on those difficult experiences that have taught you the most. List some ideas, both short- and long-term, that could inspire something similar for groups with whom you work.

#12. Clarify your values and define your philosophy of teaching

In January 1941 Great Britain introduced food rationing and coupon books to inspire sacrifice and conserve resources needed for the war effort. Much effort had to go into explaining to the public why rationing was necessary and why resources had to be saved. Given the threats to their survival as a free people, everyone understood the need for sacrifice. The following "tip" is adapted from #5 in *147 Practical Tips for Using Experiential Learning*.

Writing down your philosophy of teaching can be a valuable exercise in critical reflection and values clarification. This can be a catalyst for you to check-in with your beliefs, values and understandings that you have created over time and where experiential learning could fit. This can also serve as an opportunity to ask yourself about any assumptions that you may have. Read Parker Palmer's (1998) *The Courage to Teach*, and consider these questions:

- How do I see the learner?
  - o Is the learner active or passive?
  - o What assets and liabilities does the learner bring?
  - o Is it my job to motivate the learner?

- What is knowledge?
  - o Does knowledge exist to be discovered or do we create

knowledge?

- o What is the nature of knowledge in my discipline?
- o Is it my job to impart knowledge or facilitate the learner's interaction with it?
- o Is knowledge static or dynamic; for example, does history change depending on the historian's perspective?

- What is my role as an instructor?
  - o Where do I sit in the "power paradigm" in relation to knowledge and the learner?
  - o What are my responsibilities and what are the learner's responsibilities?

- What is my philosophical orientation (behavioral, constructivist, cognitive, etc.)?
  - o How did I get to this orientation?
  - o Did it emerge from personal experiences or was it adopted from external sources?
  - o Does it still fit for learners today?

- How do I know that I am an effective facilitator of learning?
  - o How am I evaluated; and more importantly, is this evaluation a valid representation of my teaching?
  - o Do I invite constructive criticism from my learners, peers, and experts?
  - o Am I open to integrating this feedback into my instruction?

By developing your philosophy of teaching or presenting and keeping it updated, you will engage in critical reflection about yourself as a facilitator of learning and as a leader. You will also be open to seeing where you could grow, what new experiences might inspire you. Ask yourself these questions and write out a draft of your philosophy of teaching.

FEBRUARY
Tips #13-24

In February of 1956 eighty participants in the Montgomery bus boycott were arrested including Martin Luther King, Jr. and Rosa Parks, sacrifices that helped to push the U.S. Supreme Court to later mandate the desegregation of those buses and eventually all other institutions that served the public. In 1964 Bob Dylan inspired us to think differently with his song, *The times they are a-changing*. In 1990 South African President F. W. de Klerk lifted the ban on the African National Congress and quickly freed Nelson Mandela from prison. By 2010 two-thirds of the world's population were using mobile phones. Positive lights can be pushed into the darkest corners.

#13. Make the case for possibility

From daring and disasters can arise both great sorrow and valuable insights, even inspiration. On February 1, 2003 the Space Shuttle Columbia disintegrated upon reentering the Earth's atmosphere, killing all seven crew members. Future plans had the space shuttles flying only to the International Space Station so that the crews could have a secure base if something prevented the orbiter from a safe reentry. There is always great risk when taking on great challenges. What humans are doing to the environment and its natural resources will require new thinking, collective resolve and action to even begin to redress. Unfortunately, it may take numerous crises and setbacks to arouse the necessary political will. The following idea is adapted from "tip" #6 in *147 Practical Tips for Teaching Sustainability*.

> Information overload and the constant drumbeat of negative news in mainstream media can overwhelm even the most informed citizen. Referencing important historic transformations can help people see what can be done.

> Lester Brown (2003) is president of the Earth Policy Institute and author of *Plan B: Rescuing a Planet under Stress and a Civilization in Trouble*. In response to all those who seem paralyzed by the chang-

es needed to support a truly sustainable culture, he reminds us of the transformation of U.S. industry after the Japanese attacks on Pearl Harbor and the American entry into World War II: "In retrospect, the speed of the conversion from a peacetime to a wartime economy was stunning…. The harnessing of U.S. industrial power tipped the scales decisively toward the Allied Forces, reversing the tide of war…The mobilization of resources within a matter of months demonstrates that an economy and, indeed, the world can restructure its economy quickly if it is convinced of the need to do so…" (pp. 205–206).

Brainstorm ways in which people can be convinced of the need for a more sustainable way of life. Remember that to convince some people of something, it is often necessary to answer the question they will inevitably ask: "What's in it for me?"

#14. Add missing voices

On February 3, 1821, Elizabeth Blackwell was born. She later became the first female physician in the United States. Attempting to study medicine in the Philadelphia area, Blackwell met with resistance almost everywhere she went. Most physicians recommended that she go to Paris to study or that she take up a disguise as a man. The reasons she was given included her supposed intellectual "inferiority" as a woman or, perhaps more telling, the threat she would pose to their livelihoods if she proved capable. After receiving her medical degree from the Geneva Medical College in upstate New York, Blackwell remained active in reform efforts to open the medical profession to women in the U.S., England and Europe.

In the face of growing challenges in every arena, from climate change to exploding population growth, from the spread of pollution to the conflicts that continually arise over natural resources, from the tensions of growing inequalities to both the opportunities and challenges of increasing dependence on technology, our collective well-being cannot afford to exclude segments of the population whose talents could inspire us toward answers we might otherwise miss. The following "tip" is adapted from #7 in *147 Practical Tips for Teaching Sustainability*.

Teaching and learning are dynamic activities that can be energized by making traditional content more relevant to today's concerns about sustainability. Be sure to look through the classics as well as unpublished or neglected sources when you look for new ideas. Know that Aldo Leopold (a forester), Rachel Carson (a biologist), Ralph Waldo Emerson (a minister), John Muir (a naturalist), and many others who advocated for conservation early on were once in the minority in their thinking.

Read passages from classics like *Sand County Almanac, Silent Spring, Nature, My Summer in the Sierras,* and others for ideas that may be missing from today's conversations. Also identify those individuals, those metaphorical "canaries" who have been warning us about unsustainability in the "mines" of our lives and offering new solutions. Encourage students to read these works as well, and infuse your talks with new insights and discoveries.

Discuss how people with different backgrounds could draw such similar conclusions. Analyze why their message eventually resonated with others, and consider who will emerge as a conservation leader from today's thinkers, scholars, writers, and community leaders.

#15. Revisit big questions

In February of 1976 a major earthquake in Guatemala and Honduras killed more than 22,000. Striking in the early morning when most people were asleep contributed to the high death toll. International assistance helped repair the roads and villages. While earthquakes offer inspired appeals for aid, other environmental problems are "slow burning," less dramatic and a problem for raising concern. Climate change, for example, represents the additive impact of human activities that continue to pump pollutants into the air, adding to the slow rise of temperatures world-wide. Weather changes and sea level rise are only two of many effects that are now gathering increasing amounts of both scientific and public attention. The following concept is adapted from "tip" #8 in *147 Practical Tips for Teaching Sustainability.*

In *Collapse,* his compelling and sobering review of societies that faced challenges and adapted or perished, Jared Diamond (2005) asks us to study the record of human response and reflect on those environmental issues, in particular, that we face today. How will history judge our actions or inactions? "Greenland provides us with our closest approximation to a controlled experiment in collapse: two societies (Norse and Inuit) sharing the same island, but with very different cultures, such that one of those societies survived while the other was dying. Thus, Greenland history conveys the message that, even in a harsh environment, collapse isn't inevitable but depends on a society's choices" (p. 21). According to Diamond, the Norse were so secure in their superiority over the Inuit that they refused to adopt the Inuit's time-tested but presumed to be more primitive practices for survival.

As a more recent example, the Worldwatch Institute's 2005 Annual Edition of *State of the World* features Mikhail Gorbachev's plea to remember what was considered very possible when the Cold War was dismantled. "Humankind has a unique opportunity to make the twenty-first century one of peace and security. Yet the many possibilities opened up to us by the end of the cold war appear to have been partially squandered already. Where has the 'peace dividend' gone that we worked so hard for? Why have regional conflict and terrorism become so dominant in today's world" (p. xvii)?

Ask yourself, your students and colleagues, friends, family and others: What is happening today that history someday will judge foolish or dangerous to our very survival? What would have been possible if some percentage of funds spent on the military world-wide had gone to sponsoring more sustainable solutions?

#16. Examine policies and court decisions

In February of 1960 sit-ins at segregated Woolworth lunch counters began in Greensboro, North Carolina and quickly inspired action across the South. These were tactical efforts to attract media and governmental attention and use the nonviolent tactics being promulgated by Dr. Martin Luther King, Jr. and others to shame the established racist power structure of segregated communities into changing their policies and practices. Eventually support built nationally and especially after the assassination of President John F. Kennedy in 1963, newly elected President Lyndon Johnson was able to garner political support needed to get the 1964 Civil Rights Act approved, mandating desegregation in all public accommodations. The following "tip" is adapted from #5 in *147 Practical Tips for Teaching Diversity*.

> Beyond the rhetoric of acceptance and tolerance are the hard facts of life for many diverse peoples within a dominant culture. A focus on laws, policies, and primary sources can help remove the haze of denial that often shrouds brutal reality. For example, on June 23, 2016, Anemona Hartocollis reported for the *New York Times* that the Supreme Court upheld a University of Texas admissions plan that allows race and ethnicity to be considered as one of many factors in admission at public universities. In contrast, several states have banned affirmative action. Against Harvard, a private university, there is also another kind of complaint, that affirmative action policies have had the effect of discriminating against high-achieving Asian-American applicants.

Identify legal and public policy issues at your local college or university, public or private. Ask students how these are impacted by questions of culture, social class and political values.

#17. Introduce new ways of thinking

On February 15, 1820, Susan B. Anthony was born into a Quaker family that helped shape her lifetime of commitment to new ways of thinking about needed social reforms, about the abolition of slavery and a woman's right to vote. An early advocate for equal rights for all women and African Americans, Anthony was far ahead of the nation in inspiring changes that would later be embraced. She worked tirelessly across the U.S. and internationally, giving 75-100 speeches per year and working on many state campaigns. Ridiculed and attacked, Anthony was eventually celebrated at the White House on her 80th birthday. The following "tip" is adapted from #10 in *147 Practical Tips for Teaching Diversity*.

> Roe Bubar and Irene Vernon (2003) have drawn on their legal training for materials, approaches, and language as they confront years of discriminatory policies and practices toward Native Americans. "First, we begin teaching by helping students understand the 'study of law.' Law is a difficult subject matter, with an 'elitist' jargon that typically requires students to purchase a separate legal dictionary to complete reading assignments. It involves a new way of thinking.... We expect students to learn this new legal language, to brief legal cases, and to participate in moot court arguments" (p. 162).

> Progress often hinges on overturning old and problematic concepts and finding new, creative ways forward. Perry (1999) points to these abilities as the high end of cognitive development where people learn to stretch to understand different perspectives, reexamine their own ideas and, in general, to better handle the complexities and ambiguities of real world issues and projects.

Rethink some of the concepts you or your texts have been using and explore the possibilities of new language.

#18. Celebrate growth, development and a desire to speak the truth

In February of 1965, Malcolm X was gunned down in New York by members of the Nation of Islam. His parents, Earl and Louise Little, were outspoken advocates of "Negro self-reliance" but because of threats from the Ku Klux Klan they relocated from Omaha to Milwaukee and then Lansing. His father died when Malcom was six and his mother, dogged by financial pressures, later had a nervous breakdown and was committed to a state mental hospital. Malcolm and the other children were farmed out to various foster homes. Eventually Malcolm became immersed in petty crimes and theft. Arrested in 1945 he began serving an eight-to-ten year sentence for larceny and breaking and entering. In prison, Malcolm studied and then converted to the Nation of Islam after which he formally changed his name from Malcolm Little to Malcolm X.

With a powerful and inspiring presence, he became successful at recruiting converts to the Nation of Islam and was publically critical of the leaders of the Civil Rights Movement who advocated integration. Speaking about all "whites as devils" and that John F. Kennedy's assassination was a reflection of the "chickens coming home to roost," he also came under surveillance by the FBI. Travelling to Mecca in 1964, however, he saw people of all shades of skin color worshipping Allah together and soon broke from the Nation of Islam. The following "tip" is adapted from #12 in *147 Practical Tips for Teaching Diversity*.

> Personal initiative, in terms of the framework established by Perry (1981, Cognitive and ethical growth: the making of meaning, in *The modern American college: Responding to the new realities of diverse students and a changing society*; and 1999, *Forms of intellectual and ethical development in the college years: A scheme*), develops as students progress from thinking in terms of dichotomies (right/wrong, yes/no), a stage in which agency (authority) is external (in the teacher and the texts), toward accepting different opinions and becoming more able to handle complexity and ambiguity, a stage in which agency is internal (within themselves) (see: 2003,Timpson, Canetto, Borrayo and Yang).

> Consider the case of Will Williams (2006), an African American who grew up in the deep South when segregation was the norm and racism ran deep. Williams seethed with anger and hatred for what he had seen done to Black people but he later realized that he grew up in the army in Vietnam when he began to see his own racism. "When I first got there, I didn't see them as Vietnamese. I'd been brainwashed. I saw them as the enemy. I had no regard for their life. I used to call them 'gooks,' the word that I hate to hear now. It bothers me when people use it. But back then, I was

doing it. It took a lot of years for me to realize that I was doing to them the same thing that had been done to me in Mississippi verbally. That word 'gook' is the same as being called 'nigger' in Mississippi, and I was guilty of it. So it just reinforced the fact that I was brainwashed, that I was used as other veterans are used. I hadn't realized that the system had beaten my brain to that point where I didn't see people as people until many years later" (p. 82).

Personal initiative—and courage—may be necessary for learning to go deeper, especially when the content may be sensitive, complex, personal, and emotional. Consider sharing instances from your own life, such as when your initiative helped you break down some of your own prejudices and allowed you to grow and develop further.

#19. Map peace, non-peace and violence

On February 12, 1809, Abraham Lincoln was born. As President he led the nation through the horrors of a Civil War that subdued the rebellious South, freed the slaves but cost the nation 600,000 plus military deaths, 400,000 plus wounded, and upwards of a million civilians dead. All romantic notions of a quick and glorious conflict evaporated in year one with the war grinding on for another four years. While peace was finally attained through Robert E. Lee's surrender, efforts at reconciliation are still needed as the descendants of formerly enslaved people continue to lag behind whites in school, income, wealth, health and more. The map of Civil War casualties would scar the country for decades to come. Peace had come at a horrific price and Lincoln deserves much credit for his inspired leadership through the darkest hours. The following "tip" is adapted from #5 in *147 Practical Tips for Teaching Peace and Reconciliation.*

> Everyday understandings of peace and non-peace can vary from one socio-cultural context to another given the unique realities and dynamics of those contexts and histories. Mapping everyday understandings of peace and violence is a research technique that can be used to determine both conceptions of peace and non-peace; it can be used to identify peaceful and non-peaceful attitudes and behaviors in various contexts, historic and now. These conceptions and identifications can then be used to engage local,

cultural actors in transformative change processes (Brantmeier, 2008).

As a warm up, make a list on a sheet of paper of words that "go with peace" and then words that "go with non-peace." Begin with an analysis of the Civil War in the U.S. and its legacy for us today. Circle the two most important words that identified peaceful attitudes and behaviors in everyday life (classroom, school, community, church, city, etc.) after that war ended. Now identify non-peaceful attitudes and behaviors. Circle the two most important. If you are leading a group, record the most important responses on a flip chart or chalk board. You can also share stories about today, either your own or what you've observed, both peaceful and non-peaceful. Take notes or record the stories that are shared. Ask some of the following questions: How did peaceful attitudes and behaviors multiply after the Civil War? How can the war's legacy of non-peaceful attitudes and violent behaviors be changed? From this list, create action plans that could enhance what is peaceful and change what's not.

#20. Make meaningful contact and reduce conflict

In February of 1990, Nelson Mandela walked out of the Robben Island Prison off Cape Town, South Africa after 27 years as a prisoner. He could have been angrily bitter but instead brought an inspired grace and humanity to his critique of the apartheid system that had dehumanized so many. After winning the Nobel Peace Prize in 1993, he went on to win the general election in 1994 as President and served until 1999, articulating a hope for a "rainbow nation" that would be inclusive of all colors. In an effort to help the nation recover from the ravages of a brutal and racist past, Mandela also pushed for a Truth and Reconciliation Commission (TRC) that would surface confessions of the truth of that dark past and calls for forgiveness in return for considerations of amnesty and reparations, all covered on television and broadcast world-wide. South Africa, it must be said, has avoided the bloodbath that many thought would follow the end of apartheid. The following "tip" is adapted from #7 in *147 Practical Tips for Teaching Peace and Reconciliation.*

In conflict-ridden societies much investment is often made in educational contact schemes designed to bring young people from the divided groups together in short- and long-term encounters with the aim of reducing prejudice towards the 'other' and hopefully thus ameliorating conflict. This approach draws on contact theory (Allport, 1954), the notion that working together on a common goal will do the most to reduce hostile feelings and build appreciation, and a subsequent litany of conditions for success. In Northern Ireland, for example, contact theory underpins much peace education efforts, both in the formal and informal education sectors.

After many years of extensive empirical research into the efficacy of inter-group contact in Israel and elsewhere, Gavriel Salomon (2007) concluded that there are two fundamental success criteria. First there must be a very important common goal for the two groups to work towards together and second there must be the opportunity for sustainable friendships to emerge from the contact.

Consider the work that Mandela, Bishop Desmond Tutu and others in the ANC did to bring together people with little experience of the 'other' and address their dark past in open and honest ways through the TRC. How might Salomon's main criteria influence the way in which you design educational policy and practice today with regards to reducing inter-group prejudices that currently exist in your school or on your campus or community. What kind of common goals would be appropriate and how, as an educator, can you support the development of inter-group friendships?

#21. Reconsider old beliefs and promote inspired, transformative leadership

On February 21, 1972, President Nixon arrived in China for meetings with Communist Party Chairman MaoTse-tung and Premier Chou En-lai. This was an important step in beginning to normalize relationships between the U.S. and the People's Republic of China, calming the waters of the Cold War, ideological differences and the legacy of a Korean War still not completely resolved. Somehow, Richard Nixon was an ideal emissary for the U.S. given his lifelong and fierce critique of everything Communist. Many Americans believed that he could be trusted to deal with the Chinese. The following concept is adapted from "tip" #10 in *147 Practical Tips for Teaching Peace and Reconciliation.*

Betty Reardon (1999, pp. 14-15) describes a system of values and capacities that can be fostered in future teachers to support peace building efforts. It could be argued that these values and capacities are also needed in all leaders who are desirous of peace. The framework includes the value of environmental responsibility, cultural diversity, human solidarity, social responsibility, and gender equality. Corresponding to these values are capacities for transforming societies into cultures of peace through ecological awareness, cultural competency, conflict proficiency, and gender sensitivity.

Individually or in groups, you can begin with an analysis of the Nixon's visit on U.S. and Chinese relationships. You can then consider a self-examination on these criteria. Write the values of environmental responsibility, cultural diversity, human solidarity, social responsibility, and gender equality on a flip chart, board, or piece of paper. Think of specific behaviors that you or others do that are related to each of the listed values. Identify everyone's strengths as peace leaders according to this value framework. Identify areas for improvement. Discuss the possibilities and constraints for improvement. Complete the above exercise in the context of ecological awareness, cultural competency, conflict proficiency, and gender sensitivity. What behaviors correlate with these capacities? Strengths? Areas of improvement? Develop action plans for peace leadership. Could we in the U.S. use Nixon's visit to open direct contact with North Korea or Iran where relationships have been sorely strained for many years? How does Reardon's framework of values and capacities help your analysis?

#22. Scaffold the experience

On February 11, 1847, American inventor Thomas Edison was born. Through his tireless experimentation and tinkering, the inventions, both small and transformative, rolled out of his mind and hands. In his 84 years, Edison acquired a phenomenal record of 1,000 plus patents and was the driving force behind innovations like the phonograph, the incandescent light bulb and one of the earliest motion picture cameras. Beyond this genius at innovation, Edison was also very successful as a businessman, making himself wealthy and popular with the general public.

As a young man, Edison was imaginative and inquisitive. However, because he had difficulty hearing, he was bored and labelled a misfit. Reading became his passion. At the age of twelve he quit school to work on the railroad and took advantage of an opportunity to be an apprentice telegrapher to learn and consider improvements, especially as his hearing problems limited him otherwise. Later in life he would build and lead a research laboratory that at its time was the world's most complete. While he scoffed at formal education, he celebrated the benefits of hard work and ceaseless experimentation in pursuit of insights, inspiration and applications. The following "tip" is adapted from #7 in *147 Practical Tips for Using Experiential Learning*.

> Scaffolding a learning experience is similar to having training wheels on a bike when a child is learning to ride (Bruner, 1975). If simply given the "bike without training wheels" the learning curve can be steep and dangerous. Think of it as the "science of learning" that we can apply to any situation and deepen our understanding of what would give greater substance to our desire for inspiration.
>
> In Edison's case, much of what he needed he learned on his own or through apprenticeship with others when he was young. As instructors we can do much by adding a supportive structure for students so that their success can come more quickly. As people move toward mastery we—and they—can remove part or all of the scaffolding.
>
> The support that you offer during the initial learning stages can include many of the following, features that Edison must have discovered for himself.
>
> - Breaking the task into smaller pieces;
> - Seeing for himself new ideas or skills and helping others to do the same;
> - Experimenting with resource material in different forms to meet his own learning needs and helping others do the same;
> - Using groups and using the interactions to improve on a design;
> - Outlining steps so that everyone could see and others could

measure progress toward a goal.

An inventor can help people become self-directed and independent, in part by increasing the level of risk and difficulty with each successive activity.

Use scaffolding when planning your next project or presentation activity.

#23. Embrace risk

On February 20, 1962 John Glenn became the first American to orbit the earth. Before joining NASA, he had been a distinguished fighter pilot. He later won a seat in the U.S. Senate and served four full terms or 24 years in all representing Ohio. Born in 1921, he later became the oldest person at age of 77 to fly in space when he served as a crew member for the Discovery space shuttle. Glenn's early years as an engineering student were interrupted by the Japanese attack on Perl Harbor. He quickly volunteered and eventually served in combat as a fighter pilot in the Pacific. After another tour as a fighter pilot during the Korean War, Glenn became a test pilot for the Navy. While the military has very clear training protocols, combat and space travel push pilots beyond their training where experience becomes a central teacher. Think of risk as the energy that can help surface inspiration. The following "tip" is adapted from #11 in *147 Practical Tips for Using Experiential Learning.*

> Risk is at the core of what fighter pilots and astronauts must face. By definition, some risk is inherent to learning since we stagnate without mistakes, feedback and correction. That risk, however, can take on many forms. One form is physical and has the potential for bodily harm. A second form of risk is emotional or psychological (Brown, 1999). This form of risk often goes unnoticed. Having a range of personalities in a group, from those who are risk seekers to those we could consider risk adaptive and others who are risk adverse, will challenge any instructor. Think about the following lines from Rumi, a 13th-century Persian Muslim poet, jurist, theologian, and Sufi mystic:

> *Refuse to play it safe,*
> *for it is from the wavering edge of risk*
> *that the sweetest honey of freedom drips.*

Covey (2004) argues that we need to help learners take a proactive approach to confronting the challenges they face. As instructors we can help students be more proactive, to reflect, plan and practice new responses in the face of uncertainty. Otherwise people are likely to be reactive and continue old, dysfunctional or counterproductive habits. Typically, some form of scaffolding (progressive levels of difficulty or complexity) in designing a learning sequence can be helpful. This allows people to challenge themselves at a "safe" level before moving up to a more difficult level.

Risk can add or detract from a learning experience depending on the type, level, and intensity of the risk. As a facilitator or instructor you can use risk as a tool to enhance potential outcomes but you'll need an understanding of the concept and a plan for how to use it.

Identify the levels of physical and emotional risk in John Glenn's life as a fighter pilot and astronaut. Then identify the risks you have faced in your own life as well as what your friends, family members or work colleagues have faced. What could have helped your learning? What have your students or others learned? List ways in which you could introduce risk into an upcoming presentation, session or activity and best help those present to grow.

#24. Develop your own learning cycle

On February 19, 1473, Nicolaus Copernicus was born in Prussia. Growing into a variety of roles—a mathematician, astronomer, physician, classics scholar, translator, governor, diplomat and economist, a truly Renaissance man—he published his most famous work just before his death in 1543 and reasoned that the earth rotated around the sun, thus ushering in the "Copernican Revolution" and altering the trajectory of science. Speaking several languages he seems to have been able to pursue a range of studies across different fields that allowed him to see through the established perceptions of the earth as the center for the universe. Inspired insight? Indeed. The following "tip" is adapted from #16 in *147 Practical Tips for Using Experiential Learning.*

> Learning cycles are models that can help guide your planning and facilitation of experiential learning. Copernicus had a learning cycle that took him through a range of different studies. As another example, David Kolb's (1984) learning cycle (concrete experience -> reflective observation -> abstract conceptualization -> active experimentation) has been foundational for many texts in adult education and training, in particular. But these are generalized concepts and can lack the specificity your students and audiences may need for a specific context. So consider creating your own learning cycle. You can take the best from the life of Copernicus, the Kolb model or others who inspire you, integrate these into the uniqueness of your context, the environment in which you work and the specific learning outcomes you have in mind, to create a cycle or process that best serves your needs and the needs of those with whom you work.

Here are some questions to consider: What are some of the underlying assumptions and experiences of your class, organization, business or group? Do you want to focus on the process, the end product, or both? How much active participation will you expect? How can group members assist and support each other, creating a learning community that can help everyone? From responses to these questions, try to create your own learning cycle and use that model to inspire others.

MARCH
Tips #25-36

In March of 1475 legendary artist Michelangelo was born in Italy and gave a lifetime of inspired art to the world. In March of 1933 President Franklin D. Roosevelt offered his challenge to a demoralized America deep in the throes of the Great Depression—"Let me assert my firm belief that the only thing we have to fear is fear itself." In March of 1961, at a time when most people associated the word "Corps" with the U.S. Marines, President John F. Kennedy followed up his inspirational challenge—"Ask not what your country can do for you but what you can do for your country"—with the establishment of the Peace Corps.

#25. View the world through a systems lens

Completed in March of 1936, the Hoover Dam on the Colorado River in Nevada was a massive public works project during the Great Depression in the United States. The dam was intended to help control floods, provide irrigation water and produce hydroelectric power, all potentially positive factors in something sustainable, i.e., that would contribute to the interconnected health of the environment, society and the economy, the "triple bottom line." A concrete structure of this size had never been built before and some of the techniques used were unproven. However, once completed problems with impacts on the environment became clear. For six years as Lake Mead filled, virtually no water reached the mouth of the river in Mexico and real damage was done to the downriver surroundings including plants and native fish species. The following "tip" is adapted from #12 in *147 Practical Tips for Teaching Sustainability.*

> Think about the Hoover Dam and its impact. What could have been anticipated? What could not have been known and what options exist for remediation of the damage done. David Schaller, formerly with the Environmental Protection Agency, notes that everything in nature is connected and that nature is constantly making itself anew and taking itself apart again for the benefit of the larger system. He insists that there is never any waste or

unemployment in nature and that in nature, change is constant
but the time scales are often long and the feedback loops difficult
to observe. Schaller wants us to slow down and observe so that
we can see the causes and effects of the change that is going on
around and under us, and thus understand better the richness of
the systems framework. He also wants us to challenge narrow,
disciplinary, short-term approaches with systems thinking and
inspiration can follow.

Adapt exercises to stretch and build learning and systems thinking capabilities by using
Booth Sweeney and Meadows (2010) The Systems Thinking Playbook. *Have people*
practice using interdisciplinary thinking. Develop assignments that have them draw on
ideas, principles, theories, metaphors and more from their various subjects.

#26. Take a bigger perspective

In March of 1974 work began on the Trans-Alaska Pipeline which was built under very difficult conditions to augment U.S. energy supplies and transport North
Slope oil at Prudhoe Bay to an ice free port at Valdez some 800 miles to the south.
In most places it is about five feet above ground to allow passage of wildlife underneath. Several incidents of oil leakage have occurred including damage from
sabotage, maintenance failures, natural disasters, and bullet holes. Since the start-
up, seven incidents and accidents have caused the pipeline to be shut down. The
overall impact of the pipeline has been enormous including economic, physical
and social repercussions. Native peoples have complained that the pipeline cross-
es some of their traditional lands yet no economic benefits would come their way.
Their complaints have served to inspire others. The following "Tip" is adapted
from #10 in *147 Practical Tips for Teaching Sustainability.*

> Given the history of the Trans-Alaska Pipeline, consider that the
> last hundred years has been a time of unprecedented growth and
> change. Over this short time period, we have seen the emergence
> of cars and planes as well as flights to the moon and beyond. We
> now live in a time of rapidly evolving technologies: computers, the
> internet, e-mail, social media (Facebook, Twitter, Instagram), cell

phones, television, radio, and more. We are constantly stretched to handle all this information in an increasingly fast world. What do all these advances in technology say, if anything, about a project like this pipeline? For example, even in hindsight, could advances in solar technology have offered a viable alternative to the costs of this project with much less risk to the environment?

Take a "bigger perspective" and discuss what has changed for you with respect to what is truly sustainable in your community. Identify what has changed in your field. Consider the gains and losses. Has the growth and change been sustainable? What has inspired you?

#27. Connect the dots

On March 23, 2010 the Affordable Care Act (ACA) was signed into law by President Barack Obama, what many consider to have been an inspired step in the right direction toward a more inclusive and effective national health care system. The ACA—or "Obamacare" as its opponents termed it, working feverishly to tar and feather its passage—extended health care to 20-24 million more Americans and expanded access to Medicaid for the poor. The following "tip" is adapted from #13 in *147 Practical Tips for Teaching Sustainability*.

The "cancer alley" of Louisiana's petrochemical industries has left many in the poorest, African-American communities there facing the deadliest environmental and health hazards with few apparent economic possibilities for sustainable solutions. Robert Bullard (2005) has worked at Clark Atlanta University's Environmental Justice Resource Center. In the immediate aftermath of Hurricane Katrina in 2005, he noted that problems of social class, ethnicity and environmental threats were clearly evident in the 1970's when his study unearthed the fact that "every one of the city-owned landfills was located in a predominantly black neighborhood even though blacks made up a quarter of the population.... The hurricane highlighted some glaring inequities that most people would not see just by visiting the French Quarter. The fact is New Orleans is 67 percent black, and almost half the children live

below the poverty level. The issues of race and poverty are out of
the closet, and we can no longer deny that we've done a lousy job
addressing the environmental, as well as economic and social issues, in this country…. Katrina supports what environmental-jus-
tice activists have been saying for more than three decades: When
you connect the dots and look at the facts, it's irrefutable that all
communities are not created equal. If a community happens to be
poor, or a community of color, or located on the wrong side of the
tracks, it gets unequal protection" (pp. 28-29).

*Identify the interplay of factors that underlie these problems and possible
solutions. Concerns about environmental justice force us to see the mix of
related factors that constrain any solution.*

#28. Emphasize critical and creative thinking

In March of 1991, officers from the Los Angeles Police Department stopped Rodney King after a high speed chase and then several beat him savagely as others
watched. A witness videotaped the incident from a nearby balcony and sent the
footage to a local news station. Parts of the footage then went viral world-wide, inspiring protests of rage, especially among the African American residents of LA. In
the aftermath, four officers were charged with assault with a deadly weapon and
use of excessive force and three were acquitted of all charges while the Jury de-
liberated about the charges against the fourth officer. The 1992 LA riots exploded
from the ensuing outrage, lasting six days and costing the lives of 55 people with
more than 2,000 injured. The rioting ended when the governor sent in the state's
National Guard. When the federal government then stepped in to prosecute on the
grounds of civil rights violations, two of the four officers were found guilty and
sentenced to prison. The following "Tip" is adapted from #13 in *147 Practical Tips
for Teaching Diversity.*

At its core, a college or university education has often meant
questioning even the most cherished of traditional beliefs, searching for better explanations, and being open to the dictates of evidence, logic, and argument. Learning will deepen as students

move beyond simplistic, dichotomous expectations about right/ wrong answers and become better able to accept varied opinions and multiple perspectives. Learning will deepen when students can go beyond merely accepting differences and ask about the coherent logic of underlying explanations and theories. In the Rodney King case, history has shown how routinely juries and judges side with police officers when challenges are raised.

Working with students in a course on Native American history in its all too frequent tragic collision with U.S. courts, laws and enforcement, Roe Bubar and Irene Vernon (2003) emphasize critical thinking: "We encourage students to support their statements with logical arguments, and to take responsibility for what they say. This helps them master the complexities associated with learning and speaking intelligently. Students are taught that they must be able to explain how they come to their conclusions. They must examine their thought processes, including their own preconceived notions and biases" (p.161).

Encourage your students, colleagues, friends, family and neighbors to think critically. For example, you could have people write down a particular point they want to make and then list the support that exists for that point. Then have them pair off and each partner critique the other's arguments. Ask for people to volunteer to have others critique their arguments. Affirm the value of this kind of critical analysis for inspiring improvement for any issue of importance, especially when emotions run high.

#29. Make use of different perspectives and rethink reactions

In March of 1956, the U.S. Supreme Court upheld a ban on racial segregation in state schools, colleges and universities. The University of North Carolina had appealed a 1954 ruling that ordered college officials to admit three black students to what was previously an all-white institution. The court ruling, that the principle of "separate but equal" had no place in the field of public education, inspired many to challenge segregation and the legacy of slavery and state-enshrined racism. The following "tip" is adapted from #14 in *147 Practical Tips for Teaching Diversity*.

As Roe Bubar and Irene Vernon (2003) write, "Students who represent worldviews that differ from the majority challenge others to re-examine their perspectives and ideas that most simply take for granted as true. All of our students seem to benefit from the introduction of other paradigms and diverse world views" (p.159).

In a *New York Times* article on November 11, 2015 that chronicles issues of race and discrimination on college campuses across America, Hartocollis and Bidgoodnov provide context and insight for the resurgence of college student activism and nonviolent public protest. While the ultimate effects of these student-led demonstrations are as yet undetermined, many college administrators and leaders have been compelled to take notice and action. The leadership, grassroots organizing, and civil disobedience of students have created a groundswell of protests that have emboldened and empowered many to call into question political correctness, systemic discrimination, and the conscious and unconscious biases and practices that advantage some while marginalizing others.

Finally, in the *Book of Joy* (Lama and Tutu, 2016), Bishop Desmond Tutu, a victim of apartheid in South Africa but a tireless proponent of forgiveness and reconciliation, challenges us when we look back at events to see the progress being made despite the continuing controversies that persist: "You can be helped to look at the world and see a different perspective … Where some people see a half-empty cup, you can see it as half-full" (pp. 241-242).

People often value the opportunity to share their perspectives with each other. Find ways to surface differing reactions, beliefs, and perspectives. For example, use role-playing to surface alternative views. Ask individuals to represent certain groups whose perspectives have not surfaced.

#30. Help students stretch and develop a compassionate concern for others

In March of 1930, Mohandas Gandhi set out on his march of nonviolent civil disobedience to harvest sea salt from the ocean and protest British rule in India that had reserved all salt mining to its own enterprise and profit. This march covered 240 miles, attracted great publicity and inspired nearly 60,000 to allow themselves to be arrested. Ultimately Britain ceded independence in 1947 just prior to Gandhi's death at the hands of an assassin. World-wide compassion and concern emerged as a key ally in challenging longstanding British claims to "rightful controls in their empire." The following concept is adapted from "tip" #17 in *147 Practical Tips for Teaching Diversity.*

> Roe Bubar and Irene Vernon (2003) offer an example of helping their students stretch: "By encouraging students to reach out beyond their own ethnocentricity and culture, beyond their own sense of worldview, we try to encourage students to develop a better understanding of each other. For example, when a student says she herself did not steal Native lands and does not see why tribes should have any right to get those lands back a hundred years later, we pose questions for the class about the ethics and values of our society, world opinion, and our own justice system.... Regardless of how the colonials and Founding Fathers chose to act, we encourage our students to consider how legal decisions could have been decided, how society should conduct itself, and what values and morals we should advocate" (pp. 163-164). In turn people of British descent can be challenged to rethink their history of empire, exploitation and profit.

> The Dalai Lama (Lama & Tutu, 2016) goes further and insists that a preoccupation with the self can be very damaging to a wider perspective. He argues that "[too] much self-centered thinking is the source of suffering. A compassionate concern for others' well-being is the source of happiness." Desmond Tutu adds: "We are growing and learning how to be compassionate, how to be caring, how to be human" (p. 251).

In their chapter in *Social Work: A Profession of Many Faces*, Morales, Sheafor and Scott (2012, pp. 421-422) provide contexts for their students to critically reflect on the values that are central to their profession while simultaneously promoting the general welfare of people generally. Reminding students of the core values of service, social justice, dignity, and the worth of the person, of the importance of human relationships, integrity and competence, combines to provide a foundation for essential reflection and comparison, what everyone needs to rethink earlier time periods and how we can move forward.

At the end of a discussion, ask everyone to assess the stretching that British and Indian people needed to do to undo generations of colonial controls. Then ask what "stretching" needs to be done today and by each individual. Discuss how well everyone was able to understand the different perspectives expressed. Did their images about themselves interfere with their analyses? Did a concern for others and compassion for their well-being enter into their thinking?

#31. Inspire and learn through international service

In March of 1961, as the Cold War continued with many fearing the inevitability of a nuclear exchange between the U.S. and the U.S.S.R., President John F. Kennedy established the Peace Corps by executive order, beginning a tradition of international service that inspired thousands of Americans to volunteer and learn more about people in the far reaches of the planet, especially those in poor and developing areas. Since its inception some 200,000 volunteers have now served in 139 countries. Today the call of the Peace Corps continues to expand, now resonating more with older and more specialized volunteers. The appeal of this program over so many years provides another model for increasing global understanding in our increasingly interdependent world. The following "tip" is adapted from #13 in *147 Practical Tips for Peace and Reconciliation*.

Peace scholar and professor, Jing Lin (2006, p. 315), advocates for a global ethic of universal love, forgiveness, and reconciliation; she provides a constructive, optimistic critique of the very purposes of education in the United States and around the world when the daily reports of violence and conflict indicate such a clear need for increased understanding and appreciation among countries and populations. In her co-edited book, *Transforming Education for Peace*, Lin (2006) argues for a paradigm shift where the teaching of love comprises the central purpose of education. Lin maintains, "I envision our future schools will shift from a mechanical, function-alistic perspective that primarily emphasizes tests and efficiency, to a constructive, transformative paradigm where students' intel-lectual, moral, emotional, spiritual, and ecological abilities are de-veloped in order to promote understanding of the world and help nurture love and respect for all human beings and nature. In all, constructing a loving world should be the central purpose of edu-cation in the twenty-first century." Pairing that ethic with service in the Peace Corps, for example, provides a context for reaching Lin's vision in a realistic manner.

Ask everyone to envision the ideal program, school, community, nation, or world where love serves as the foundational means and ends of education. Can Peace Corps serve that role? Describe the curriculum, how teaching is conducted, how people are assessed on their capacities for providing needed services as well as love, and how the policy context and rule of law shape the containers in which cultural actors engage in everyday actions.

#32. Learn from those who have had experience with occupation and violence

Inspired to break free of European colonial controls in the mid-twentieth century, Ghana gained its independence from England in March of 1957. The Portuguese had been the first Europeans to arrive in the late 15th century and eventually built up trade for gold, ivory and pepper. Captured in local wars, slaves had long been used as labor and for trade between African tribes within the region and eventual-ly for sale to various colonizers. With a growing population of 28 million plus and a robust economic growth, Ghana is considered to be one of the more stable coun-tries in West Africa since its transition to a multi-party democracy in 1992. There is so much we can all learn from Ghanaians and their struggles for independence and self-determination. The following "tip" is adapted from #36 in *147 Practical Tips for Peace and Reconciliation*.

> After World War Two, the super powers were serving as occupying forces. In *Long Shadows* (Giffey, 2006), Cold War veteran Don Kliese remembers being stationed in Germany during the 1980's when international tensions between East and West were high, when the "sword rattling" between the U.S. and the U.S.S.R., in particular, was intense and unnerving, when national security was encased within a nuclear arms race, and talk of "mutually assured destruction" was at the core of U.S. defense thinking. As an infantry man, Kliese often patrolled the border between East and West Germany, at times a few feet apart from East German troops. Yet, he remembers how kind the German people were, the horrors of their own experience in war so very recent and raw. "They always expressed such a deep sadness to see young men such as us primed for war. They had lived it. They lived it in such ways that we could never even begin to comprehend. So many of them were really sad and angry. They would say to us: 'We don't want to see you live what we did, and we're so afraid that's what's going to happen again.' . . . It's a mixed feeling when you serve in the military. It's that sense of pride of having served, but also a sense of despair about what you did" (p. 254).

Many scholars believe that the televised images of the Vietnam War had much to do with the eventual decline in U.S. public support and why the Pentagon has been so intent on managing the news coming out of subsequent wars and military operations. When have you seen the devastation of war or a struggle for independence like what occurred in Ghana? How did it affect you? Others? How can the "experience" of war or independence be built into the education we need for inspiring efforts for peace and reconciliation? Can we make better use of film clips, documentaries, and theater productions? Atwood Publishing has produced a DVD of several of these veterans speaking about their contributions to the Long Shadows book. Visit their website (http://www.atwoodpublishing.com) and look under "Bookshelf" and "Social Justice."

#33. Employ patience, perspective and perseverance for peace

In March of 1939, the Spanish Civil War ended when the Republican defenders of Madrid raised the white flag over the city, bringing to an end the bloody three-year civil war and presaging the rise of Fascist military threats all over Europe. Having won the election of 1931 to abolish the monarchy in favor of a liberal republic, Spain saw many liberal reforms enacted by a coalition of organized labor, progressives, socialists and others. However, wealthy land owners, the church and a large faction in the military began to employ violence and in July 1936 General Francisco Franco led a right-wing army revolt. Franco soon consolidated forces under Spain's fascist party and courted aid from Hitler's Germany and Mussolini's Italy. While the Soviet Union provided assistance to the Republic the other European nations and the United States imposed an embargo in an effort to "contain the fighting." However, inspired by a call to defeat fascism, volunteers from around the world came to Spain's defense as members of the International Brigades that included 1,200 from the U.S. organized as the Lincoln Brigade. They hoped that their sacrifices might rally support others. Sadly, their sacrifices were ignored and in 1941 the world exploded into a world war that would take more than 70 million lives.

After World War Two ended, Spain continued to be ruled by Franco and former Republicans were hunted, executed or otherwise disappeared. Schools and teachers were on notice to ignore this history and teach only what Franco and his allies wanted to hear. As an opponent to Communism, Franco was quick to earn the support of the U.S. and other Western allies during the Cold War that quickly pushed into that vacuum when Germany, Italy and Japan surrendered.

After Franco died in 1975, Spain began a transition to democracy and eventually joined the European Economic Community and NATO. Obviously, patience and persistence were keys to this journey out of civil war and dictatorship. The following idea is adapted from "tip" #38 in *147 Practical Tips for Peace and Reconciliation.*

> Visiting the Grand Canyon in the U.S. invariably evokes feelings of awe. Standing on the north rim, Bill Timpson noted how small the Colorado River appeared off in the distance far below. "It's mind boggling to imagine the workings of weather and water over the past two billion years combining their forces to whittle

the smallest crevices into gigantic canyons, the sturdiest boulders eventually into pebbles and sand. As a peace scholar who is frequently frustrated at the slow pace of change, a visit to this canyon is a helpful reminder about the importance of patience and perseverance in supporting positive change and sustaining the peace movement, that small and personal contributions in different communities across the planet will, in time, chisel out the dark overhangs of violence and dissolve them into a free flowing and life affirming river of peace and reconciliation."

Find photographs and descriptions of the Grand Canyon. Where do you find the patience and inspiration you need to promote positive change, peace and reconciliation?

#34. Celebrate exploration, invention and failures

Born in March of 1847, Alexander Graham Bell was a Scottish-born scientist, inventor, engineer and champion of innovation who is credited with patenting the first practical telephone in 1876. Because of deafness in his own family and his own struggles with hearing, Bell began early on to research hearing and speech and experiment with various devices. His other patents included work on the telegraph, the phonograph, alternative fuels, a form of air conditioner that blew air over melting ice, and an attempt to put sound onto magnetic tape, an idea that later became the foundation for the tape recorder, the hard and floppy disc drives and other magnetic media. A voracious reader, Bell was constantly inspired to explore new frontiers and experiment with various inventions, persevering through every false start toward something of progress. The following "tip" is adapted from #17 in *147 Practical Tips for Using Experiential Learning*.

Jacqueline McGinty makes a case for allowing students to learn from their experiences. "As educators, we can direct our classes in many different ways. When designing course projects and assessments, we want to ensure the greatest possibility for students to be successful. We can be clear in our instructions, allow time for students to ask questions, and give them the tools that they will need. However, if you can remove some of the pressure for 'getting it right' or 'earning an A', then you can provide space for students to try out new ideas and take some necessary risks."

In his riveting book and video for *The Last Lecture*, Randy Pausch (2008), knowing that he was dying from cancer, offers the following advice: "Experience is what you get when you didn't get what you wanted. That's an expression I learned when I took a sabbatical at Electronic Arts, the video-game maker. It just stuck with me, and I've ended up repeating it again and again to students. It's a phrase worth considering at every brick wall we encounter, and at every disappointment. It's also a reminder that failure is not just acceptable, it's often essential" (p.148).

Identify those experiences that you initially thought were failures but later proved to be inspirational. List the various ways you could build this kind of experience and insight into an upcoming class, presentation or discussion. As a teacher or presenter you can create assignments that allow students and others to make revisions based on your feedback.

#35. Promote divergent thinking

In March of 2003 President George W. Bush announced that war had begun against Iraq. Bush recruited participation from 35 other countries for this preemptive attack despite the warnings from the United Nations weapons inspectors that there was no evidence of the weapons of mass destruction that the U.S. President claimed. In hindsight, this attack seemed to have been inspired by the experiences of the September 11th attacks on the World Trade Center and the Pentagon when the shock gave way to a desire for quick revenge by many of the more hawkish Americans. The following "tip" is adapted from #18 in *147 Practical Tips for Using Experiential Learning*.

A 1968 study by George Land and Beth Jarman (1992) gave 1,600 3-5 year olds a creativity test used by NASA to measure divergent thinking in engineers and scientists. They then re-tested the same children at 10 years of age and then again at 15 years of age. Their findings were alarming. While 98% of children 3-5 years of age scored at the genius level on the creativity test, only 32% of the same children did so at ages 8-10, and then only 10% did do at 13-15 years of age. Moreover, the researchers gave the same test to a large group of adults over the age of 25 and only 2% of those participants scored at the genius level. One thing these people had in common was that they had all been through the modern educational system. The essential question for Americans and others is whether a democracy can remain healthy without dissent, without the scrutiny that comes with practice in critical thinking?

Divergent thinking is the ability to see many possible answers to a question and to see many possible ways to interpret a question. Sir Ken Robinson, an internationally recognized leader in connecting education, creativity and innovation, gave a famous TED speech in 2006 on the changing paradigms in these areas. He believes that modern education is depressing divergent thinking and creativity, an essential capacity for divergent thinking. A high IQ alone does not guarantee creativity. Instead, personality traits that promote divergent thinking are more important. Divergent thinking is found among people with personalities which have traits such as nonconformity, curiosity, a willingness to take risks, and persistence (Wade & Tavris, 2017). We will need students who are divergent thinkers to confront the issues and solve the problems of the 21st century. Once the patriotic euphoria waned, public opinion slowly turned as the evidence emerged about the lack of any connection between the 9-11 attacks and Iraq. The rush by many Americans to enact revenge had tragic consequences with enormous, enduring chaos within Iraq and far too many deaths on both sides. Our only hope is that this tragedy will inspire more careful scrutiny of perceived threats in the future as well as the emotional intelligence to avoid the pitfalls of angry overreactions.

Reflect on the various ways in which your own divergent thinking has been nurtured or stifled. List what you could do to promote divergent thinking in an upcoming presentation or activity. What other examples can you see where emotions clouded reason and led to tragic consequences?

#36. Walk in their shoes

On March 26, 1979, the Egypt-Israel Peace Treaty was signed in Washington, D.C. following the 1978 Camp David Accords. Having been invited to these talks by U.S. President Jimmy Carter, Egyptian President Anwar Sadat and Israeli Prime Minister Menachem Begin signed their names and the world was inspired by what had seemed impossible. Israel returned land it had seized during the Six-Day War while Egypt agreed to allow Israel free passage of ships through the Suez Canal. It is notable that with this act Egypt became the first Arab state to officially recognize Israel. We have to believe that having these experiences on neutral ground in the U.S. and mediated by a U.S. President eager for results had much to do with the ultimate success of these talks. Far from the glare of their own nations, Sadat and Begin could feel more free to "walk in each other's shoes" and better understand each other. The following "tip" is adapted from #20 in *147 Practical Tips for Using Experiential Learning*.

As a teacher of adults, Jacqueline McGinty understands that there are many things that teachers need to attend to in their classrooms. "I deliver subject matter, provide feedback and assessments, and engage students in the course material. Yet I also know that we as instructors spend much of our lives rooted in our role as experts, paying homage to our own disciplinary paradigms and then presenting our ideas in class. There we see students but do we ever stop to ask ourselves who they really are and what it might be like to live their lives? How do they see the course content and our teaching style? We often reflect upon ourselves and our own beliefs; how often do we take time to reflect upon the experience of each learner" (pp. 43-44)? How often do we ask ourselves what life is like in their shoes?

McGinty continues: "In a course that I am teaching I decided to give the students a questionnaire about themselves. I was noticing that in class they often appeared tired or preoccupied. I began to wonder what aspects of their lives outside of class may be affecting their experiences in class. I asked them where they worked and how far they had to drive to get to class? The course is late in the evening and many of the students have another class before-hand. I wondered if they had a chance to eat dinner. Were they full time students? Parents? What else is going on that could impact their learning (p. 44)?

"When I look at my students holistically, I think I can uncover hidden dimensions that allow for greater synthesis and transformation. Reading the answers to the student questionnaires gave me the opportunity to 'walk for a moment in their shoes.' It provided me with valuable perspectives on their realities. It also provided me with an opportunity to look beyond myself and my own experiences. This helped me to see my students more as individuals and less as a sea of people before me. In the *Pedagogy of the Oppressed*, Paulo Freire (2007) wrote: 'Revolutionary leaders commit many errors and miscalculations by not taking into account something so real as the people's view of the world: a view which explicitly and implicitly contains their concerns, their doubts, their hopes, their way of seeing the leaders, their perceptions of themselves and of the oppressors, their religious beliefs (almost always syncretic), their fatalism, their rebellious reactions. None of these elements can be seen separately, for in interaction all of them compose a totality'"(p. 182).

List the various ways by which you could better know your students, co-workers, friends and neighbors, what interests them and who they are as individuals. What would you learn by "walking in their shoes"? Why is this kind of imagined experience so effective?

APRIL
Tips #37-48

The changes in climate assure us that warmer weather is indeed coming to the northern hemisphere with new growth while those in the southern hemisphere may be preparing for the coming cold and the Fall harvests. Particular innovations may only succeed for a short time yet some will endure and have inspired a kind of folklore through the ages. In April of 1860, the Pony Express burst on the scene in the West to get mail across a landscape that had no other means of communication. For five dollars an ounce, letters could be delivered in ten days across the 2,000 miles from Missouri to California. The famed riders each rode 75-100 miles before handing off the letters to the next rider. This service only lasted ten years when it was replaced by the completion of the overland telegraph.

#37. Study hard for a sustainable future

In April of 1635, Puritans established the Boston Latin School (BLS) as the first school in the U.S. so that the male offspring of those early colonists could read the Bible and receive spiritual and moral instruction. Modeled after similar schools in Europe, BLS emphasized the learning of religion, Latin and classical literature. Currently, BLS is an exam-based public school and continues to receive much recognition for the achievements of its graduates. Given the enormity of the environmental impacts that humans are having, we will need more schools that produce high performing graduates. A commitment to study all these interrelated effects, to cooperate with others and to share the results will go far and surface constructive possibilities. The following idea is adapted from "tip" #17 in *147 Practical Tips for Teaching Sustainability*

> Many communities have the opportunity to remake themselves in a different mold following the damage caused by natural disasters. What would happen if your own community were impacted? Work with people to imagine how it could be redesigned to be more in harmony with the environment, more supportive of healthy communities and more equitable in its distribution of

resources. How would focused and extended study help?

One educator is fond of repeating: "The stone age didn't end because of the lack of rocks! In advocating for new ways to think and act, it's easy to hang on to what you fear might be lost in the transition. However, the benefits of a sustainable economy and healthy environment will only happen when we move past the 'unsustainable stones' of waste, exploitation and unfairness." And figuring out how to moving past those "stones" will require committed study.

Ask yourself and others: What "stones" need to be removed for your own area or community to repair damages from the past and inspire a move forward toward sustainability? Where can you study those "stones" and develop alternative plans?

38. Assign a voice for the future

On April 26, 1986 the nuclear power plant experienced a horrific accident at Chernobyl in the Ukraine in what was then the USSR. An explosion in the core occurred during an emergency shutdown of the reactor while undergoing power failure safety experiments. The problems seem to have arisen from basic design flaws as well as human error that sparked uncontrolled reactions conditions. Fires produced updrafts which carried plumes of fission products into the atmosphere, eventually leading to fall-out of radioactive material over much of the surface of the western Soviet Union and Europe. The remains of the Number 4 reactor were enclosed in a large radiation shield. This accident inspired safety upgrades on all remaining Soviet-designed reactors although seven of these plants continued to power electric grids.

As for the environmental damage, we now estimate that over four hundred times more radioactive material was released from Chernobyl than by the atomic bombing of Hiroshima. Weather impacted the spread and rain was purposely seeded over Belorussia in an effort to remove radioactive particles. Questions about safety and disposal of radioactive waste remain. As of 2017, thirty countries around the world are operating 449 nuclear reactors for the generation of electricity and 60 new plants were under construction in 15 countries. In 2014 nuclear power plants provided 11 percent of total electricity production. The following "tip" is adapted from #18 in *147 Practical Tips for Teaching Sustainability.*

> Accountability is an essential component of any discussion about sustainability. As a business, program, or organization, it is tempting to grow fast or big. That growth can have adverse economic, social and ecological impacts, especially when there are safety concerns for a volatile commodity and unresolved, long-term storage issues. Yet energy demands are growing relentlessly. Putting someone in the role of "defender of future generations" can give the future a voice for asking about the impact of various decisions on our economy, community and natural environment years from now. When someone is given the license to look ahead and serve as a spokesperson for the planet, the insights that arise are often remarkable.

In a discussion or debate, assign one individual to be the "advocate" or "watchdog" for future generations, offering perspectives and inspiration that might otherwise be missed. Does the "pre-cautionary principle" hold, i.e., that we should err on the side of caution when there are serious questions and doubts to be addressed?

#39. Consult visionary frameworks

In April of 2010, the Deepwater Horizon drilling rig, owned by Transocean and leased to British Petroleum (BP), exploded from an uncontrolled blowout in the Gulf of Mexico and ignited a massive fireball that killed several crew members. The fire could not be extinguished and two days later the rig sank, leaving the well gushing oil and causing the largest oil spill in U.S. history. During its 10-year lifetime, the rig had received 5 citations for non-compliance, 4 of which were in 2002 and included problems with safety and blowout protection. Industry and regulatory "experts", however, seemed to agree that this rig had a "strong" record of safety. Ultimately Transocean agreed to pay $1.4 billion for violations of the U.S. Clean Water Act. Other fines to BP followed as well as settlements from BP and Halliburton, a project contractor.

Globally, offshore oil production accounted for approximately 30% of total oil production. While advances in technology make deep water drilling more accessible, shallow water drilling dominates because of the fewer unknowns. The U.S. and Brazil account for more than 90% of global ultra-deep water production. Given the press and competition for sources of energy, how do we step back and consult with what we see as visionary for the health of life on earth? The following "tip" is adapted from #19 in *147 Practical Tips for Teaching Sustainability.*

> The Earth Charter: Responding to a call by the United Nations in 1987, a declaration of fundamental principles was authored for building a just, sustainable, and peaceful global society in the 21st century. It seeks to inspire in all peoples a new sense of global interdependence and shared responsibility for the well-being of the human family and the larger living world. It is an expression of hope and a call to help create a global partnership at a critical juncture in history." See: earthcharter.org

> The Natural Step: Founded in Sweden in 1989, this organization supports science and systems-based approaches to organizational planning for sustainability that provide a practical set of design criteria which can be used to direct social, environmental, and economic actions. See: thenaturalstep.org

> The Talloires Declaration: With discussions beginning in 1990, this was a ten-point action plan for incorporating sustainability and environmental literacy in teaching, research, operations and outreach at colleges and universities. It was assigned by over 300 university presidents and chancellors in over 40 countries. See: ulsf.org/talloires-declaration

Take a breather from the details and the numbers, the data and the critiques. Consult these visionary statements as well as others for reflection, discussion and inspiration.

#40. Invite new thinking

In April of 1968, Martin Luther, Jr. was shot and killed while he stood on the balcony of the Lorraine Motel in Memphis, Tennessee. James Earl Ray, a fugitive from the Missouri State Penitentiary, was arrested on June 8 and sentenced to 99 years in prison after pleading guilty in October of 1969. Ray made several unsuccessful attempts to withdraw his guilty plea, implying that others had been involved, and later died in prison at the age of 70. The King family alleged a conspiracy involving the government.

Because of his prominence in the Civil Rights Movement and later after his denunciation of the Vietnam War, King had received many death threats. Bravely he carried on, emphasizing how the movement would endure. He had gone to Memphis to support the striking African American sanitation workers who were paid considerably less than white workers and suffered from unsafe conditions. On his flight there to speak, King's plane had received a bomb threat, inspiring King in his famous but ominous address "I've been to the Mountaintop" (1968) where he said, "Like anybody, I would like to live a long life. Longevity has its place. But I'm not concerned about that now. I just want to do God's will. And He's allowed me to go to the mountaintop. And I've looked over. And I've seen the promised land. I may not get there with you. But I want you to know tonight, that we, as a people, will get to the promised land. And so I'm happy, tonight. I'm not worried about anything. I'm not fearing any man. My eyes have seen the glory of the Lord."

For some, King's assassination meant the end of the strategy of nonviolence as riots broke out in major cities across America. As time passes, how do we continue to learn from this tragedy? How do we rethink our current values, policies and practices and move more confidently into the future? The following "tip" is adapted from #16 in *147 Practical Tips for Teaching Diversity*.

> Every moment can be a gift for learning. In their book, the Dalai Lama and Bishop Desmond Tutu (2016) reference the comments by David Steindl-Rast, a Catholic Benedictine monk with a long-standing commitment to interfaith dialogue: "Every moment is a gift. There is no certainty that you will have another moment, with all the opportunity that it contains. The gift within every gift

is the opportunity it offers us. More often it is the opportunity to enjoy it, but sometimes a difficult gift is given to us and that can be an opportunity to rise to the challenge" (pp. 242-243). However difficult to see in the context of an assassination of a revered leader, the joys and tensions that come with work on diversity can be both gift and challenge. King himself believed that the work for equal rights, justice and a better future for all Americans would continue.

Consider how Rosemary Kreston (2003, in Timpson, et al.) invites new thinking: "I begin the course by explaining that my interest is to give students an opportunity to 'think' about disability differently. The students are invited to be open-minded and to contribute what they know from their own experiences, recognizing that each person may have a somewhat different familiarity with disability but a piece that can contribute to a more complete understanding" (pp. 173-174).

Change demands innovation. Without pretending to know all the answers, we can design our classes and discussions to explore a range of possibilities. We are all captives of limited experiences and belief systems. Revisit the ground rules you have for class or other groups and ask those participating to understand perspectives very different from their own. Utilize case studies similar to what we referenced here about the life of Martin Luther King, Jr. where students get to play different roles and develop empathy for different perspectives in an effort to sustain momentum toward a "promised land."

#41. Develop leadership skills

In April of 1887 the first woman mayor was elected in the U.S. in Argonia, Kansas. In 2018, there were more women than ever before running for the U.S. Congress. Some 374 female candidates were seeking seats in the House of Representatives—smashing the previous high of 298 in 2012—and 42 are trying to reach the Senate. Much of the surge comes from Democratic women seeking to unseat Republican incumbents after Hillary Clinton failed to become the first female president in 2016. There are hopes of recreating the so-called "Year of the Woman" in 1992, when scandal in Washington D.C. and a national debate about sexism triggered a jump in the number of congresswomen. Inspired by these changes, the number of women running for Congress has been rising over recent years, but we can already see a dramatic jump. The following "tip" is adapted from #66 in *147 Practical Tips for Teaching Diversity.*

> Learning is always a shared journey. The more you can help students—and others—develop the skills they need to communicate effectively, the more they should be willing to assume greater responsibility for their own learning and the more likely they can learn the lessons of diversity and the benefits for themselves (Timpson, Canetto, Borrayo and Yang (Eds.), 2003). Moreover, the research on cooperative learning is extensive and clear, i.e., the prosocial skills of effective communication, cooperation, negotiation and consensus make group learning more successful (Timpson and Doe, 2008).
>
> In addition, we can encourage students and others to select issues of critical importance to them, cases that reflect one of their more salient identities. Ask them to share the privilege and/or challenges related to this identity with others. On occasion in his social work classes, Malcolm Scott has used a grounding framework for students to explore their visible and invisible identities. This provides an opportunity for honesty, openness, and transparency within our class while simultaneously allowing students to practice leadership, responsibility, and effective communication.

Spend some time early on, drafting ground rules about effective, open and respectful communication. How can you inspire people to be more responsible for their own learning? Periodically revisit these rules, assess what has occurred since you adopted them, and consider any modifications needed. Build in opportunities for people to practice and then assess their use of these skills. Group work can be a very effective laboratory for highlighting needs, exploring various responses and providing opportunities for practice.

#42. Be alert to problems and then challenge stereotypes and assumptions

In April of 2001 same sex marriage became legal in the Netherlands, the first country to allow it. It was not until the U.S. Supreme Court ruled on June 26, 2015 that state-level bans on same-sex marriages were ruled unconstitutional. The court ruled that Due Process and the Equal Protection clauses of the Fourteenth Amendment had been violated by these bans. Although "Gay and Lesbian Rights" had been a loud rallying cry for activists for many years, positive public opinion had been slowly shifting upward and reached almost 60% by 2015. The call for equal treatment under the law and the accommodation of same-sex partners for purposes of health care proved decisive. The following "tip" is adapted from #21 in *147 Practical Tips for Teaching Diversity.*

> In an August 11, 2016, article for the *New York Times,* Jan Hoffman reports that the first nationwide study to ask high school students about their sexuality found that gay, lesbian and bisexual teenagers were at far greater risk for depression, bullying and many types of violence than their straight peers. More than 40 percent of these students reported that they had seriously considered suicide, and 29 percent had made attempts to do so in the previous year. The percentage of those who used illegal drugs was much higher than their heterosexual peers. Some 15,600 students across the country, ages 14 to 17, took the survey. The population who identified as a sexual minority is in line with estimates from other state or local surveys, and with national studies of young adults. While the figures paint a portrait of loneliness and discrimination that is longstanding and sadly familiar, they are important because they now establish a national databank. While these data may overwhelm an inexperienced instructor, others will see opportunities to challenge assumptions and promote new thinking.

> James Banning, who taught in the School of Education at Colorado State University for many years, recommends two exercises for challenging the way that students think.

> For the first activity, ask people to identify as many associations

as they can between animals and personality characteristics or behaviors. For example, stubborn as an ox, cute as a bug, soft as a
kitten, brave as a lion, and so on. Record their contributions on the
board. It usually takes about 15-30 minutes for people to exhaust
the possibilities. Then, them which sex is usually associated with
each of the animals listed.

In our culture we stereotypically associate kittens as female, oxen
as male, dogs as male, and so on. Once everyone has assigned the
label of male or female to each of the animals, then the person-
ality/behavior characteristics associated with the animals can be
summarized by sex. This exercise brings out the point that our
culture has taught us stereotypical ways of viewing masculine
and feminine characteristics even in the simple descriptions of
animal traits.

For the second activity, Banning reads the following list of "cultural" sayings and asks participants to shout out the words to fill
in the blanks:

- "Big boys don't _____."
- "A woman's place is in the _____."
- "Boys don't play with _____."
- "Sugar and spice and everything nice: that's what little
  _____ are made of."
- "Someday you'll meet Prince _____."
- "Nice girls know how to keep their mouths _____."
- "You should learn to take it like a _____."
- "Nice guys finish _____."
- "Boys don't like smart _____."
- "Don't act like a _____."
- "Boys will be _____."
- "Girls grow up to be mommies, nurses, and _____."

You can then ask the group to generate additional sayings. The
point of the exercise is that, despite the differences in backgrounds, the places where people have grown up, and their fami-

lies, they all have learned the same cultural gender stereotypes of what boys and girls are "supposed" to be like.

This is not only about challenging the assumptions that people make. You can also challenge your own assumptions. Here's another example. Teaching a graduate course about diversity and special populations in rural Colorado, Angie Paccione (2003), tried some opening activities to define terms like *race, racism, discrimination, oppression, ethnicity, and culture*. It didn't work. This class broke down into heated exchanges and emotional withdrawal. Rethinking that first class, Paccione realized that she had made some mistakes: "I had to suppress the urge to make assumptions about the students' readiness, closeness, openness, and experiences. I fell back on the basic triad that forms a foundation for diversity work: knowing self, knowing others, and making the connection" (p. 149).

Think back over the assumptions or stereotypes you have held about homosexuals or heterosexuals. What has been true in your community? Reflect on a class session or discussion that went poorly and speculate about what would have been different if you had taken more time to unpack stereotypical thinking—your own and theirs.

#43. Make peace with fears and get involved

In April of 1933, Nazi Germany began the persecution of Jews by declaring a boycott of Jewish owned businesses. At that time, there were approximately 600,000 Jews in Germany, less than one percent of the total population. Notably, most Jews were proud of their German heritage and over 100,000 had served in the German army during World War I. Jews were also well represented in positions of leadership in government and universities. Of the 38 Nobel Prizes won by German writers and scientists between 1905 and 1936, 14 went to Jews. Marriage between Jews and non-Jews was becoming more common.

On the day of the boycott, Storm Troopers stood in front of Jewish businesses and put signs up saying "Don't Buy from Jews" and "The Jews Are Our Misfortune."

Throughout Germany acts of violence against Jews and Jewish property occurred but the police rarely intervened. Although this boycott lasted only one day, it ushered in other restrictions in later weeks and Jewish government workers and teachers were quickly fired. Fear grew and the average German citizen grew increasingly withdrawn. What would inspire dissent?

One quick response came in the form of an Anti-Nazi Boycott of German products which was soon organized in the United States, the United Kingdom and other places by those alarmed by Hitler's anti-Semitic policies. German reprisals continued as did the Anti-Nazi Boycott until the entrance of the U.S. into World War Two. The following idea is adapted from "tip" #39 in *147 Practical Tips for Teaching Peace and Reconciliation.*

> Daniel Reinholz is a graduate teaching assistant who understands what it takes for students to make peace with their fears and demonstrate the kind of confidence needed to master higher-level concepts. "Focusing on positives rather than negatives can go a long way. Especially when someone is feeling nervous or uncertain, a small amount of praise or an expression of appreciation can make a huge difference. I have learned that such acknowledgments will be seen as more sincere if they are made directly. These efforts don't require much effort and can go a long way toward building personal connections. I try to model these kinds of responses and encourage students to do likewise." Think of how important the leadership of teachers can be at all levels. Not surprisingly, attacking and firing Jewish teachers sent chills throughout the German educational system and quickly muted any dissent.

> Many people never encounter the needs of others in a first hand, face-to-face, personal manner. It is easier to discuss an issue or injustice from the safety of our office, school, or home. It takes less of our valuable time to give money to a good cause. It is much safer, less invasive, and impersonal to address injustice from a distance. But, when we actually take a little time to get our hands dirty in working toward a solution or when we take a little time to make ourselves present amidst other people, we may take a big

step toward understanding, justice, and love.

In *Growing up Generous*, Roehlkepartain, et al. (1989) commented "humanizing and personalizing the issues can have an immediate, significant impact on young people" (p. 112). Engaging youth (and adults!) in the needs of those around them will help humanize the people, the problems, and the injustice that others may encounter regularly. By humanizing the issues, the people and problems become real, and youth can personalize the issue. Collective action can also inspire courage in the face of brutality. Make the experience tangible, unforgettable, engaging by providing opportunities for authentic engagement between two very different people. Get involved: humanize; personalize; inspire others to do the right thing!

Describe your own fears during previous historical conflicts. Have you carried fears into your own learning, for example, avoiding what you thought would be difficult subjects? What subject areas are the most challenging for you and why? When have praise and appreciations helped you make peace with those fears? How have you helped others reconcile their struggles to learn?

#44. Build empathy for intercultural peace

In April of 1994 civil war erupted in Rwanda. In approximately three months, Hutu extremists brutally murdered an estimated 500,000 to one million Tutsis and moderate Hutus in the worst episode of genocide since the Nazi's "final solution" for the Jews. While many were quick to point to "tribalism" as the explanation, it was the legacy of first German and then Belgian colonization that put the minority Tutsis in power and dependent on colonial forces to maintain control. While the Tutsis enjoyed a range of privileges, they were also deemed inherently superior as people. Over the next hundred plus years, this imposed hierarchy left a deep bitterness that later emerged after independence through conflict and violence. A memorial to the victims of this genocide will hopefully help to inspire others to see how the damage done can be repaired. The Quakers, for example, have hosted a series of reconciliation workshops for victims and perpetrators, stories of healing

that have been captured in a fascinating documentary film titled *Hope*. (See: www.
natcom.org/communication-currents/post-rwandan-genocide-documentary-de-
picts-reconciliation-and-hope)

The following "tip" is adapted from #41 in *147 Practical Tips for Teaching Peace and
Reconciliation*.

> Deep listening and position-taking through an empathetic pro-
> cess are crucial for improving relationships that foster a positive
> environment. Nothing can be more challenging—and inspir-
> ing—than repairing the damage caused by genocidal rage and
> murder. In the context of intercultural communication, empathy
> is understood as "...the imaginative, intellectual and emotional
> participation in another person's experience" (Bennett, 1979, p.
> 418). Through self-to-other dialogic interactions and position-tak-
> ing, one can participate, both intellectually and emotionally, in the
> experience of the "other." By doing so, one begins to understand
> the existence of multiple perspectives and emotions experienced
> in a diverse world. Complexity and the relativism of different
> viewpoints and emotions might emerge from such position-tak-
> ing (Brantmeier, 2008).
>
> Typically, at the beginning of a group meeting, individuals intro-
> duce themselves. Position-taking is a different ice-breaking ap-
> proach that promotes intercultural empathy for peace—a theme
> to be touched upon again and again in peacemaking and peace-
> building work. In the film *Hope,* Rwandans from the same village
> sit and listen to their stories of slaughter and fear, despair and
> guilt. One victim tells how she lost her husband to a mob. A per-
> petrator tells how he was forced to join that murderous mob or be
> killed himself there on the spot. After some time in prison, he is
> back in that same village living with his guilt and a fear of further
> retribution. The victim, in turn, is "re-victimized" every time she
> has been seeing one of the killers. In time through this guided
> reconciliation workshop, each begins to see the humanity in the
> other. Forgiveness and co-existence may be possible.

In a group, ask people to pick a partner they do not know. Give them a script or collectively generate a script of typical and atypical questions: educational background; hometown/ state/country; favorite childhood memory; something extraordinary and inspirational about the person; experience of "diversity"; most outlandish wish, etc. Have them interview one another while writing down their partner's response. During oral introductions, have the interviewer stand in the foreground and the interviewee in the background. The interviewer speaks from the first person perspective, as if he or she were the person interviewed. Have both people introduce each other from this first person perspective. Have them ask: How did it feel to speak as if you were someone else? How did it feel to be represented by someone else? What did you learn from this process? Can you imagine how this might inspire two people who are trying to overcome the memories of real conflicts and tragedies?

#45. Listen to veterans talk about peace

A growing wave of anti-war protests had led President Lyndon Johnson to quit his re-election bid in 1968 in the face of challenges from the pro-peace wing of the Democratic Party that included first Eugene McCarthy and then Robert Kennedy. The "leaking" of the Pentagon Papers by Daniel Ellsberg revealed the secrets of the U.S. Government's involvement in propping up the French colonial ambitions in Vietnam and later attempts to disguise the American role. The tragedies of this war inspired many to get involved in the peace process, to confront those who had been in power and rethink what it was that took the country down this path.

In 1969, as this anger about the Vietnam War continued to build, a series of coordinated demonstrations and parades were held on April 5 and 6 in major cities across the U.S.—New York, San Francisco, Los Angeles, Washington, D.C. and others. Those with longstanding involvement in the peace movement had their ranks swell with participation from African Americans and Latinos in the Civil Rights Movement, for example, who were seeing a disproportionate number of military casualties coming from their communities and while the defense budget continued to climb, funds for social welfare programs were being cut. Teach-ins became common on campuses as "business as usual" was suspended in order to focus on these larger issues. Veterans were inspired to organize and protest. Some young men left the country to avoid the draft. The following idea is adapted from Tip #102 in *147 Practical Tips for Teaching Peace and Reconciliation*.

In *Long Shadows*, Vietnam veteran David Giffey (2006) offers us a collection of autobiographical essays by veterans who are active in the peace movement, although few see themselves as pacifists. Instead, they cry out to stop unnecessary violence perpetrated by politicians and senior commanders far distant from combat but eager for power and honor. From the Spanish Civil War up through the War in Iraq, first-hand experiences in warfare make for heartfelt commitments to an ethic of honest and courageous resistance to what is all too often only the deadly sword rattling bravado of greed exploding into violence.

Robert Kimbrough, for example, was a front line marine officer during the Korean War. Listen to his description of what he faced and the conclusions he has had. "For example, and this kind of thing happened more than once, from battalion, we got an assignment that filtered down to one squad of my platoon that had us going deeply behind some strong points of land shooting out toward our lines from the hills where the Chinese were. It was a full moon. There wasn't a cloud in the sky. We had to go out on rice paddies. So I did what most platoon leaders were doing: We went out slowly in a spaced single line. Hunkered down in front of our own lines, I said. 'Okay, everybody be at ease. Be alert.' After an hour or so, I said, 'Okay, fire.' Everybody fired his rifle and trooped back in. I called in a report that we had carried out our mission of assault. 'No casualties. Many enemy killed.' Strictly speaking, I had disobeyed an order. But the order was insane. . . You've got to watch out for your troops. . . And those guys would do anything that I would ask them to do, which was very humbling. . . Again, the senior people plan for their own glory" (pp. 46, 47, 49).

How do you connect Kimbrough's experience to your life today? What have you read that offers an inside and deeper perspective on what those in the military have experienced and believed? Describe those situations when you have encountered significant diversity of thought? When differences seemed to be stifled?

#46. Consider more experiential learning

In April of 1940, Wangari Maathai was born in Kenya. She would later rise to lead the Green Belt Movement which sparked the planting of over 30 million trees across Africa. Through these efforts toward making peace with the planet, she was recognized with the Nobel Peace Prize in 2004, the first African woman so honored. In many ways her grassroots movement emerged from her challenge to conventional practices of abdicating initiative and waiting for government officials to take action. Maathai was also eager to inspire teachers to go beyond textbook learning. The following "tip" is adapted from #1 in *147 Tips for Using Experiential Learning*.

> In *Academically Adrift*, their provocative critique of higher education in the U.S., Arum and Roksa (2011) identify a striking shift in student time on campus away from studies and into work, friends, and recreation. "In addition to attending classes and studying, students are spending time working, volunteering, and participating in college clubs, fraternities, and sororities...A recent study of University of California undergraduates reported that while students spent thirteen hours a week studying, they also spent twelve hours socializing with friends, eleven hours using computers for fun, six hours watching television, six hours exercising, five hours on hobbies, and three hours on other forms of entertainment. Students were thus spending on average 43 hours per week outside the classroom on these activities—that is, over three times more hours than the time they spent studying...Given that students are spending very little time studying or attending classes, in both absolute and relative terms, we should not be surprised that on average they are not learning much" (p. 98).

Without sacrificing standards, list ways that you could tap the natural draw of experiences outside the formal school or work environment. Identify how hands-on activities inspired your own learning in the past and how it could boost engagement in an upcoming presentation.

#47. Tap into multiple intelligences

In April of 1896 the modern Olympic Games were reborn, 1500 years after they were banned by the Roman Emperor Theodosius I. At the reopening, 60,000 spectators welcomed athletes from 13 nations to this international competition. The history of the games dates back to 776 B.C. and probably 500 years before then. Initially the games were limited to foot races but later a number of other events were added, including wrestling, boxing, horse and chariot racing, and various military competitions. After being banned as part of an effort to suppress paganism, the games reemerged when the Renaissance in Europe inspired interests in the gifts—philosophical, political, cultural and athletic—of ancient Greece, a true celebration of the "multiple intelligences" of this early civilization. Everyone seems to value the experience of coming together every four years for friendly competition. The following "tip" is adapted from #27 in *147 Tips for Using Experiential Learning.*

> Among the many arguments for experiential learning is the writing of Howard Gardner (1999, p. 202) on multiple intelligences. Especially popular among elementary and secondary school teachers, this work describes eight "intelligences." The "linguistic" and "logical-mathematical" are the two that schools typically emphasize and test. However, there are six others that Gardner insists are essential to what makes us human and of these, several are essential to experiential learning. "Bodily-kinesthetic intelligence" is the most obvious. However, "intrapersonal intelligence" or self-awareness is also essential to experiential learning as is "interpersonal intelligence" or how individuals interrelate with others. "Naturalistic intelligence" reflects those talents that connect us to the environment. Finally, "existential or spiritual intelligence" permits us to consider those larger metaphysical questions of meaning.
>
> Compared to traditional classroom instruction, experiential learning offers us a broader perspective of human abilities. As Gardner describes it: "Deviating from established wisdom, I do not believe that there is a single best representation for any core idea or set of ideas. The notion of such a representation is an illusion, usually derived from a particular history of contact with a concept—how

the teacher has first encountered it, or how it was initially presented or written about." The challenge for all teachers, then, is to go
beyond how they learned in school and explore the many varied
ways that ideas can be presented, studied, experienced, and explored. The Greeks pioneered the early, broad-based education;
we should not retreat from that inspired model for narrow, test-
able knowledge alone.

Reflect on the "intelligences" that underlie learning in your own experience. List the var-
ious ways you could tap into a "broader" perspective for an upcoming presentation. In an
ideal world, what would your classroom be? What experiences would you love to include?

#48. Use the five senses

On April 12, 1961 Soviet pilot and cosmonaut, Yuri Gagarin, became the first human to orbit the earth, inspiring many world-wide about the possibilities beyond
earth's atmosphere. Every explorer must ultimately rely on all the senses to augment what was studied and practiced for entering unchartered terrain. Along with
other recruits, Gagarin had completed a series of experiments designed to test
his physical and psychological endurance. He was seen by colleagues as someone
who had a sharp and far-ranging sense of attention to his surroundings along with
quick reactions. He persevered. He prepared himself painstakingly for his activities and training exercises. The following concept is adapted from Tip #28 in *147*
Tips for Using Experiential Learning.

> Activities such as Gagarin's space exploits allow people to learn
> by engaging all their senses. In *Leadership and the New Science,* Meg
> Wheatley (2001, *Leadership and the New Science: Discovering order*
> *in a chaotic world)* makes this claim: "Information provides true
> nourishment; it enables people to do their jobs responsibly and
> well" (p. 107). Experience, in turn, offers additional insights be-
> yond what can be studied in classrooms.

Think back to those experiences that fully engaged your senses while inspiring you with the
"nourishment" you needed to explore new possibilities, areas or relationships. Rethink an
upcoming event and list how a multi-sensory experience might add real value.

MAY
Tips #49-60

In 1607 the first permanent English settlement in America was established at Jamestown, Virginia. Two hundred years later Lewis and Clark embarked on what would be a 6,000-mile journey of exploration of the American Northwest. Through the eyes of the Native people who lived in the Americas during those times, however, we see inspired struggle to withstand the European onslaught. And then, in the Spring some 140 or so years on, World War Two ended in Europe and signaled a new season of hope and possibility. Americans had joined with the other Allies to beat back a brutal Nazi onslaught. Soon thereafter, in May of 1954, the French were defeated in Vietnam ending their colonial ambitions and signaling new possibilities for Southeast Asia. The world was witnessing a rebirth of challenge to colonial power and asserting a clear desire for independence.

#49. What about a living economy?

May Day has ancient roots in pagan and Christian traditions, inspired by the arrival of Spring and celebrated with dances and feasts. In the late 19th century, it would also become a celebration for working people with parades, especially in socialist countries, inspired by the Haymarket Square "Affair." On May 4, 1886 in Chicago, a peaceful rally in support of workers striking for an eight-hour day and in support of workers killed the previous day by police exploded into tragedy. An unknown person threw a dynamite bomb that killed seven police officers and four civilians with many more wounded. Eight anarchists were later convicted of building the bomb; four were eventually hanged, another committed suicide and the rest spent their days in prison. The following "tip" is adapted from #21 in *147 Tips for Teaching Sustainability*.

> "A living economy is comprised of fair-profit [in contrast to profit maximizing] and not-for-profit living enterprises that are place-based, human-scale, stakeholder-owned, democratically accountable, and life-serving. In contrast to the publicly-traded, limited-liability corporation, which is best described as a pool of

money dedicated to its self-replication, living enterprises function as communities of people engaged in the business of creating just, sustainable, and fulfilling livelihoods for themselves while contributing to the economic health and prosperity of the community." (Korten, D. (2002, March). *Living economies for a living planet – a web essay.* Retrieved from <u>davidkorten.org/living-economies-for-a-living-planet</u>)

We study living systems in nature that respond to the seasons and, for example, typically bloom every Spring but, we have to ask, how does this apply to human creations and institutions and what can we create that will inspire exploration and innovation? Solicit ideas on what would inspire a "living economy" that represents environmental, societal and economic health. Consider where current systems meet this goal and where they fall short. Explore the web site for the Business Alliance for Living Economies for inspiration: https://bealocalist.org/ .

#50. Consider the wealth of a nation

The 1930's witnessed a brutal "Dust Bowl" in the U.S. when drought mixed with outright greed as well as a lack of understanding about the ecology of the Great Plains, i.e., the importance of deep-rooted grasses to maintaining topsoil health and the increasing mechanization of farming which dug deep into the grasslands. May 11, 1934 was so intense that it was proclaimed the day of the "black blizzard." Periodic wind storms lifted this newly dislodged topsoil into dust and horrific brown clouds would spread far and wide, driving many out of the region. The devastation inspired Congress to enact new legislation and researchers to recommend new principles and techniques. By facing problems we can always benefit from lifting our heads up to take that broader look, to see how our actions in the here and now fit with a longer perspective on sustainability, i.e., the interconnected health of the land, the people and the economy. The following "tip" is adapted from #20 in *147 Tips for Teaching Sustainability.*

David Suzuki is a Canadian academic, science broadcaster and environmental activist who gave birth to a Foundation in his own name in 1990 that is dedicated to the propositions that there is one nature and that, in essence, we are nature—all people and all species. Their goals are ambitious. See: davidsuzuki.org

(1) Establish the legal right for all Canadians to live in a healthy environment, able to breathe fresh air, drink clean water and eat safe food and that this right should be constitutionally protected. That's why we are pursuing legal protections for environmental rights, and in so doing, taking responsibility as stewards for the natural world on which we depend.

(2) Accelerate the transition to a low-carbon future. Climate change threatens the planet's life-support systems. In 2016, ratification of the United Nations' Paris Agreement — signed by 195 countries, including Canada, and the European Union — was a product of the mounting urgency to act on the defining issue of our time. The agreement requires Canada and other industrialized nations to transition from fossil fuels to 100 per cent renewable energy by 2050. We will help shift the climate narrative from despair to possibility, and create real opportunities for Canadians to be part of the solution.

(3) Protect and restore nature. Human beings — like all biological organisms — depend on clean air, water and soil. We are a part of nature and must live within its limits. Our vision for biodiversity is that Canadians improve the way they interact with the natural environment and become engaged in protecting the creatures and places they love. We also recognize Indigenous peoples as biodiversity stewards in their territories. We work to resolve rights and title issues, and we advance Indigenous governance of their lands and waters.

In our classes, communities and organizations we can inspire a broader definition of genuine wealth focusing on five key asset areas: human, natural, social, manufactured, and financial capital. Discuss how the budget of your campus, community, or country would have to change to reflect all assets.

#51. Consider the cost paradigm

On May 12, 2008 a devastating earthquake struck central China, claiming more than 69,000 lives, injuring more than 374,000 and leaving some 4.8 million people homeless. General Secretary and President Hu Jintao announced that the disaster response would be rapid. Just 90 minutes after the earthquake, Premier Wen Jiabao, who has an academic background in geo-mechanics, flew to the earthquake area to oversee the rescue work.

The Internet was extensively used for passing information to aid rescue and recovery efforts. For example, the official news agency Xinhua set up an online rescue request center in order to find the blind spots of disaster recovery. After knowing that rescue helicopters had trouble landing into the epicenter area in Wenchuan, a student proposed a landing spot online and it was chosen as the first touchdown place for the helicopters. Volunteers also set up several websites to help organize contact information for victims and those needing evacuation.

Natural disasters can inspire new thinking about relief and rescue efforts as well as about building designs that can better withstand earthquake shocks. The costs of recovery from natural disasters can also be devastating and bring into sharp focus the dangers of short-cuts that undermine building safety. The following idea is adapted from "tip" #23 in *147 Tips for Teaching Sustainability*.

> The Institute for the Built Environment at Colorado State University (CSU) has helped bring new "green" design school buildings in on budget even though the design and materials used had to meet the highest standards. Fossil Ridge High School, for example, was awarded Leadership in Energy and Environmental Design (LEED) silver certification and saves the Poudre School District in Colorado, over $100,000 per year in utility costs, using sixty percent less energy when compared to other modern high schools. The state of Ohio has taken the bold step of requiring LEED for all new public schools due to the significant savings enjoyed by most certified schools.

> CSU's Danny Birmingham focuses on ways in which the STEM

disciplines—Science, Technology, Engineering and Mathematics—can be connected to the communities that surround schools. He writes: As an example, "we had middle school youth interview elders in their community about the appliances and technologies they used that required fossil fuels when they were young. Next the middle school students had to compare usage over time (between elders and themselves) and write about the implications for future behaviors." In China the schools could be charged with reviewing the disaster for lessons to be learned.

From teachers and campus administrators to students living on campus or renting nearby, from everyone in nearby communities, people are involved in the built environment every day. There is a general misconception that using sustainable practices in building projects automatically equates to increased costs. Investigate local projects. Find architects and builders who can make the case for sustainable, yet more cost effective, designs. Have people research the "cost" implications of other ideas for enhancing sustainability and durability.

#52. Encourage self-examination and self-acceptance

Margaret Thatcher, the "Iron Lady", was Prime Minister of Great Britain from her instillation in May of 1979 until 1990, making her the first woman to have held that office as well as the longest-serving leader in that role in the twentieth century, a legacy that would inspire many. A concern for diversity seems to have defined much of her life. As a twelve-year old, she remembered helping to save money to support a teenage Jewish girl escaping Nazi Germany, describing this as among the significant events of her early years. Her study of chemistry in college meant that she would also become first prime minister with a science degree, an accomplishment she reportedly prized. Because of that early immersion in science, Thatcher came to support an active climate protection policy and played a central role in the passage of the Environmental Protection Act of 1990. Thatcher had talent and drive but doubted that a woman could be chosen as Prime Minister because of what she saw as the entrenched prejudices of the male population. The following "Tip" is adapted from #23 in *147 Tips for Teaching Diversity*.

There is no substitute for self-reflection as a mechanism for finding a better alignment of values, beliefs, and actions, especially when issues surface that touch on diversity. While difficult to assess objectively, reflective journals and open discussions can set the stage for deeper learning and transformation.

In their book on joy, the Dalai Lama and Bishop Desmond Tutu (2016) describe the benefits of meditation, that much of "traditional Buddhist practice is directed toward the ability to see life accurately, beyond all the expectations, projections, and distortions we typically bring to it. Meditative practice allows us to quiet the distracting thoughts and feelings so that we can perceive reality, and respond to it more skillfully. The ability to be present in each moment is nothing more or less than the ability to accept the vulnerability, discomfort, and anxiety of everyday life" (p. 225).

In his human behavior theory classes, Malcolm Scott encourages students to reflect on their individual cultures and identities through the creation of a pictorial collage. Students can use personal or magazine photos, personal drawings, cultural artifacts, and other visual representations of themselves and their multiple identities. Early in the semester students get the opportunity to share their collages with the class in the context of discussions over course content. This practice has been a richly informative and creative way to promote student engagement and expression. Moreover, students often experience deepened insights and revelations about themselves and their cultural influences, while being exposed to the cultures of others in the classroom in an affirming and culturally responsive way.

Experiment with a short reflective free write or meditation on diversity as a prelude for a group discussion. You can then ask people to each share with someone nearby to see where their agreements might lie. You should be able to get everyone participating more once they have had this opportunity to prepare their thoughts and talk them through in smaller, more intimate settings first. To be truly effective and inspirational, leaders in this increasingly diverse and interdependent world will certainly need this kind of self-awareness.

#53. Use response sheets

The Chinese Exclusion Act was a United States federal law signed by President Chester A. Arthur in May of 1882, prohibiting all immigration of Chinese laborers. At times welcomed for their cheap labor, these immigrants became vulnerable during economic downturns when competition for jobs intensified. White supremacy organizations also sprang up. For example, in California during this same era we can find the Supreme Order of Caucasians with some 60 chapters statewide. Once the Chinese Exclusion Act was finally passed, California pushed to pass additional restrictive laws that were later held to be unconstitutional. After the act was passed, most Chinese were faced with the difficult choice of staying in the United States alone or returning to China to reunite with their families. Ironically, while these Chinese immigrant workers provided cheap labor they rarely used publicly funded infrastructure (schools, hospitals, etc.) because they were predominantly made up of healthy male adults.

Although some 10,000 Chinese appealed to federal court against negative immigration decisions between 1882 and 1905, for all practical purposes, the Exclusion Act, along with the restrictions that followed it, froze the Chinese community in place during these years. All of this also gave rise to a great wave of commercial human smuggling, illegal activities that later spread to include other national and ethnic groups. However, limited immigration from China did continue until the repeal of this Act in 1943 during a time when China had become an ally of the U.S. against Japan in World War II. With all the heated anti-Nazi rhetoric that emerged, many in the U.S. wanted to embody a greater image of fairness and justice during a time when the Japanese were becoming vilified.

Despite the fact that the exclusion act was repealed in 1943, the California law that prohibited non-whites from marrying whites was not struck down until 1948. Much later, on June 18, 2012, the U.S. House of Representatives was inspired to pass a resolution that formally expressed regret for the Chinese Exclusion Act. This resolution had already been approved by the U.S. Senate in October 2011. In 2014, the California Legislature then passed additional measures that formally recognized the many proud accomplishments of Chinese-Americans in California and to call upon Congress to formally apologize for the 1882 adoption of the Chinese Exclusion Act. Looking back we are reminded of the reoccurring tendency in the United States for minorities to be punished in times of economic or political crises, a history that can be difficult for students and other audiences to address honestly. The following concept is adapted from "tip" #24 in *147 Tips for Teaching Diversity*.

> Find ways to allow students and others to ask those difficult and sensitive questions they do not want to ask in class and respond to them in private until there is enough trust to bring these issues into the open for public discussion. Try the following activity that Roe Bubar (Bubar & Vernon, 2003, p. 161) uses with her students:

Pass a response envelope around and encourage students or other audiences to ask about or comment on any issue from class. Then plan to write a response. Be sure to thank those who were willing to respond even if they go unnamed. Offer an empathetic comment about the inspiration often required to ask a difficult question or raise a sensitive issue.

#54. Develop and use empathy

Asked about May Day celebrations, many people will think of festivals while some will remember images of children dancing around a May Pole. Others will recall televised news footage of endless formations of soldiers, tanks and missiles parading through Red Square in Moscow when the Soviet Union would celebrate its commitment to the proletariat, the "workers of the world." Few Americans, however, know that the origins of this focus on workers had its origins in the U.S. at the culmination of years of struggle by unions and their members for recognition and improved working conditions.

As industrialization, spread across America, the need for ever more labor grew. At the same time large numbers of immigrants were entering the country and the workforce. Ideas that had been hatched in Europe about worker's rights pushed up against historic U.S. values for individual initiative, private property rights and the prerogatives of unfettered capitalism. Yet the reality was that the work place was often brutal in its demands on workers and the lack of basic safety with countless injuries and some deaths reported at certain worksites across the country. A ten to sixteen-hour work day under very dangerous conditions was common in the late nineteenth century in some industries made all too possible by cheap immigrant labor and the absence of reasonable regulations and political pressure to hold owners accountable for decent working conditions, in particular.

In response to this reality, a variety of organizations and ideas emerged to represent workers and champion a range of changes, from the eight-hour work day to the legal rights of workers to withhold their labor and strike for improvements. Socialism, for example, made a strong argument for collective ownership, protections, accountability, a share of political power and the wealth produced at these worksites. On May 1, 1886, more than 300,000 workers in more than 10,000 businesses across the United States walked off their jobs in the first May Day celebration in history. In Chicago, the center for the push for the 8-hour day, 40,000 went out on strike.

In the days, weeks and years that followed, workers would gain increasing influence through their unions and a willingness to withhold their labor and strike for better conditions. May Day celebrations would grow in popularity and spread world-wide. Through their struggles and sacrifices, workers would achieve greater political power and secure a place amid the days that are devoted annually to national celebrations. As we look back on this history we can tap our own abilities to empathize with those who were forced to labor under these conditions and recognize their courage in challenging a powerful system of private privilege, what has become an inspiration for so many far and wide. The following "tip" is adapted from #25 in *147 Tips for Teaching Diversity*.

> Know that students often need help and support when wrestling with difficult, complex ideas. Addressing racism, sexism, sexual orientation, class issues, unfair working conditions and other forms of oppression will challenge them to face tough issues that have long divided cultures worldwide. Feeling sorry for someone else, however well-intentioned that reaction may be, can easily transform into pity and block a deeper connection or understanding of those who are supposedly less fortunate. An expression of empathy, however, might convey at the very least an attempt to understand the emotions that a particular experience could engender for someone else, how earlier generations, for example, could fight for a stronger political voice to redress oppressive

working conditions.

Rose Kreston (2003, in Timpson, et al.) describes what she faces in her classes. "Unfortunately, the typical emotional response to disability seems to be rooted in sympathy, a 'feeling sorry for,' as opposed to empathy or an understanding of how someone might feel. The former tends to distance people while the latter tends to connect. One of the central goals of my class is to help students develop empathy for the disability experience, to understand it as a human condition and not an abnormality" (p. 177). It is not that long of a leap to connect this classroom with the ways in which some might pity or sympathize with workers from an earlier day and stop short of changing their own beliefs about political rights and needed regulations.

We can help students develop some depth of understanding about all this. In their book on joy, the Dalai Lama and Bishop Desmond Tutu (2016) distinguish between empathy and compassion. "(While) empathy is simply experiencing another's emotion, compassion is a more empowered state where we want what is best for the other person. As the Dalai Lama has described it, if we see a person who is being crushed by a rock, the goal is not to get under the rock and feel what they are feeling; it is to help to remove the rock" (p.259). In the case of the history of the labor movement in the U.S., the goal would be to "remove the rock" of oppressive owner power and prerogative.

Periodically stop a lecture, presentation or a discussion, whenever sharp differences of opinion or belief are evident, and ask if everyone can really understand the perspective of someone who thinks that differently. Focus on what the feelings might be. Then ask whether there is more to be done beyond empathy, and where there are struggles today that can inspire us to rethink our ideas and actions.

#55. Confront violence and build the capacity for peace

In May of 1970, unarmed college students protesting the Vietnam War at Kent State University were confronted by members of the Ohio National Guard some of whom seemed to panic and fired 67 bullets in 13 seconds. Four students died, nine were wounded, one of whom suffered permanent paralysis. Inspired by these events, one veteran of the fighting in Vietnam insisted that it was one thing to fight in Southeast Asia against what everyone was told was a real foreign threat but it was something else when U.S. troops began killing Americans. The following "tip" is adapted from #44 in *147 Tips for Teaching Peace and Reconciliation*.

> In an editorial for the *International Herald Tribune* entitled "Taking the Responsibility to Protect," South African Bishop Desmond Tutu (February 19, 2008) argued for both proactive intervention and prevention "when a government is unwilling or unable to stop mass atrocities being committed within its borders?" He writes: "The Universal Declaration was adopted in the aftermath of World War II, the Holocaust and the use of nuclear weapons. World opinion came together then to say, 'never again.' Yet in the past six decades, we have witnessed mass atrocities committed against others across the globe. We all share a responsibility to do whatever we can to help prevent and protect one another from such violence. The place to start is with prevention: through measures aimed in particular at building state capacity, remedying grievances, and ensuring the rule of law. My hope is that in the future, the *Responsibility to Protect* will be exercised not after the murder and rape of innocent people, but when community tensions and political unrest begin. It is by preventing, rather than reacting, that we can truly fulfill our shared responsibility to end the worst forms of human rights abuses."

Describe a conflict that has impacted your school, organization, family or community. What prevention efforts and "capacity building" would have inspired a positive difference?

#56. Eat together and celebrate common ground for peaceful coexistence

Celebrated on the eighth of May, 1945, Victory in Europe (VE) Day marks the formal surrender of the armed forces of Germany's Third Reich, Hitler and the Nazi Party's push for military power, political domination, colonial exploitation and ethnic cleansing. Estimates of total deaths from World War Two range from 50 million to more than 80 million human beings when war-related diseases and famine are considered. It can be inspiring to find the time to reflect on past events, the reasons for celebrating in the present and what can be done to support changes in the future. The following "tip" is adapted from #42 in *147 Tips for Teaching Peace and Reconciliation.*

> A Denver based non-profit group, Common Tables, believes that peaceful coexistence among people can emerge when they get to know each other better. Their strategy is simple: use common meals to offer people a starting point for finding some greater understanding, tolerance, and appreciation. They bring people together from diverse faiths, backgrounds and cultures in an attempt to overcome barriers, misconceptions, and fear-based thinking about those things that make them different.
>
> The former Denver, Colorado initiative Common Tables once noted on their now defunct website: "Each of us can think differently about diversity and inclusion by recognizing one important truth—we have much more in common than we do in difference. Common Tables members are making great friends while satisfying their yearning for learning, growing—and great food. In a short time, these small group interactions will generate the momentum needed for respect and understanding to circle the world." (See: www.commontables.org) Meredith Laine, an experienced college instructor of business, says, "I read about this in *The Healing Path* (March/April, 2008). Our local communities and neighborhoods could benefit from organizing small groups like these. By starting where we live, we can begin to learn to understand our cultural differences and become more of a global family."

Reflect on experiences you have had when "breaking bread together" inspired you to connect with people different from yourself. Organize a dinner or potluck and invite people from different faith groups, cultures, social classes, age groups or areas of your community. Have some questions or prompts in mind to stimulate sharing of experiences of crossing boundaries and developing new appreciations, especially on those days that should be remembered.

#57. Promote an anti-bias (ABC) approach

The Good Friday Agreement was a culmination of the peace process in Northern Ireland and approved by voters across the island of Ireland in May of 1998. Signed by representatives of government as well as non-governmental agencies, it contained proposals for a Northern Ireland Assembly with a power-sharing executive that included both Catholic and Protestant representatives, new cross-border institutions as well as formal linkages between Britain and Ireland. Importantly, there were also proposals on the decommissioning of paramilitary weapons, how policing would be organized in Northern Ireland as well as new agreements about the early release of paramilitary prisoners. After 800 years of conflict between the colonizing forces of Great Britain, their descendants and the native Irish, this peace accord has proven inspirational for anyone despairing about supposedly "intractable" conflicts. The following idea is adapted from "tip" #83 in *147 Tips for Teaching Peace and Reconciliation.*

> During the worst of the recent conflict in Northern Ireland, a common perception among educators was that schools should be 'oases of calm' from societal violence and that, in particular, issues of religion, identity and politics should be avoided. By contrast, the integrated school sector, which was started in 1981 by a parent pressure group who wished to see Catholic and Protestant children educated together (rather than the traditional separate provision), advocated a more upfront approach to these topics. Emerging from more than twenty five years of experience in the integrated schools sector is a curriculum approach that explicitly tackles these sensitive topics head-on and is unashamedly anti-bias with regards to culture, religion, ethnicity, social background,

gender, sexual orientation and disability.

The handbook *ABC: Promoting an anti-bias approach to education in Northern Ireland* (N.I.C.I.E., 2014) outlines the approach recommended. Such an approach may involve challenging previously unquestioned practices and behaviours and may meet with resistance from students, teachers, parents, support staff, administrators, and politicians. However, positive action is required in order to challenge bias. The Northern Ireland Council for Integrated Education (2014) identifies a number of characteristics that are important for engaging in anti-bias work, namely:

- a willingness to develop a positive self-identity;
- an open-mindedness and awareness of one's own bias, behaviour, motivation, and limitation;
- an understanding of issues of gender, sexual orientation, ethnicity, culture, religion, class, physical and learning ability, and how these interact; and
- a readiness to incorporate an anti-bias approach throughout the school community.

Consider the types of anti-bias approaches with which you are familiar. How do they compare with the Northern Ireland examples and what are their strengths and limitations? Explore the implications of an anti-bias approach for policies and practices, experiences and activities, language used with students and teachers, and for the physical environment of the classroom and its surroundings. What role can anti-bias work play in peace and reconciliation education?

#58. Ask yourself: Is this place holy?

In May of 1937 San Francisco's Golden Gate Bridge opened to the public. Construction had begun during the worst of the Great Depression and workers had to overcome many challenges: the strong tides, frequent storms and those classic Bay Area fogs as well as the problem of dynamiting rock many feet below the water in order to establish a foundation that would hopefully be earthquake-proof. A total of eleven men died during construction. After five years of construction, the completion of the bridge became inspirational as a symbol of progress in the Bay Area during a time of deep national economic crisis and is now routinely photographed as an iconic and revered architectural treasure. At 4,200 feet, it was the longest bridge in the world for many years. The following "tip" is adapted from #40 in *147 Tips for Using Experiential Learning.*

> Science teacher and consultant Lisa Pitot likes to provoke a deeper conversation about place by referencing Wes Jackson (1994, *Becoming Native to this Place*) and his insistence that *either all places are holy, or none of them are.* She writes: "When I shared this with adult learners, the word 'holy' was instantly challenged. In the discussion that ensued, we explored individual meanings of the word 'holy' and almost everyone was okay with that but not with any general 'truth'" (p. 59).

Consider the following meditation: Find a place to be by yourself. Get centered within your body and become aware of your breath. Your eyes may be open or closed, whichever is more comfortable for you. Begin to connect with this place. What could make this place feel holy to you? Take another deep breath and relax your mind as you exhale. Close your eyes if they are not already closed and place yourself in the midst of your everyday environment, where you spend the majority of your time. It might be your classroom, your car or your kitchen—whatever comes to mind, just place yourself there for this moment. Breathe in this place. Breathe out this place. Feel the holiness that is here. Hold onto that holiness as you return to your place here and when you are ready to open your eyes. Now shift your focus to an "unholy" place and find the holiness that you could not see before. Being in touch with the holiness of all places can be helpful grounding for embarking on place based education.

#59. Adopt new names and identities

Born into a sharecropper's family, Jesse Owens moved with this family to Cleveland, Ohio as part of that great migration of African Americans from the south. He attracted national attention with his performances in the sprints and long jump. Moving on to Ohio State University brought him international recognition in May of 1935 when he set three world records and tied a fourth during 45 minutes at the Big Ten track meet. Later at the 1936 Berlin Olympics, Owens inspired millions, especially among people of color, by winning four gold medals in the face of the racist ideology of Hitler and other Nazi disciples. This new identity, however, was not able to carry him past the racist limitations of his own country for long and provide financial stability until years later. The following "tip" is adapted from #41 in *147 Tips for Using Experiential Learning*.

> When anyone enters a new environment there is the opportunity to have a new identity. Too often we are known by our histories, i.e., the behaviors, skills, and abilities we have exhibited in the past. Some of these attributes may be positive and helpful, for example, our openness to new experiences. However; some may be limiting, for example, the inhibitions that can restrict our learning. Instead, we can give people the opportunity to re-create themselves in a new situation. At the beginning of a session, you can frame the challenges that lie ahead as opportunities for people to re-create themselves, especially if others in the group do not know them. This invitation can empower people to bring forward the positive traits, skills, and abilities that they want to exhibit. You can also suggest that people can adopt new names or nicknames. New identities may then mean new traits, behaviors, and skills that they can practice (Northouse, 2010).

Once in a new environment, ask people what positive traits, behaviors, and skills they want to bring forward and how they could leave the rest behind. What talents might get them wider recognition? What would inspire them to make the sacrifices that a Jesse Owens had to make to find success?

#60. Understand the stages of group development

Located in the Himalayas, Mount Everest is the earth's highest mountain and has inspired climbers for generations. The first pair, Tom Bourdillon and Charles Evans, came within 330 feet of the summit in May of 1953, but turned back after running into oxygen problems. As planned, their work in route finding and breaking trail and their oxygen caches made the final ascent—and a place in history—possible for others.

Two days later, the expedition made its second and final assault on the summit with its second climbing pair, the New Zealander Edmund Hillary and Tenzing Norgay, a Nepali Sherpa climber from Darjeeling, India. At the time, both acknowledged it as a team effort by the whole expedition. They paused at the summit to take photographs and buried a few sweets and a small cross in the snow before descending.

However, the challenges—including the limits of human endurance, the weather and technological advances—have always remained. In May of 1996 eight climbers died after several expeditions were caught in a blizzard high up on the mountain. During that 1996 season, 15 people died while climbing on Mount Everest. These were the highest death tolls for a single event, and for a single season, until the sixteen deaths in the 2014 Mount Everest avalanche. The disaster gained wide publicity and raised questions about the commercialization of climbing the world's highest peak. With this as a reference, it can be helpful to examine all aspects of a group's preparation including their bonding as a real team and the nature of the risks that they could face. The following "tip" is adapted from #43 in *147 Tips for Using Experiential Learning.*

> Bruce Tuckman (1965) introduced a group formation model to explain the four stages of group development, i.e., forming, storming, norming, and performing. In the *forming* stage there is a high degree of dependence on the facilitator since the group is establishing initial roles and relationships and often needs direction. In the *storming* stage, while group members define individual roles and positions, sub-groups of similar beliefs may form and everyone must compromise to move forward. In the *norming* stage agreement and consensus become more important when the group starts functioning more as a whole to solve its problems. In the *performing* stage the team develops a shared vision, a high degree of autonomy, and its own leadership.
>
> A facilitator will want to be conscious of the stage of a group and align the challenges and tasks accordingly. For example, if you use a high level task to challenge a group that is in the storming

stage, you may overshoot their ability at that point in time. But if you adapt the task difficulty to the stages of a group, you can ensure greater success and help build the group's ability to become a healthy, high functioning and vibrant learning community.

Reflect on your own experiences in groups in the context of these stages of development, especially if you are facing a very high stakes project. As you prepare to facilitate experiential learning, reference these stages to assess a group's collective abilities to meet its challenges, accurately assess the risks, what inspiration will be needed and adapt your plans accordingly. How can understanding this help in your preparation as a team?

JUNE
Tips #61-72

In June of 1215, the signing for the Magna Carta by the English King John helped spark the evolution of modern democracies around the world. In June of 1872 Susan B. Anthony was fined for voting in a presidential election in Rochester, NY only a temporary setback in the long drive for the full expansion of voting rights. In June of 1944 Allied troops liberated Rome, inspiring millions to sustain the push to defeat the Nazi tyranny and terror. Born in June 1922, Judy Garland's rendition of the song, *Over the Rainbow,* in *The Wizard of Oz* became an instant classic about the possibility of hope even during the darkest hours.

#61. Follow the Finns for innovation and inclusive prosperity

The Treaty of Versailles brought an end to World War I between Germany and the Allied Powers. It was signed on the 28th of June in 1919, exactly five years after the assassination of Archduke Franz Ferdinand that had sparked five years of brutal bloodshed across Europe with over 18 million dead and 23 million wounded. The treaty forced Germany to disarm, make territorial concessions, and pay reparations. While some claimed that this treaty was too weak, many historians believe that its punishing terms were unsustainable and soon led to a chaos that Hitler and the Nazis fed on to grab power on promises of returning Germany to its military greatness. Could the tragic consequences that followed in World War II have been avoided with a more inspired and sustainable treaty that recognized the interconnections between the health of the economy, society and the environment? The following "tip" is adapted from #27 in *147 Tips for Teaching Sustainability.*

> In an analysis of the successes of the Finnish people in crafting government policy that requires heavy taxes but ensures a healthy foundation for ongoing innovation, Peter Ford (2005, "Egalitarian Finland Most Competitive, too," *Christian Science Monitor*, Oct. 26.) describes their collective belief: "High level education is the key to what Pekka Himanen, a brilliant young philosopher who advises the Finnish government, calls his country's 'virtuous cir-

cle.' 'When people can fulfill their potential, they become innovators.... The innovative economy is competitive and makes it
possible to finance the welfare state, which is not just a cost, but
a sustainable basis for the economy, producing new innovators
with social protection.' In the end, says Jorma Sipila, the Chancellor of Tampere University, Finland's inclusive social model is
its best guarantee for the future. 'The conditions for a flourishing
economy are so demanding that the state has to make social in-
vestments to raise competent people and take care of dropouts so
that they carry their share of the burden.'... Marrying prosperity
and social protection is the only sustainable future" (pp. 6–7).

*Ask yourself: How could the Allies have followed the lead of the Finns in designing a trea-
ty? How could your community be inspired by these same principles?*

#62. Recognize the power of consumers as agents of change

It was in June of 1997, that the crown colony of Hong Kong officially reverted to
Chinese control, ending 156 years of British rule. The agreement stipulated that
Hong Kong would enjoy a high degree of autonomy, except in matters of foreign
relations and defense, and that the social and economic systems as well as the lifestyle in Hong Kong would remain unchanged for the next 50 years. Many observers, however, expressed considerable skepticism about China's pledge to abide by
the "one country, two systems" plan outlined in the agreement. They feared that
China would drastically curtail the rights and freedoms of Hong Kong residents.
The questions have to be asked: Will the residents of Hong Kong be inspired to
defend their values in the face of their new Chinese overlords? Will the material
successes of the people in Hong Kong give them real power? The following concept is adapted from "tip" #26 in *147 Tips for Teaching Sustainability.*

If consumers demanded more products and services that contributed to sustainability, the private sector and government would
respond accordingly. Recycling plastic, for example, is not an
economically viable option in much of the United States because
there is insufficient consumer demand for goods made from re-

cycled plastic. Moreover, too many are willing to look past the real costs of waste and landfills. Our choices as consumers and responsible citizens of planet earth can drive the economy and our communities and, therefore, the health of the environment. What choices can students make and encourage others to make for a more sustainable community and planet?

Calculate the ecological, economic, and social impact consumers can make through purchasing choice and the pressure they can exert on politicians.

#63. Address disparities

In June of 1876 a regiment of the U.S. Seventh Cavalry numbering some 647 men under the command of Lieutenant Colonel George S Custer faced off against a much larger force of Lakota, Dakota, Cheyenne and Arapahoe warriors along the Little Big Horn River in the Crow Indian Reservation in southeastern Montana territory. This proved to be a major victory for the Indian coalition and sent shock waves across the country. Five of the seventh Cavalry's twelve companies were annihilated and Custer was killed. This battle proved to be the beginning of the end of the Indian Wars. Native peoples everywhere had been forced into ever smaller reservations as settlers and gold prospectors pushed ever deeper across reservation lines in violation of signed treaties. Eventually these encroachments would inspire others to honor treaty boundaries and agreements. The poverty and problems that beset many Native communities today are a legacy of these violations and conflicts. The following "tip" is adapted from #29 in *147 Practical Tips for Teaching Sustainability.*

> In *No Future Without Forgiveness*, Bishop Desmond Tutu (1999) recognizes the threats to healing in post-apartheid South Africa when serious attention is not paid to the enduring privileges of so many in the minority white community when contrasted with the persistent poverty and limitations on so many in the majority black community: "In South Africa the whole process of reconciliation has been placed in very considerable jeopardy by the enormous disparities between the rich, mainly the whites, and

the poor, mainly the blacks. The huge gap between the haves and the have-nots, which was largely created and maintained by racism and apartheid, poses the greatest threat to reconciliation and stability in our country.... For unless houses replace the hovels and shacks in which most blacks live, unless blacks gain access to clean water, electricity, affordable health care, decent education, good jobs, and a safe environment—things which the vast majority of whites have taken for granted for so long—we can just as well kiss reconciliation goodbye" (pp. 273–274).

Brainstorm a list of inequities in your own culture and/or community and how they prevent sustainability on all levels. Discuss the enduring inequities that undermine movement toward a more sustainable future. What will inspire more people to intervene in the search for constructive and equitable ways forward?

#64. Build supportive communities

Born on June 27, 1946 in Cleveland, Ohio, Sally Priesand eventually became the first ordained rabbi in Jewish history. Even though her parents were not strictly and religiously observant, they were active in Jewish organizations, Priesand began to show a commitment to Judaism as a teenager. At the age of 16 she was inspired to be a rabbi. Her eventual ordination was considered to be historic. The following "tip" is adapted from #26 in *147 Practical Tips for Teaching Diversity.*

Here's an activity that Angie Paccione (2003) used. "Students select a bag to carry artifacts that are representative of their identities. In the past these have included pictures, diplomas, tools of their trades, mementos, and heirlooms. Each student is given ten minutes to tell the group about the items in his or her 'people bag.' I always do the first one as a model" (p. 149).

Pay attention to the potential benefits of the time invested in this kind of activity when you ask for responses to a question, spark a discussion or begin a small group activity. As a mechanism for reflecting on self, understanding individual uniqueness, and building a supportive community, you could also experiment with expanded versions of the usual introductions. Ask people to emphasize three features of their identities: cultural, personal, and professional as well as what inspired them about their future lives and contributions.

#65. Connect to the personal

In June of 1811 Harriet Beecher Stowe was born in Litchfield, Connecticut, into a famous religious family and inspired many to the cause of the abolitionists with her vivid description of the harsh conditions of slavery in *Uncle Tom's Cabin*. In her twenties she lived in Cincinnati and got to know several African Americans who had been attacked by ethnic Irish over the jobs that were available. Later she married a professor and ardent critic of slavery himself and together they supported the underground railroad, harboring several fugitive slaves temporarily in their home before these slaves moved on toward Canada and freedom. In June 1851 the first installment of her *Uncle Tom's Cabin* first appeared in serial form with an emotional portrayal of the effects of slavery on individuals that captured the nation's attention while arousing condemnation in the South. The following "tip" is adapted from #27 in *147 Practical Tips for Teaching Diversity*.

> Rose Kreston (2003, in Timpson, et al.) shares her strategies for keeping conversations grounded in possibility. "Simply providing information about the ills of society may merely reinforce the perceived status (inferior) of disabled people through their 'struggle to overcome.' Yet, having a disability is both a personal experience as well as a societal one. A connection to that personal side is necessary if disability is to be perceived as part of the human condition and not deviant. The continuing challenge is to focus on the personal aspects of disability without further stigmatizing it" (p. 178).

Regularly look at the personal stories of individuals under study, what they live(d), and what their interests are or were. This kind of activity can help humanize a curriculum. But keep in mind that the various "oppressions" of society—historic racism, sexism, privilege and power—can overwhelm and paralyze students and other audience members. Beware of shattering hope and only feeling despair, seeing victims everywhere and losing sight of the actions, individual and collective, that can be constructive, inspirational and transformative.

#66. Encourage participation and stir the soul

In June of 1964, three civil rights workers were abducted and murdered in Mississippi. James Chaney, Andrew Goodman and Michael Schwerner had talked with congregation members at a church that had been burned. They then were arrested after a traffic stop for speeding. Held for a number of hours at a local jail they were followed by law enforcement and others when they drove away. Soon thereafter they were pulled over again, abducted, driven to another location, shot at close range and buried. After a massive search the FBI was tipped off and the bodies were found. The murder of these activists inspired national outrage and helped build support for the passage of the Voting Rights Act of 1965. Eventually it was revealed that the Ku Klux Klan had colluded with local law enforcement in targeting these three young men. Forty-one years after the murders took place, one of the perpetrators was convicted on three counts of manslaughter. Disturbing events like this can prove difficult to process, both emotionally and intellectually, especially when racial tensions have been running high between members of a minority community and the police. The following "tip" is adapted from #29 in *147 Practical Tips for Teaching Diversity.*

> We can learn much from traditional American Indian practices that create open spaces for members to reflect and contribute without having to compete in the larger group for talk time. Roe Bubar and Irene Vernon (2003) write: "In many ways, we conduct class in the same manner that tribal groups have made important decisions. Open tribal meetings have been an integral part of tribal life from time immemorial.... We respectfully call on quiet students and provide small-group work to encourage the participation of those students who are reluctant to speak up in the larger classroom environment" (p. 160) They then add: "We have also noticed that issues that come from the heart have been the ones that students are able to speak about with ease. When students are able to identify issues that stir their soul and consciousness, we find that their confidence to speak out increases" (p. 161).

Discussions will suffer if participation is limited to a few assertive or extroverted individuals who dominate. Valuing wide participation and a range of ideas can help you find different ways to encourage the quieter, introverted or minority view points to surface, especially when events have been deeply troubling. In order to get more perspectives in discussions, experiment with calling on individuals by name, especially after you have given everyone a few moments to get their thoughts down on paper in a free-write or through a brief discussion with someone nearby. Be sure to take a few minutes to get some feedback about this from both those involved when you get the chance to ask. These comments can prove very valuable when you reflect and rethink future classes.

#67. Create "Hands of Heroes" and share ideas for a peaceful future

In June of 1968 Robert Kennedy was fatally shot after giving a campaign speech in his bid for the Democratic nomination for president. One of his often repeated sayings continues to inspire people today: "Some men see things as they are and say why. I dream things that never were and say why not." The following concept is adapted from "tip" #45 in *147 Practical Tips for Teaching Peace and Reconciliation.*

> Rooted in connectivity and creativity, the activity "Hands of Heroes" allows people an opportunity to share honestly about the pain that they see in their worlds as well as the ideas that they have for peaceful futures. When asked about a source for this activity, Cassandra Poncelow had this to say: "I don't have a source for it. I've used it a lot with youth groups and ministry teams over the years and it is something that was developed out of several different activities that I rolled into one. It has been a really powerful experience for students and I just modified it to focus more on the peace element versus a prayer practice that I traditionally use" (pp. 56-57).

For this activity you will need paper and writing utensils for everyone. Younger people may want a variety of colors or markers, pens, or pencils. After distributing the materials, explain that there are really no set requirements in this activity other than to allow people an opportunity to reflect on themselves and their communities as well as provide a place to dream about things that they long for in their world.

Begin by tracing your hands on the sheet of paper. Then draw or write things in your hands-spaces that are items of "non-peace" or violence. Think of some examples. You can use words or pictures to represent "hate, anger, and violence" or you may have specific stories from your own life and community that you want to put into the "hand." Allow for a period of silence for this.

After people have completed this part of the activity, you can ask yourself or others: "What did you feel while you were filling in your hand?" or "What types of things did you write down or draw?" Understand that no one has an obligation to share but everyone is welcome to offer comments or reactions.

After this, look outside the tracing of your hand. Here people can write or draw things that represent "peace" to them. These might be words such as "love, balance, and community" or they may be specific aspects of family members or personal experiences. This can also be a place to write down dreams that they have for their own lives, communities, or the world. An example might be, "I dream that someday war will not be an option for solving conflict." Allow for some time for participants to complete this. You can also invite a conversation about what participants included by using the earlier questions or some of your own.

When people have completed their "hands," ask them to put their hand back over what they had originally traced. Discuss the significance of this "gesture" that covers all items of non-peace and that their hands are surrounded only by peaceful dreams, words, and experiences. If people are comfortable, you may take some time to have them cover another participant's "hand" and read about the dreams of that individual. This is a good time to acknowledge the role that we have in working together. If there is an area where these hands can be displayed, encourage everyone to explore possibilities for greater sharing and inspiration, for example, "covering" each other's hands and seeing other visions of a peaceful future.

#68. Build something out of the ashes of violence

On D-Day, June of 1944, Allied forces mounted the largest seaborne invasion in history when 156,000 troops from the U.S., Britain, Canada and France landed on the coast of Normandy, France that was defended by more than 50,000 German troops in bunkers above beaches that were bristling with barbed wire, mines and other barriers. In total over 875,000 men disembarked by the end of June, inspiring the end of Nazi control in Europe and foretelling the end of the war some eleven months later. The following "tip" is adapted from #54 in *147 Practical Tips for Teaching Peace and Reconciliation.*

Claire McGlynn (2009) is a peace education scholar at Queen's University in Belfast, Northern Ireland. She writes: "In the fall of 2008 I was busy taking a workshop on Diversity and Inclusion with a new group of Catholic and Protestant student teachers. This is demanding because it involves discussion of issues relating to religion, politics and identity that are usually avoided because of their divisive nature. As the students began their first activity I received a text message to say that my local Gaelic games club (a predominantly Catholic organisation committed to sustaining Gaelic sports and culture) had been destroyed by fire. Instinctively I knew that this was not accidental and by the time I returned home that night and inspected the damage for myself it was abundantly clear that this was an arson attack, most likely in retaliation for the daubing of IRA (Irish Republican Army) graffiti on a local Orange Order (Protestant) meeting hall. It was terribly sad to see a recently refurbished community centre in ashes, along with many historical artefacts including photographs of the team with whom my son won the championship. There was a palpable sense of disbelief and fear, not least because people had finally been starting to accept that the 'bad old days' were over. There was also a sense of relief that no-one had been hurt.

"I was struck by the tentative nature of peace and how easily sectarian sentiments could be aroused and mobilised in such a way. It was hard to reconcile this hurtful act of vandalism with the hopes that my students expressed for the future. However out of the ashes of this fire came a number of positive aspects. First, the response to the club from right across Northern Ireland was strongly supportive, denouncing violence and providing strong leadership in all quarters to resist further acts of retaliation. Second, the Gaelic club renewed its efforts to be more inclusive of all members of the local community, redoubling its attempts to reach out particularly to young Protestant people. Third, there was a

groundswell of support for building a new centre that is open to
all, irrespective of religious background and plans are already taking shape for a bigger and better community centre" (pp. 63-64).

*What can we learn about the precarious condition of peace from this story? From D-Day?
What does it teach us about the mobilization of forces and how resistance can be overcome?
What inspirational examples of hope emerging out of violence can you share with each
other?*

#69. Create your own Nobel Peace Prize

Born in June of 1929 Anne Frank's tragic story of her family's ultimately failed
attempt to hide from Nazi persecution continued to inspire others after her diary was found at the end of World War Two. Born in Germany, Anne lived most
of her life in or near Amsterdam, Netherlands where her family moved when
the Nazis gained control over Germany. By May 1940, the Franks were confronted by the German occupation of the Netherlands. As persecutions of the Jewish
population increased in July 1942, the family went into hiding in some concealed
rooms behind a bookcase in the building where Anne's father worked. From then
until the family's arrest by the Gestapo in August 1944, Anne – just 15 years old
– kept a diary she had received as a birthday present, and wrote in it regularly.
Following their arrest, the Franks were transported to concentration camps. Anne
and her sister died in Bergen-Belsen camp.

Inspired to become a journalist, Anne would chronicle the daily interactions, pressures, reactions, hopes and fears of her family. She wrote about wanting to become
a writer and hoping that she had the talent needed. She wanted more than what
then was the fate for most women, i.e., a husband, children and a home to keep.
She wanted to leave a legacy and her tragic life propelled a dream that became very
real although she would not live to see it. Could Anne Frank have been awarded
the Nobel Peace Prize? Should she have been? The following idea is adapted from
"tip" #56 in *147 Practical Tips for Teaching Peace and Reconciliation*.

Have you ever considered offering your own version of the Noble
Peace Prize? We could recognize when a student, faculty, staff or

community member acts like a peacemaker, like someone who is committed to resolving conflicts in constructive and creative ways, restoring lost harmony and healing any hurts. We need to reinforce and highlight these kinds of positive behaviors.

Kim Watchorn, an experienced teacher who leads staff development efforts, wants to see the idea of a Nobel Peace Prize replicated on a local level. "All too often, too much attention goes to those who cause problems or conflicts — the drama kings and queens, the bullies, the cranks. However, rather than awarding people who are performing their 'jobs' in a professional manner, we could make a public acknowledgement of those special actions that honor the work of those who have stepped beyond their roles and acted with nobility in a quest for peace and reconciliation. By adding a ceremony and award we educate others about the value we place on peacemaking, the kinds of actions we will celebrate" (p. 66).

#70. Push for the tipping point

Jacques-Yves Cousteau was born in June of 1910 to live a life exploring the wonders of the sea, sharing his findings through books and film that inspired millions world-wide. His study and experiments produced improvements in underwater scuba gear and the cameras needed to make the ocean's wonders accessible to the general public. In hindsight we can see all those places where Cousteau's experiments and explorations had an impact. The following "tip" is adapted from #53 in *147 Practical Tips for Using Experiential Learning*.

Experiences can have a multiplier effect as participants share their successes and setbacks and then discuss what they have learned. The settings, the changes, and the challenges often combine to bond a group together through shared experiences—and it can happen quickly. Knowing about Malcolm Gladwell's (2000) argument for a "Tipping Point" can help group leaders take full advantage of the time together. "These three characteristics—one, contagiousness; two, the fact that little causes can have big effects; and three, that change happens not gradually but at one dramatic moment—are the same principles that define how measles move through grade-school classroom or the flu attacks every winter.

Of the three, the third trait—the idea that epidemics can rise or fall in one dramatic moment—is the most important, because it is the principle that makes sense of the first two and that permits the greatest insight into why modern change happens the way it does. The name given to that one dramatic moment in an epidemic when everything can change all at once is the Tipping Point" (p. 9).

Bill Timpson took his doctoral capstone class to a mountain retreat center. After the first afternoon of orientation talks, blindfolded "trust walks" and other group problem solving challenges, the second day began with a hike. By noon they had eaten and some of the group turned around but others wanted to press on to the snow fields two to three hours ahead. Navigating all the water runoff from that Spring's thaw, the log bridges in various states of repair and disrepair, the newly fallen trees and limbs made for a memorable full day that quickly pulled the class members together, experiences that they talked about and thought about in the days, months and even years that followed.

Reflect on those experiences that proved to be "Tipping Points" for you. Identify strategies for getting a future group inspired by that transformational point.

#71. Get the right people on the bus and have them help move in the right direction

In June of 1963, Soviet Cosmonaut Valentina Tereshkova became the first woman to travel into space aboard Vostok 6, completing 48 orbits over 71 hours, more time in space than all U.S. astronauts combined up to that date. Before becoming a cosmonaut, Tereshkova was a textile-factory assembly worker who was inspired by her experiences as an amateur skydiver. She could have been overlooked for the Soviet space program for any number of reasons including her gender. The following "tip" is adapted from #55 in *147 Practical Tips for Using Experiential Learning*.

Much can be invested in professional development but having

the best teachers, presenters or candidates is the first and most important place to begin. For business, we appreciate the recommendation by Jim Collins and his associates (2001) in *Good to Great* about hiring the right people and getting them in the right positions. "The good to great leaders began the transformation by first getting the right people on the bus (and the wrong people off the bus) and then figured out where to drive it" (p. 63). We want to take this one step further, however, and make a claim for a commitment to development as well. Quality recruitment and placement is, we believe, only the beginning. Getting everyone involved in the experience of designing and building a better bus as well as helping to guide its direction taps into a high level of intelligence, innovation, inspiration and energy.

A general manager in the restaurant business thought about it this way: "We need to find motivated people who can multi-task. I think we should recruit more from the ranks of student athletes who have the ability to handle competing high-level challenges. They are inherently competitive, energetic and team players. We also need people who are self-reflective, who can direct their own learning." His regional vice president added: "In sports, teams will attempt to improve with trades, signing free agents or players who have been released and are on the waiver wire, or developing young talent from within. It's the same in our business."

Make a list of the "best" passengers on your organization's "bus." Are you or others blocked by preexisting assumptions or prejudices? Identify ways in which you could involve them more in determining the best design and direction for this "bus." How could you recruit and inspire greater use of the "right kind of passenger"?

#72. Understand the impact of "climate" on learning

In June of 1983, Sally Ride became the first American woman to fly in space when the space shuttle Challenger launched. As one of the three specialists on the STS-7 mission, she played a vital role in helping the crew deploy communications satellites, and conduct experiments. She was reported to have said that when she was getting ready to launch into space, it felt like sitting on a big explosion waiting to happen. She had to reach a level of comfort to find that kind of a risk inspiring.

Sally Ride was born in Los Angeles, California 1951. As a teenager, she was inspired by the challenges that came with sports such as running, volleyball, softball and, especially, tennis. She loved to excel. After receiving undergraduate degrees in physics and in English from Stanford University in 1973, she went on to earn her Ph.D. in physics. She worked for two years at Stanford University's Center for International Security and Arms Control, then at the University of California, San Diego as a professor of physics.

While Ride was studying physics in 1977, NASA was looking for women astronauts. Drawing on her love of challenges, she was one of 8,000 people who answered an advertisement in the Stanford student newspaper seeking applicants for the space program. Eventually she would be one of six women chosen as an astronaut candidate. However, because she was a woman, she faced additional challenges. For example, during one press conference, she was asked if she wept when things went wrong on the job. Here, everyone can be more attentive to the climate in schools, colleges and organizations—i.e., how people are treated, what assumptions or prejudices exist, what needs to be challenged and changed. The following "tip" is adapted from #56 in *147 Practical Tips for Using Experiential Learning*.

> Much research on classroom climate identifies the importance of trust, support, mutual respect, open communication, and problem solving for student morale and learning. In *Concepts and Choices for Learning*, Timpson and Doe (2008) describe the physical aspects of a positive classroom environment: "It matters that our classes meet in rooms that are comfortable for students, providing them with adequate space and good lighting where they can easily hear their instructors. Operable windows are important for fresh air and natural lighting…Climate knowledge of this sort… impacts the variety of teaching methods that an instructor can employ, while, in turn, varying the teaching methods helps to reduce student boredom…The underpinnings of classroom climate reach back many years and offer us a number of useful reference points for improvements" (pp. 34-35). While climate factors work well in formal classrooms, experiential learning often moves out of doors

where the benefits of fresh air, natural lighting, and shared adventure can inspire that much more. The challenges of space travel
and her successes would eventually prove Sally Ride's doubters
wrong.

Rethink an upcoming presentation to incorporate more that is experiential. Add in some measure of challenge to see if you can boost morale, engagement, inspiration and learning. Identify those factors that might be barriers.

JULY
Tips #73-84

In July of 1776 the Declaration of Independence announced the intent of American colonists who were inspired to free themselves from British control. In July of 1863 secessionist Confederate forces were defeated over three days in Gettysburg, Pennsylvania, an event that many historians believe was a turning point in the war to preserve the American Union and end slavery. In July of 1964, the Civil Rights Act was signed into law. Three years later Thurgood Marshall became the first African American to serve on the U.S. Supreme Court. In the midst of the worst of times, we can look back and see those points of inspiration that pushed and pulled people forward.

#73. Compare needs with wants

In July of 1956, U.S. President Eisenhower called for the construction of an interstate highway system and helped to usher in an explosive expansion of automobile, truck and bus travel in the U.S. By the turn of the twenty-first century the impact of fossil fuel exhaust on air pollution in the U.S. and world-wide would continue to "fuel" the threat of climate change. While most people want to enjoy the benefits of modern comforts, the world lacks the natural resources for everyone to live as many do in the industrialized world. The following idea is adapted from "tip" #30 in *147 Practical Tips for Teaching Sustainability.*

> Many people in the developed world want—and have—much more than they need. Advertising feeds these wants in order to increase corporate profits. Have people reflect on their own needs and wants within a context of sustainability. A disposable consumer society is like a never-ending conveyer belt of the latest and greatest, with the old and supposedly useless too often tossed aside, contributing to the already overflowing level of waste. Historically our necessities meant air, water, food, and protection (from the elements). However, developed societies have created a fifth need, fed by advertising—the need for novelty (Ewen, 1986).

The American public seems to have been conditioned to expect new products each year in the pursuit of better living. What is behind this need? What factors make it unsustainable? Should it be addressed and, if so, how? To what degree are you, or your students, friends, co-workers or community leaders a part of this disposable, consumer society?

Have your students, employees, staff, friends or family members track their behaviors over a week, month or semester and report back. How did they contribute to the problem? What could inspire them to change?

#74. Explore Community-Based Social Marketing

Henry David Thoreau was born in July of 1817, one of the most influential writers on the natural world and human responsibility to safeguard their collective inheritance. His classic book, *Walden,* made a strong case for living simply and appreciating nature. His essay, "Civil Disobedience" laid the foundation for citizen resistance to governmental actions. Together they continue to inspire the actions of people concerned about waste and conservation, pollution and climate change. The following concept is adapted from "tip" #31 in *147 Practical Tips for Teaching Sustainability.*

Students, coworkers and family members can create sustainable programs using ideas that reflect the kinds of citizen input that Thoreau would have applauded. For example, Doug McKenzie-Mohr and William Smith (1999) discuss the profound effectiveness of Community-Based Social Marketing (CBSM) in their book, *Fostering Sustainable Behavior: An Introduction to Community-Based Social Marketing.* They write, "This approach involves: identifying barriers and benefits to a sustainable behavior, designing a strategy that utilizes behavior change tools, piloting strategy with a small segment of a community, and finally, evaluating the impact of the program once it has been implemented across a community" (p. 15).

The beauty of CBSM is that it is not limited to a certain group of people or type of behavior. Businesses, non-profits, teachers, and local, city, and state governments can use it to help inspire a more responsible citizenry. Challenge individuals to use this tool and these ideas to rethink projects in their communities or on their campuses.

#75. Rethink basic rights

Born in July of 1912, the American singer, songwriter Woody Guthrie was a life-long activist for social justice, the land and the dispossessed, and whose songs inspired generations of musicians who would follow. His immortal ballad, *This Land is Your Land,* was written in 1940 in response to repeated airing of *God Bless America* on the radio and later became an anthem for the civil rights and peace movements of the 1960's and 1970's. He frequently performed with the slogan *"This machine kills fascists"* displayed on his guitar. Many of his songs addressed that triple bottom line of sustainability—the interconnected health of society, the economy and the environment:

> *This land is your land, this land is my land*
> *From the California to the New York island*
> *From the Redwood Forest, to the gulf stream waters*
> *This land was made for you and me*
>
> *As I went walking that ribbon of highway*
> *I saw above me that endless skyway*
> *And saw below me that golden valley*
> *This land was made for you and me*
>
> *I roamed and rambled and I followed my footsteps*
> *To the sparkling sands of her diamond deserts*
> *And all around me, a voice was sounding*
> *This land was made for you and me*
>
> *When the sun comes shining, then I was strolling*
> *In the wheat fields waving and dust clouds rolling*
> *The voice was chanting as the fog was lifting*
> *This land was made for you and me*

As I went walking I saw a sign there
And on the sign it said "No Trespassing."
But on the other side it didn't say nothing,
That side was made for you and me.

In the shadow of the steeple I saw my people,
By the relief office I seen my people;
As they stood there hungry, I stood there asking
Is this land made for you and me?

Nobody living can ever stop me,
As I go walking that freedom highway;
Nobody living can ever make me turn back
This land was made for you and me.

This land is your land and this land is my land
From the California to the New York island
From the Redwood Forest, to the gulf stream waters
This land was made for you and me

The following "tip" is adapted from #41 in *147 Practical Tips for Teaching Sustainability.*

History will judge everyone harshly—especially our educators—if too few are willing to respond to the threats to maintaining a sustainable, collective existence. Examine the basic assumptions in your own field for barriers to greater environmental responsibility, societal well-being, and economic fairness. Allow your conclusions to be a starting point for discussion. Begin these examinations with yourself but then challenge students to join in and offer their insights.

Winona LaDuke, Native American author, activist, and one-time Green Party candidate for vice president, has written about the need for a "seventh generation" constitutional amendment to protect our common property. Such an amendment would inject an intergenerational perspective concerning oceans, air, forests, rivers, water, and public lands into our policies and practices.

Explore the virtues and shortcomings of a culture based on private property or common property or a combination of both, and how each impacts sustainability. How do such matters mesh or conflict with our notions of capitalism, property, democracy, and so forth? What will inspire new ideas to reduce waste and, conserve resources to promote the interconnected health of the environment, society and the economy?

#76. Avoid easy answers and embrace complexity

In July of 2005 the Provisional Irish Republican Army called an end to their 30-year long war against the British occupiers and Protestant loyalists in Northern Ireland After the tragic events of "Bloody Sunday" in 1972 when British soldiers fired into a demonstration of civilians in Derry, killing 14 and wounding 16 more, bombings and revenge killings spiked while a grass roots peace movement, led by women, slowly took shape in the thirty years that followed. As Nobel Peace Prize recipient, Mairead Corrigan Maguire said, "bombs and bullets" were used for 400 or so years and the violence only continued. It was past time for ordinary citizens to inspire others with a vision of a new more inclusive direction toward a future that would not be Catholic or Protestant but a dynamic, healthy mix of both. As peace took hold, integrated schools would also emerge as a place that could identify common ground in a shared history, not favoring one side or the other. The following "tip" is adapted from #19 in *147 Practical Tips for Teaching Diversity.*

> All too often, instructors reinforce dichotomous thinking by focusing too much on correct answers. It would be foolish for us to claim that there are simple answers to the complexities inherent in teaching about human diversity. Issues of diversity contain an overlay of factors that requires real sophistication to address, especially where there has been conflict.

Consider what Suzanne Tochterman (2003) recommends: "When introducing new material, I frequently will remind my students of any competing theories, perspectives, interpretations or ideas. All too often, they may otherwise be inclined to think that there is one final authority on some matter or another" (p. 143).

#77. Allow time

In July of 1964 the Civil Rights Act was signed into law by President Lyndon Johnson, making it illegal to discriminate on race, color, religion, sex, or national origin. It prohibited unequal voter registration practices as well as racial segregation in schools, employment, and public accommodations. The passage of what became a landmark legislation had been inspired by President John F. Kennedy in response to demonstrations and protests across the U.S. in 1963. Its passage was almost assured after Kennedy was assassinated in Dallas and some time had passed. The following "tip" is adapted from #31 in *147 Practical Tips for Teaching Diversity*.

> It usually takes time to reevaluate long and deeply held beliefs—beliefs that have developed and taken root over many years. In their book on teaching peace and reconciliation, Timpson et al. (2009) offer various examples for ways in which teachers and others can begin to counter these stereotypes and biases that too often are bolstered by shared histories and community traditions that target and indict the "other." Change is possible but often requires focused effort, guidance and ongoing support.

Have people write a self-reflective prologue to a particular prompt or project as well as a self-reflective epilogue that is more feeling-based. Encourage the sharing of these reflections. What do people find inspiring in the stories of others? In their own reflections?

#78. Emphasize constructivist learning

Leroy Robert "Satchel" Paige was born in July of 1906. Beginning his career as a professional baseball pitcher, first in the Negro League and then late in his career in Major League Baseball. Long before Jackie Robinson broke the color line, Paige became a legend in his own lifetime because of his talents, his longevity in the game, and by drawing record crowds wherever he pitched. At age 42 in 1948, he was the oldest major league rookie while playing for the Cleveland Indians. He played with the St. Louis Browns until age 47, and represented them in the All-Star Game in 1952 and 1953. In 1948 he was the first player who had played in the Negro leagues to pitch in the World Series and in 1971 Satchel was the first player from those early

Negro Leagues to be inducted in the National Baseball Hall of Fame. Paige inspired generations of African American players, in particular, to step through and over those earlier color barriers, both in baseball and beyond.

In hindsight we can see how those racial barriers had been constructed to maintain the power and privileges of white populations who had allowed those systems to persist long after slavery had been abolished. Moreover, the constructed mythology of the American melting pot was obviously flawed with respect to people of color as was the mythology that the "American Dream" was achievable by anyone through talent and hard work. The following "tip" is adapted from #32 in *147 Practical Tips for Teaching Diversity.*

> Constructivism is a philosophy of learning based on the premise that we construct our understanding of the world through reflecting on our experiences. We each develop mental models and rules to make sense of our experiences. Learning is the process of adjusting these models and rules to accommodate our new experiences.
>
> Constructivism can mean two things, in particular, especially to educators. One, there is no knowledge independent of the meaning that the learner constructs from his or her experience; we do not absorb knowledge passively, but rather we develop it actively. Two, when we think about learning, we must focus on the learner, not on the subject matter to be taught (Timpson & Doe, 2008). Unlearning dysfunctional biases while forming new concepts typically requires much more than is possible from a lecture and information-based approach to instruction. Satchel Paige was able to challenge traditional prejudices about race and talent and then inspire new thinking.

Rethink an upcoming lecture, presentation or discussion topic that touches on some aspect of human diversity and frame it as a problem or case study. This approach centers on those attending, on their discoveries, their experiences. Ask them for feedback during your concluding debrief. As part of your assessment, reflect on their understanding and the quality of participation.

#79. Transform motivation into constructive change

The Battle of Gettysburg was fought in early July of 1863 and proved to be a pivotal engagement in the American Civil War. General Robert E. Lee had marched his Army of Northern Virginia into Pennsylvania and faced off with the Union's Army of the Potomac, commanded by General George G. Meade, at the crossroads town of Gettysburg. Between 46,000 and 51,000 soldiers from both armies were casualties in the three-day battle, the most costly in U.S. history. On November 19, President Lincoln used the dedication ceremony for a cemetery there in his historic, two-minute Gettysburg Address whose opening lines have inspired generations ever since:

> *"Four score and seven years ago our fathers brought forth on this continent, a new nation, conceived in Liberty, and dedicated to the proposition that all men are created equal...The world will little note, nor long remember what we say here, but it can never forget what they did here. It is for us the living, rather, to be dedicated here to the unfinished work which they who fought here have thus far so nobly advanced. It is rather for us to be here dedicated to the great task remaining before us, that from these honored dead we take increased devotion to that cause for which they gave the last full measure of devotion, that we here highly resolve that these dead shall not have died in vain, that this nation, under God, shall have a new birth of freedom—and that government of the people, by the people, for the people, shall not perish from the earth."*

The following concept is adapted from "tip" #100 in *147 Practical Tips for Teaching Peace and Reconciliation*.

> In the video series on nonviolence for PBS, *A Force More Powerful* (2000), movements for freedom and social justice from around the world and in different historical contexts are connected to the pioneering efforts of Gandhi to introduce nonviolence as a mechanism for change. In one program, the origins of the Civil Rights Movement in the U.S. are traced to efforts at desegregation in Nashville, Tennessee. We see the African-American students at Fisk University, one of the country's prominent, historically black colleges and universities (HBCU). Early scenes depict leaders in

the black community holding workshops to explain how a campaign of nonviolence could confront racist power and control. Attempting to integrate a downtown lunch counter, volunteers take the abuse of whites without resorting to revenge. The media is alerted so that the attention that ensues arouses support locally and nationally. Throughout this campaign, nonviolence was framed as a courageous act and the antithesis of the weakness or inadequacy that some associate with pacifism.

The work of Rudolph Dreikurs (1968), in particular, offers a useful framework for understanding violence and rethinking responses. In his work on classroom conflicts and student misbehavior in schools, Dreikurs hypothesized that without being taught or shown how to get their needs met in positive ways, students may escalate from wanting attention to seeking power and control, and, then, to feeling inadequate.

Explore the value of the Dreikurs' framework for other programs in the six-part PBS series on nonviolent change, A Force More Powerful—Chile, South Africa, India, Poland, and Denmark. Identify another film, videotape or DVD that contains examples of violence. Draw on the work of Dreikurs to analyze the behaviors of those in conflict, i.e., (1) Attention, (2) Power and Control, (3) Revenge, and (4) Helplessness and Inadequacy. Analyze the events portrayed on the screen within this framework and explore how responses could be reframed in a constructive manner that encourages peace and reconciliation.

#80. Acknowledge grief, invite connection

In July of 2017, Bill Timpson joined a study tour group from the U.S. that met at the Palestinian Museum of Natural History and the Palestine Institute of Biodiversity and Sustainability at the Bethlehem University. The Director of both organizations, Dr. Mazin Qumsiyeh, inspired everyone with the breadth and depth of his commitment to the health of the lands and its people.

Dr. Qumsiyeh was born in 1957 near Bethlehem in the area now occupied by Israel since 1967. With a Ph.D. in molecular and cell biology, he previously served on the faculties of the University of Tennessee, Duke, and Yale Universities and has published over 130 scientific papers on topics ranging from biodiversity to cancer. His books range from *The Bats of Egypt* (1985) and *Mammals of the Holy Land* (1996) to *Sharing the Land of Canaan: Human Rights and the Israeli-Palestinian Struggle* (2004) and *Popular Resistance in Palestine: A History of Hope and Empowerment* (2011).

From the website of the Palestine Museum of Natural History and the Palestine Institute of Biodiversity and Sustainability are these institutional mission statements: "Work to research, educate about, and conserve our natural world, culture and heritage and use knowledge to promote responsible human interactions with our environment. Our Goals are: (1) Explore and research the diversity of the fauna, flora, and human ethnography via collections and research; (2) Support environmental protection and responsible interaction between people and the environment; (3) Use the knowledge gained and the books and databases and collections to promote science education; (4) Catalogue and build a physical and an electronic data base of all animal and plant species existing; (5) Develop respect (a) for ourselves (self-empowerment), (b) for our fellow human beings (regardless of background), and (c) for all living creatures and our shared earth." See: https://www.palestinenature.org/

The history of this region at the crossroads of civilizations has been dominated by powerful military forces, from the early Greeks to the Romans, the Ottoman, the British, and now the Israeli. It was inspiring to hear of such broad and inclusive goals at these two institutions that encompass both the natural and human worlds, the hallmark of work toward sustainable solutions that builds on recognizing these deep interconnections. The following idea is adapted from Tip #48 in *147 Practical Tips for Teaching Sustainability*.

> We live in times of loss—loss of species, loss of cultures, and loss of languages. Introducing rituals for acknowledging the associated grief can help release energy for new, sustainable commitments. In *The Ecology of Commerce*, Paul Hawken (1993) writes, "At the present rate of extinction—estimates range from 20,000 to over 100,000 species every year...the loss of evolutionary potential is being called the 'death of birth.' This is tantamount to marching backward through the Cenozoic Era, losing millions of years of evolutionary development in a matter of decades" (p. 29).

Consider these activities: Sit in a circle. Light a candle. Play soothing music. Create a center hearth for photos, words, prayers, stones, and mementoes. Pass a "talking stick" to help hearts speak one by one as others only listen. Speak of grief. Speak of joy. Speak of fear. Speak of love for all living beings and the health of the earth. If culturally appropriate, practice eye contact. Encourage genuine emotion. Invite honesty with kindness. Honor silence. End by sharing food, smiles, and gratefulness. Think of one resource in the area that has been lost and perform a grief ceremony for it. Think of another reason to inspire and celebrate a positive step.

#81. Build and sustain peaceful networks

In July of 2017, a tour group of Americans was visiting sacred sites and organizations committed to building peace in the Middle East, an area of the world mired in conflict and occupying forces for centuries. Yet these ashes of past and continuing conflicts can inspire new and creative ways toward something better, more peaceful. Parents Circle - Families Forum (PCFF) is a grassroots organization of bereaved Palestinians and Israelis. The PCFF promotes reconciliation as an alternative to hatred and revenge. Their website posts the following: "The Parents Circle - Families Forum (PCFF) is a joint Palestinian Israeli organization of over 600 families, all of whom have lost a close family member as a result of the prolonged conflict. Joint activities have shown that the reconciliation between individuals and nations is possible and it is this insight that they are trying to pass on to both sides of the conflict. Moreover, the PCFF has concluded that the process of reconciliation between nations is a prerequisite to achieving a sustainable peace. The organization thus utilizes all resources available in education, public meetings and the media, to spread these ideas."

"The Parents Circle—Families Forum is registered as an association and is managed jointly by the professional staff, Israelis and Palestinians working in two offices: the Palestinian Office is Beit Jala and the Israeli Office is in Ramat Ef'al, Tel Aviv. Although the PCFF has no stated position on the political solution of the conflict, most of its members agree that the solution must be based on free negotiations between the leadership of both sides to ensure basic human rights, the establishment of two states for two peoples, and the signing of a peace treaty. The historic reconciliation between the two nations is a necessary condition for obtaining a sustainable peace treaty."

Two representatives of PCFF met with this touring group from the U.S. in late July, 2017. Both had lost a child to the violence. "We must talk to each other," they both insisted. "We must think of others. We recognize how difficult it is for Palestinians to grow up under occupation. It's easy to understand why kids want to incite Israeli soldiers. We have seen kids as young as seven years old in jail. Some did not believe the Holocaust happened. They think it is just a movie, a big lie, and that they are the victims of a kind of revenge."

"But we cannot give up. We can behave differently. We can have dialogue in school. We can make peace with ourselves. Nonviolence is a very strong weapon but a different kind of weapon. We like to visit schools and create cracks in their thinking about what is possible. Palestinians rarely meet Jews, just the soldiers." The following "tip" is adapted from #97 in *147 Practical Tips for Teaching Peace and Reconciliation*.

> When the twentieth century came to a close and she completed *Cultures of Peace*, Elise Boulding (2000) stepped back to reflect upon what had been and what was needed. "We are in the middle of rough times as I write, and much rougher times lie ahead. The challenge is to draw on the best of the hopes and the best of the learning skills, and the relationship-building networking, and coalition-forming skills that have developed in this past century, so that the long-term future may yet birth new cultures of peace" (p. 257).

Assess the role of your own networks in supporting yourself through tough times. What have you learned about coalition building that has made a difference for you and others? What new "learning skills" have you had to develop? What "cultures of peace" have you created for yourself?

#82 Bring the classroom outside

In July of 2017 in Bethlehem, Palestine, Bill Timpson joined with seven other members of a touring group to experience going through a check point into Jerusalem with hundreds of Palestinians, mostly men, needing to get to work. The press was intense—body to body. Timpson's notes have the following entry: "I strained to stay upright as the crowd pushed us one way and then another, three to four bodies abreast across the 7-foot opening. Another member of our group talked about the panic he had felt when memories of a surging, drunken New Year's Eve crowd in Times Square pushed him up and over a parked car. It required a full hour for all of us to make our way up the 100 feet in that cage-like funnel, much like the chutes that animals have to push through on the way to the slaughter houses. Ever since the Six Day War in 1967 Israel has been occupying the West Bank in violation of the Oslo Agreements and in spite of numerous United Nations sanctions. Eventually my U.S. passport got me through although locals have to "pass" an electronic fingerprint check by an Israeli soldier. Other heavily armed soldiers are also visible at this checkpoint.

"In spite of this intense but slow process everyone on the tour talked about being inspired by the decency of these locals who have to do this daily to get to work and back again. While one guy motioned for us to take the faster "international's lane"—an offer we refused because we wanted to experience the daily grind that the locals faced—another thanked us for our being there saying, 'We rarely see white people here. We appreciate your presence.' For each of us, this experience was truly a profound way to better understand more about what we had been reading and hearing of the Palestinian experience of occupation in this their ancient homeland." The following "tip" is adapted from #35 in *147 Practical Tips for Using Experiential Learning.*

> Lisa Pitot (2002) has made good use of the Promise of Place web site, a project of the Center for Place-Based Learning and Community Engagement. (See: http://www.promiseofplace.org/) "It is a useful resource for background information, research studies and curriculum ideas for place-based education. In terms of addressing common barriers to bringing the classroom outside, they suggest the following: (1) Entice (Challenge? Inspire?) people outside; (2) Streamline logistics for getting kids outside; (3) Celebrate how invigorating the outside can be, even in cold months; (4) Simplify and economize transportation needs; (5) Develop projects and units where nature and culture blend."

Pitot also reminds us that we will need to keep in mind the char-

acteristics of a positive classroom climate, even when we are outside. We can focus on the relationship between student morale
and productivity, the intellectual excitement of our lessons and
the rapport we want to build. We can also emphasize trust and
the place for Maslow's hierarchy of needs: Physiological; safety;
love and belonging; self-esteem; and self-actualization. First and
foremost, however, in order for any lesson outside to be produc-
tive, students will need to be reminded about proper behavior.
Many students equate being outside with recess. We can also do
all of this for ourselves, deepening our own understanding and
reporting back our experiences.

*Plan for bringing a group outside for a period of time, whether it would be for a solo sit, an
hour class period or a whole day, or more. However, know that it is important to prepare
and think of the "outdoor" classroom—including the entire community or region—the
same as you would prepare the regular classroom environment. You can also bring your
own experiences into the classroom or lecture hall, augmenting your analyses with your
first-hand accounts, reports of your feelings and what was inspirational.*

#83. Engage the world and take action

New Zealand mountain climber, Edmund Hillary, was born in July of 1919 and at
the age of 34 in 1953 he joined with Nepalese Sherpa Mountaineer Tenzing Norgay to become the first team to reach the summit Mount Everest. A shy young-
ster, Hillary took refuge in books and daydreams. Learning to box increased his
self-confidence and a school trip exposed him to climbing where he found that his
natural strength and endurance set him apart from others and nurtured his love
for adventures in nature. We can never know what experiences will inspire which
people. Be sure to utilize varied approaches and observe closely how students
respond. The following "tip" is adapted from #37 in *147 Practical Tips for Using
Experiential Learning.*

In *Last Child in the Woods*, Richard Louv (2008) recognizes the
challenges we face in unhooking young people from the addic-
tive attractions of television, video games, computers and social

networking, in particular, and inspiring them to reconnect to the natural world. "No list of nature activities and community actions can be complete, but here are a few suggestions...Parents, grandparents, and other relatives are the first responders, but they cannot resolve society's nature-deficit disorder by themselves. Educators, health care professionals, policy-makers, business people, urban designers—all must lend a hand. Many of the activities presented here are adult-supervised (up close or at a distance). However, the most important goal is for our children, in their everyday lives, to experience joy and wonder, sometimes in solitude—for them to create their own nature experiences and, as they grow up, to expand the boundaries of their exploration" (p. 359).

Identify areas that you could explore and take action. Look through the 100 "Actions we can take" at the end of Louv's book for ideas and sources that could work for you and inspire others. Make a list of what you will try.

#84. Use a continuum

In July of 1969, Neil Armstrong became the first person to step on the moon, uttering that iconic one small step for man, one giant leap for mankind. Inspired by his first flight in an airplane at age six, he took that next step of flying lessons at age fourteen and was awarded his pilot's license at age sixteen. Inspired by the potential in air travel, he built a small wind tunnel in the basement of his home and used model airplanes for a variety of experiments. Armstrong was fortunate to have a neighbor with a powerful telescope and what he could see of the planets and stars fueled his fascination. All of this built into a distinguished career in aeronautics. We can clearly see the continuum in Armstrong's life experiences, from his earliest interests as a child to his accomplishments as an adult. The following "tip" is adapted from #36 in *147 Practical Tips for Using Experiential Learning.*

Lisa Pitot (2013) knows firsthand about the pressures on classroom teachers at every level: "Many of us might be thinking that place-based education is a great idea, but schedules are already bursting at the seams and demands on every teacher's time are enormous. Before saying 'I can't do it,' remember that developing and implementing place-based learning projects either at a school and/or within the community takes time, patience, and a large dollop of creativity. There is also the deadening reality of inertia—i.e., that we will continue to do what is easy, comfortable, etc." (pp. 56-57).

Csikszenthmihalyi's (1990) *Flow* is relevant here about the invigorating benefits of accepting new challenges. Know that place-based learning projects can be thought of along a continuum. Some projects will not contain every feature, nor will they be at the far end of the continuum as *the most* place-based. For example, a project may range from a broad overview of factual or procedural knowledge to a deep exploration of important concepts, from a required service learning component that connects the classroom and the community to a project that is purely academic.

Rethink an upcoming program and list ways in which you could use a project or service learning to see what sparks the imaginations of students.

AUGUST
Tips #85-96

"The arc of the moral universe is long but it bends toward freedom" was originally penned by Unitarian abolitionist minister Theodore Parker and taken up by both Abraham Lincoln and Martin Luther King Jr. to offer determined hope in the dark days of war and racial strife. Looking through history through this lens we can see other examples. In August 1961 the East German government started building the Berlin Wall in an attempt to stop the press of Germans wanting to flee to the Western section. Only thirty years later, the wall was taken down as Germany reunited and the Soviet Union collapsed. In August of 1974, facing certain impeachment for his role in approving the Watergate burglary and then obstructing justice in an attempt to cover-up the crime, Richard Nixon became the first U.S. President to resign.

#85. See enemies as potential allies

In August of 1935, President Franklin D. Roosevelt signed into law the Social Security Act. Having taken the helm of the country in 1932 in the midst of the Great Depression, the Social Security Act (SSA) followed the popularity of other "New Deal" programs such as the Works Progress Administration and the Civilian Conservation Corps, which planned to use public funds to put Americans back to work and inspire an economic recovery in the face of determined resistance to federal intervention by the previous Hoover Administration. Although it was initially created to combat unemployment, Social Security now functions primarily as a safety net for retirees and the disabled. The Social Security system has remained relatively unchanged since 1935.

In the 1930s, the U.S Supreme Court was lagging behind the populist wave that had propelled FDR into the White House. Reflecting a conservatism that had characterized Herbert Hoover's presidency, the court had struck down many pieces of Roosevelt's New Deal legislation. The President was himself inspired to do something radically different. He attempted to pack the court. On February 5, 1937, he sent a special message to Congress proposing legislation granting him new powers to add additional judges to all federal courts whenever there were sitting judges age 70 or older who refused to retire. The practical effect of this proposal was that the President would get to appoint six new Justices to the Supreme Court (and 44 judges to lower federal courts), thus instantly tipping the political balance on the Court dramatically in his favor.

The debate on this proposal lasted over six months. Eventually the seven-member court was able to defeat the court-packing by rushing pieces of New Deal legislation through and ensuring that the court's majority would uphold it. The following "tip" is adapted from #45 in *147 Practical Tips for Teaching Sustainability*.

> In *No Future Without Forgiveness*, Nobel Peace Prize recipient Bishop Desmond Tutu (1997) describes what helped to inspire the emergence of South Africa from the horrors of its brutal system of white minority rule: "The first democratically elected government of South Africa was a government of National Unity made up of members of political parties that were engaged in a life-and-death struggle. The man who headed it had been incarcerated for twenty-seven years as a dangerous terrorist. If it could happen there, surely it can happen in other places. Perhaps God chose such an unlikely place deliberately to show the world that it can be done anywhere" (p. 280).

Accepting the world the way it is may block us from seeing other and better ways forward. Use role-plays with people to surface polarized positions, but then emphasize listening, empathy, and negotiation to find common, creative and sustainable ways to move forward.

#86. Plant hope

In August of 1896 George Carmack spotted nuggets of what he thought was gold in a creek bed while salmon fishing near the Klondike River in Canada's Yukon Territory, This discovery sparked the last great gold rush in the American West. Eventually he would find a rock near the creek bed that was thick with gold deposits. News of the gold strike spread fast across Canada and the United States, and over the next two years, as many as 50,000 would-be miners arrived in the region. "Klondike Fever" reached its height in the United States in mid-July 1897 when two steamships left the Yukon carrying more than two tons of gold. Thousands of eager young men were inspired to make their way north. Few of these would find what they were looking for since most of the land in the region had already been claimed. The following concept is adapted from "tip" #46 in *147 Practical Tips for Teaching Sustainability.*

> Looking down on the glitter of Brazil's Rio de Janeiro are the inhabitants of slums (*favelas*) that cover the hillsides. Here, enterprising American students from Temple University were inspired to begin hydroponic vegetable gardens to demonstrate inexpensive rooftop solutions to the problem of a lack of locally grown fresh produce. As reporter Marion Lloyd (2005, "Gardens of Hope on the Rooftops of Rio," *The Chronicle of Higher Education*, Oct. 14) notes, "Although hydroponics does not work for root vegetables and trees, which require soil and space, the system is ideal for growing a wide variety of plants like tomatoes and beans.... The students are working with a local nongovernmental organization, Viva Rio, which directs dozens of development programs in the favelas.... The system is extremely lightweight and portable—a must for slum residents, who are constantly in the process of building new floors onto their houses as they can afford to. It can also be hung from balconies, and requires less water than conventional soil gardens. And the produce not only grows more quickly—a head of lettuce takes a month to mature, instead of the usual six weeks—but also doesn't require pesticides" (p. A56).

Review this work and discuss the merits of a positive, engaging, and hopeful approach to sustainability. Ask people to research sustainable inventions that would address inequities and injustices in their own communities, regions, or beyond. Pass along reports of ingenuity that rally the human spirit. Find stories that celebrate creative and constructive responses to the "doom and gloom" reports of environmental, societal, and economic decline that too often paralyze initiative and action.

#87. Find ways to use faith

In August of 2017, a tour group from the U.S. made a stop at the *Tent of Nations* in Palestine where a working farm and orchard now doubles as an educational enterprise with a goal of inspiring sustainable peace, reconciliation and development. Outside their gates and carved into a stone is their commitment, *We Refuse To Be Enemies*. From their website is this language, "Our mission is to build bridges between people, and between people and the land. We bring different cultures together to develop understanding and promote respect for each other and our shared environment. To realize this mission, we run educational projects at our organic farm, located in our hills southwest of Bethlehem. Our farm of 100 acres is a center where people from many different countries come together to learn, to share, and to build bridges of understanding and hope." (See http://www.tentofnations.org/)

Working with his sister and brother, Daoud Nassar serves as the Director for this project. The land itself is owned by his family who registered the property in 1924-1925 during the British Mandate period when they grew grapes, fruit, and olive trees. Despite this long history of documented ownership, the family has been fighting a legal battle to keep hold of the land since it was classified as 'Israeli State Land' and thus threatened with confiscation in 1991. Apparently, the Israeli military sees strategic value in this hilltop land.

The struggle is ongoing, however. With a commitment to peaceful resistance—remember that their slogan is "we refuse to be enemies"—and with the support from those who have visited here, Daoud insisted to Bill Timpson and the touring peacemaking study group that much has been achieved. "The Tent of Nations continues to work to protect and develop the farm as a place where people can meet, learn, work together, and inspire one another."

For a part of the world that has long felt the heavy boot of military occupiers down through history, the commitment from the *Tent of Nations* is to seek to embody a positive approach to conflict and occupation. Daoud continued, "Faced with great injustice, we know that we should not hate, despair, or flee. We can channel our pain and frustration into positive actions which will build a better future. We aim to help the oppressed and marginalized realize that they are powerful. We all have a role in creating the future we want to see. At *Tent of Nations*, we seek to work with others in the local area to lay the foundations for a future Palestine, in the belief that justice and peace will grow from the bottom up. We work to reconnect people with the land. Through mixing our hands with the soil, we learn to value and understand the significance of our environment."

This commitment has a very practical element, Daoud insisted. "We are working towards becoming completely self-sustainable in regards to food, water, and electricity, and we hope in the long-term to be able to support other local projects with proceeds from our farm. Our vision is to develop a vocational training and education center on the farm which will provide a space for children and young people to learn about alternative energy, organic farming, and community building. We hope, ultimately, to be able to prepare the young people of Palestine for a positive contribution to their future and culture by bringing values of tolerance and understanding into their life experiences, and to facilitate a respect for the environment by increasing awareness of our reliance on the land. In moving onwards with the development of this vision, we look forward to continuing to welcome many more volunteers and visitors to *Tent of Nations*, and teaching hope and faith in action to an international community."

Nassar put this project within a historical context. "The message of peace and love that started from Bethlehem more than 2000 years ago should continue to shine out from here. Our journey for justice will continue with faith, love and hope, carrying our cross, refusing to be enemies, transforming our pain into a positive energy that is able to change hearts, lives and build a better future."

However, he acknowledged that they face real challenges. "The Jewish settlers in the area have built a road through our land. They bulldozed 200 of our olive trees on this historic farm our family has owned since 1924. They have threatened us with guns." According to Nassar, there are four groups of settlers: "First, the ultra-orthodox Jews who see our land as their 'promised land' and that they are the 'chosen people.' Second, those who see the settlements as an economic investment. Third, the new immigrants from Eastern Europe who are simply seeking more affordable housing (housing in settlements is subsidized by the State of Israel). And fourth, the ideological who come with a bible and a gun and also believe that they have a divine right to the land."

But his hopes were also tied to very practical realities. "Our future is very much tied to the international guests we can invite. In Spring of 2016, 150 came from other countries to plant trees. Importantly, when we have international guests we do not get attacked by settlers. We have interns here today helping out on the farm but," he cautions, "we have no access to electricity or running water from the government. Fortunately, solar panels now provide the electricity we need. Sadly many of the best educated people in this region have been defeated and have left."

There are certain principles that Nassar insisted guide their work at the *Tent of Nations*. "First, we refuse to be victims. We act in our own collective best interests. Second, we refuse to hate in the image of God. Third, we rely on our faith to help us through. And fourth, we believe that justice will rise again. Our commitment is to actions that are nonviolent, constructive and creative."

He continued". "We are also committed to educating others. We want to connect the land and the people. Denied electricity, we find independence through different technologies and actions. For example, we save $75,000 per year on fuel costs. We collect rain water. We use composting toilets. We use bio-gas. We are committed to bringing hope to hopeless situations. In our children's camps we use music and theater to bring Martin Luther King's message in his classic 'I Have a Dream" speech into practice. We also have women empowerment programs. And a harvest camp where we collect our almond crops. And recently we are seeing more Palestinians returning to farm. There has been the threat of Israelis taking over abandoned farms. It seems that we have always lived under pressure but we know that we cannot stay in that fear. We hope for the best and prepare for the worst." The following idea is adapted from Tip #50 in *147 Practical Tips for Teaching Sustainability*.

> Identify religious allies. Find inspiration in the collective ideas and actions of Judeo-Christian, Muslim, Buddhist, and indigenous peoples and others committed to sustainability or the "triple bottom line" of environmental, economic, and societal health. For example, the National Council of Churches offers "Eco-Justice Programs. (See http://nationalcouncilofchurches. us/shared-ministry/justice-advocacy/)

Each one of us can do more to care for the creation and conservation of our natural resources and the collective health of our communities. Ask yourself and others: What are faith-based groups doing in your community and beyond that is truly inspirational?

#88. Discuss possible tensions and the lessons that can emerge from suffering

The English captured Jamaica from the Spanish in 1655. By 1662 there were some 400 black slaves on the island but as sugar cane was introduced as a potentially very profitable cash crop, the number of slaves grew to 9,504 in a little more than a decade. In another 50 years there were more than 86,000 slaves. By 1775, the year of American Independence, there were 192,787 slaves in Jamaica. In the meantime, there were movements in England pushing for the abolition of slavery. In 1807 the African slave trade was abolished by the British Parliament, effective January 1, 1808. Theoretically this meant that no more slaves could be brought from Africa to the colonies in the British West Indies, although slaves could be transported from one colony to the other.

Recognizing that the law was not being followed, the House of Commons in England passed a bill in 1815 requiring the registration of slaves, becoming effective when it was adopted by the colonial legislatures. In 1823 the British government pledged to adopt measures for the abolition of slavery in the colonies. The slaves in Jamaica by this time were very concerned about their status, as the slave trade had already been abolished. In 1824 there was a slave insurrection followed in 1831 by a more widespread revolt. The governor of Jamaica attempted to clarify the slaves' status by proclamation in June 1833. In August 1833 The British Parliament passed the Slavery Abolition Act that became effective on August 1, 1834. The Act made all slaves free, but would remain tied to their former slave masters as "apprentices." The system was a failure, and was abolished. Slaves in British colonies in the West Indies received their unrestricted freedom on August 1, 1838.

The questions remain—long before the American Civil War, Jamaica and Great Britain had abolished the slave trade. Why did it take so much longer in the U.S.? Did anything worthwhile emerge from the suffering in those intervening years and from the war itself? The following "tip" is adapted from #44 in *147 Practical Tips for Teaching Diversity*.

> In a book built around an extended dialogue between the Dalai Lama and Bishop Desmond Tutu (2016), suffering emerges as a source of growth, development and even joy. As Tutu insists,

"some suffering, maybe even intense suffering, is a necessary ingredient for life, certainly for developing compassion. You know, when Nelson Mandela went to jail he was young and, you could almost say, bloodthirsty. He was head of the armed wing of the African National Congress, his party. He spent twenty-seven years in jail and many would say, Twenty-seven years, oh, what a waste. And I think people are surprised when I say no, the twenty-seven years were necessary … The suffering in prison helped him to become more magnanimous, willing to listen to the other side. To discover that the people he regarded as his enemy, they too were human beings who had fears and expectations" (pp. 43-44).

Identify a difficult diversity issue—e.g., groups and voices that have been excluded or marginalized from previous consideration about environmental justice, how poor communities often live closest to toxic waste dumps. Explore the range of reactions that different individuals could have in contrast to any one supposedly "correct" response. How has suffering informed their understanding or undermined their growth and development? What will inspire the needed changes?

#89. Help students understand systems

The bodies of three civil rights workers—James Chaney, Michael Schwerner and Andrew Goodman—were pulled from the muck of an earthen dam on August 4, 1964. After travelling to heavily segregated Mississippi to help organize efforts on behalf of the Congress of Racial Equality (CORE), their disappearance on June 21 garnered national attention and eventually helped to inspire the nation about the righteousness of this movement.

Michael Schwerner had arrived in Mississippi as a CORE field worker in January 1964 and quickly became a target for the Ku Klux Klan after he organized a successful black boycott of a variety store in the city of Meridian and led voting registration efforts for African Americans. In May, Sam Bowers, the Imperial Wizard of the White Knights of the KKK in Mississippi, sent word that the 24-year-old Schwerner was to be killed. On June 16, twenty plus armed Klansmen had descended on Mount Zion Methodist Church, an African American church in Neshoba County, which Schwerner was using as a "Freedom School." Schwerner was not there at the time, but the Klansmen beat several African Americans who were present and then torched the church.

On June 20, Schwerner returned from a civil rights training session in Ohio with 21-year-old James Chaney and 20-year-old Andrew Goodman, a new recruit to CORE. The next day these three went to investigate the burning of the church in Neshoba. While attempting to drive back to Meridian, they were stopped by Neshoba County Deputy Sheriff Cecil Price just inside the city limits of Philadelphia, the county seat. Price, a member of the KKK who had been looking out for Schwerner or other civil rights workers, threw them in the Neshoba County jail, allegedly under suspicion for church arson.

After a few hours in jail, during which the men were not allowed to make a phone call, Price released them on bail. After escorting them out of town, the deputy returned to Philadelphia to drop off an accompanying Philadelphia police officer. As soon as he was alone, he raced down the highway in pursuit of the three civil rights workers. He caught the men just inside the county limits and loaded them into his car. Two other cars pulled up filled with Klansmen who had been alerted by Price of the capture of the CORE workers, and the three cars drove down an unmarked dirt road called Rock Cut Road. Schwerner, Goodman, and Chaney were shot to death and their bodies buried in an earthen dam a few miles from the Mount Zion Methodist Church.

The next day, the FBI began an investigation into the disappearance of the civil rights workers. On June 23, the case drew national headlines, and federal agents found the workers' burned station wagon. Under pressure from Attorney General Robert F. Kennedy, the FBI escalated the investigation, which eventually involved more than 200 FBI agents and scores of federal troops who combed the woods and swamps looking for the bodies. The incident provided the final impetus needed for the 1964 Civil Rights Act to pass Congress on July 2, and eight days later FBI Director J. Edgar Hoover came to Mississippi to open a new Bureau office. Eventually, Delmar Dennis, a Klansman and one of the participants in the murders, was paid $30,000 and offered immunity from prosecution in exchange for information. On August 4, the remains of the three young men were found. The killers were identified, but the state of Mississippi made no arrests.

Finally, on December 4, nineteen men, including Deputy Price, were indicted by the U.S. Justice Department for violating the civil rights of Schwerner, Goodman, and Chaney (charging the suspects with civil rights violations was the only way to give the federal government jurisdiction in the case). After nearly three years of legal wrangling, in which the U.S. Supreme Court ultimately defended the indictments, the men went on trial in Jackson, Mississippi. The trial was presided over by an ardent segregationist, U.S. District Judge William Cox, but under pressure from federal authorities and fearing impeachment, he took the case seriously. On October 27, 1967, an all-white jury found seven of the men guilty, including Price and KKK Imperial Wizard Bowers. Nine were acquitted, and the jury deadlocked on three others. The mixed verdict was hailed as a major civil rights victory, as no one in Mississippi had ever before been convicted for actions taken against a civil rights worker.

In December, Judge Cox sentenced the men to prison terms ranging from three to 10 years. After sentencing, he reportedly said, "They killed one nigger, one Jew, and a white man. I gave them what I thought they deserved." None of the convicted men served more than six years behind bars. On June 21, 2005, the forty-first anniversary of the three murders, Edgar Ray Killen, was found guilty of three counts of manslaughter. At eighty years of age and best known as an outspoken white supremacist and part-time Baptist minister, he was sentenced to 60 years in prison. As a deeply troubling and violent chapter in American history, this case can inspire students and other audiences to search for a deeper understanding of the systems that were in place at the time that allowed this tragedy to occur. The following "tip" is adapted from #42 in *147 Practical Tips for Teaching Diversity.*

> We all live in systems that perpetuate and even promote biases—sexism, racism, heterosexism, ableism, ageism, classism, for example. In their book on teaching sustainability, Timpson et al. (2017) describe the systems thinking that is essential when trying to attend to the interconnected health of the environment, society and the economy, the "triple bottom line." The complexities are obvious but students can be guided in developing their abilities to handle these challenges, both intellectually and emotionally.

Encourage everyone to do a deeper analysis of the systems in their disciplines that conspire

*to maintain certain biases through particular policies or practices, e.g., traditional recruit-
ment that overlooks talent in underrepresented populations, limited support for students
coming from poor communities and under resourced schools, textbooks that ignore the
contributions of various marginalized populations, the legacy of power and privilege that
was built on racist hierarchies and oppressive controls.*

#90. Know that there's a time to be objective, detached and creative

In August of 1965, President Lyndon Baines Johnson signed the Voting Rights Act,
fulfilling a promise he had made to the nation in the aftermath of President Kennedy's assassination to lead a recommitment to basic rights of citizenship. Designed
to enforce the voting rights guaranteed by the Fourteenth and Fifteenth Amend-
ments to the United States Constitution, the Act attempted to secure voting rights
for racial minorities throughout the country, especially in the South. According to
the U.S. Department of Justice, this Act is considered to be the most effective piece
of federal civil rights legislation ever enacted in the country.

In a speech to Congress in March of 1965, Johnson outlined the devious ways in
which election officials denied African-American citizens the vote. Some were told
by election officials that they had gotten the date, time or polling place wrong, that
the officials were late or absent, that they possessed insufficient literacy skills or
had filled out an application incorrectly. Some voting officials, primarily in southern states, had been known to force black voters to recite sections of the constitution from memory or explain the most complex provisions of state laws. In some
cases, even blacks with college degrees were turned away from the polls. This Act
specifically outlawed literacy tests and similar devices that were historically used
to disenfranchise racial minorities.

Although the Voting Rights Act passed, state and local enforcement of the law was
weak and often ignored, mainly in the South and in areas where the proportion of
blacks in the population was high and their vote would threaten the political status quo. Still, the Voting Rights Act gave African-American voters the legal means
to challenge voting restrictions and vastly improve voter turnout. In Mississippi
alone, voter turnout among blacks increased from 6 percent in 1964 to 59 percent
in 1969. Years later we can see how this legislation inspired change. The following

concept is adapted from "tip" #45 in *147 Practical Tips for Teaching Diversity.*

> Reflect back on various discussions you have had about diversity topics. How constrained have you been by "cultural norms", by what you think is possible based on what you have been told, what you learned through formal studies as well as from what you read and what you get through the media? When have you been inspired to "think outside the box" to imagine a new and different way forward?

> In his classic book, *The Structure of Scientific Revolution,* Thomas Kuhn (1970) used the example of Galileo to describe the difficulties of going against the teachings of a culture. Seeing new "data" about the movement of the stars and planets in the night skies through the telescopes and other devices that were used, Gallileo faced fierce condemnation and house arrest when he came to the conclusion that it was the sun that was the center of the universe, not the earth. In spite of meticulous documentation and data, Charles Darwin delayed publication of *The Origin of Species* for 22 years, knowing full well that there would be storm of criticism coming at him for theorizing about a system of evolution that seemed to challenge the prevailing belief in the earth's creation in seven days and seven nights, the literal interpretation of the biblical story.

> Learning to be objective and detached are ways to "think outside the box" when faced with data that offers new and different conclusions. There is a mix of the intellectual and the emotional when facing the need to be creative.

Make some reminders for yourself about upcoming topics. How can you be more objective and detached? More creative? More inspiring? How does a historic reference help? Identify any "prevailing paradigms" — using the words of Thomas Kuhn (1970) — that would interfere or suppress or limit a full and open consideration of new and different ideas. For example, the question of reparations for former slaves in the U.S. periodically surfaces but seems to quickly submerge under the weight of arguments that it would be too complicated. Yet, we know from the experiences of the Truth and Reconciliation Commission in South Africa that substantial reparations were provided to the "victims" of apartheid (Tutu, 1997). Pointing to this success may help those in the U.S., too many of whom seem to be stuck in their concern about what is not possible.

#91. Create soldiers of peace and reconciliation

In August of 1939 on the eve of war in Europe, Albert Einstein wrote to President Roosevelt about the prospect of Germany developing an atomic bomb. He warned FDR that this bomb would have devastating potential. Roosevelt took his advice and started the Manhattan project to develop the U.S. atom bomb. However, after he had seen the results of the use of the atomic bomb on Hiroshima and Nagasaki by the American military, Einstein was inspired to say, "Had I known that the Germans would not succeed in producing an atomic bomb, I would not have lifted a finger" (Newsweek, 10 March 1947).

Einstein was born in March of 1879 in Germany. His parents were working-class and non-observant Jews. When he was 15, his family moved to Milan, Italy where his father hoped Albert would become a mechanical engineer. However, despite the intellect and thirst for knowledge that would show forth later in life, Einstein's early school performance was unimpressive. His teachers reported that he was slow to learn. In his own defence, Albert expressed no interest in learning languages and the learning by rote that was popular at the time.

As a German Jew, Einstein was threatened by the rise of the Nazi party. In 1933, when the Nazi's seized power, they confiscated his property, and later started burning his books. Einstein, then in England, took an offer to go to Princeton University in the U.S. Over the years he was involved in many civil rights movements including the campaign to end lynching. He joined the National Association for the Advancement of Colored People (NAACP) and considered racism as America's worst disease. However, he also spoke highly of the meritocratic impulses in American society and the value for speaking freely. He famously said that he did not know how World War Three would be fought, but that in the Fourth World War, the weapons would be rocks! Ask yourself: What would happen if more people spoke up regularly about the horrors of nuclear war and inspired others to get involved? The following "tip" is adapted from #53 in *147 Practical Tips for Teaching*

Peace and Reconciliation.

> In *No Future without Forgiveness,* Bishop Desmond Tutu describes the reconciliation process adopted in South Africa to begin healing the wounds left from years of a brutal, racist policy of apartheid that kept the black majority under the iron fist of the government's security forces. On both sides of the racial divide, certain stories emerged that help explain why the country was able to avoid the bloodshed that most people predicted would occur and instead move peacefully toward democratic control.

> "Chris Hani, who was later assassinated on the eve of our historic elections (in 1994), had established his unassailable place in the hearts of the militant township youth. . . A military man himself, he could have drawn hordes to his side had he declared himself opposed to the negotiation process, if he had aligned himself to those who wanted to continue the armed struggle. Instead he took his reputation in his hands and went around the country urging the youth to be henceforth 'soldiers of peace,' and the youth responded enthusiastically to the call to work for peace and reconciliation" (p. 42).

When have you seen others resist the call to arms and instead advocate for peace? How do we inspire veterans with military experiences as well as scientists to be "soldiers for peace and reconciliation"?

#92. Practice best-case thinking about peace and reconciliation

In August of 1945, an American bomber dropped a five-ton bomb over the Japanese city of Hiroshima, a blast that was equivalent to the power of 15,000 tons of TNT reduced four square miles of the city to ruins and immediately killed 80,000 people. Tens of thousands more died in the following weeks from wounds and radiation poisoning. Three days later, another bomb was dropped on the city of Nagasaki, killing nearly 40,000 more people. A few days later, Japan announced its surrender. Despite the jubilation over the end of World War Two, these atomic bombs also inspired a parallel call for an end to the use of these weapons.

This discussion continues. In the years since the two atomic bombs were dropped, a number of historians have suggested that the weapons had a two-pronged objective. The first was to end the war with Japan and spare American lives. A second, according to some, was to demonstrate the power of the U.S. military arsenal and this new weapon of mass destruction, in particular, for the Soviet Union to see. By August 1945, relations between the U.S.S.R. and the United States had deteriorated badly and by 1949, the Soviets had developed their own atomic bomb and the nuclear arms race began. At the core of these discussions is the question about the role of the bombings in Japan's surrender. The fundamental issue that has divided scholars ever since is whether the use of the bomb was necessary to achieve victory in the war in the Pacific on terms satisfactory to the United States.

Those who oppose the bombings cite a number of other reasons as well, among them: a belief that atomic bombing is fundamentally immoral, that the bombings counted as war crimes given the number of civilian casualties, that they constituted state terrorism, and that they involved racism against and the dehumanization of the Japanese people. The bombings were part of an already fierce conventional bombing campaign that included the fire-bombing of Tokyo, for example. This, together with the naval blockade, many believe could also have eventually led to a Japanese surrender.

At the time the United States dropped its atomic bomb on Nagasaki on August 9, 1945, the Soviet Union launched a surprise attack with 1.6 million troops against the Kwantung Army in Manchuria. This attack also ended any hope that the Russians might mediate and help Japanese avoid an unconditional surrender. The following "tip" is adapted from #109 in *147 Practical Tips for Teaching Peace and Reconciliation*.

> In her book, *Cultures of Peace*, Elise Boulding (2000) makes a strong argument for a new paradigm in the way we think, individually and collectively, locally and globally. "In general, societies tend to be a blend of peaceable and warrior culture themes—the balance between the themes varying from society to society and from historical moment to historical moment. In our time, the tensions between the two themes have become a heavy social burden as a worldwide military forcing system linked to a destructive, plan-

et-harming mode of industrialization and urbanization is distorting the human capability for creative and peaceful change. No sooner did the fears of nuclear holocaust fade with the end of the Cold War than the fear of genocidal ethnic warfare reducing once proudly independent countries to a series of dusty battlegrounds rose to take the place of earlier fears. Urban violence—now manifesting itself in gun battles in the cities and neighborhoods and even the schoolyards and playgrounds of the industrial West—has unleashed other terrors. If every society is a blend of the themes of violence and peaceableness, why is the peaceableness so hard to see? It is there, but not well reported. The tendency of planners and policymakers to prepare for worst-case scenarios leaves societies unprepared for the opportunities involved in best-case scenarios" (p. 4).

Identify a problem you are having. Indulge yourself in some worst-case thinking. Now try some best-case thinking. What insights do you get about each? For many people, worst-case thinking reinforces fear-based responses, a tightening and narrowing of the hard-wired flight-or-fight response. However, when people utilize best-case thinking, they tend to see many more options, an openness to possibility in the present and hope on the horizon. In best-case thinking, there is more openness to explore new and different solutions.

#93. Use inductive thinking to re-think problems

In August of 1964, the crew of the USS destroyer Maddox received an intelligence report suggesting that three North Vietnamese patrol boats had been dispatched to attack it. The naval ship's captain, John J. Herrick, initially ordered Maddox to head out to sea, hoping to avoid confrontation. However, a few hours later, Herrick reversed his orders, and the destroyer returned to the Gulf. Within a few hours, three North Vietnamese patrol boats were fast approaching the destroyer, and Herrick ordered the ship's guns to be at the ready. He told his crew to be prepared to fire if the patrol boats came within 10,000 yards. He also called in air support from the U.S.S. Ticonderoga, which was stationed nearby. While that threat was averted, the Maddox later reported multiple torpedo attacks as well as automatic weapons fire.

The next day, in a demonstration of American resolve, President Johnson ordered the destroyer Turner Joy to join Maddox in the Gulf of Tonkin. These ships both received intelligence suggesting that another North Vietnamese attack was imminent. With visibility poor and storms approaching, Captain Herrick ordered the destroyers to take evasive measures to avoid confrontation, by moving further out to sea. Just before 9 p.m. that night, Maddox reported spotting unidentified vessels in the area. Over the next three hours, Maddox and Turner Joy were engaged in high-speed maneuvers designed to evade attack, although it was unclear whether or not North Vietnamese ships were in fact in pursuit. Still, Maddox reported multiple torpedo attacks as well as automatic weapons fire. Both destroyers returned fire, launching multiple shells at the "enemy."

U.S. President Johnson took to the airwaves to inform the American public of the attack and to announce his intention to retaliate. However, Navy Commander James Stockdale, who had overseen the air defense of Maddox two days before and was flying recognizance over the Gulf of Tonkin on August 4th, cast doubt on whether there was indeed an attack that day, noting that the destroyers were shooting at phantom targets. Captain Herrick, too, later questioned his crew's version of events, and attributed their actions on August 4th to "overeager sonar operators" and crew member error.

"Inspired" by what turned out to be a phantom attack, Congress passed the Gulf of Tonkin Resolution, which the president signed into law three days later, and used to plan a dramatic increase of U.S. military involvement in Vietnam. A few months later the United States launched Operation Rolling Thunder, a massive bombing campaign of North Vietnamese targets that would last for more than two years. The president also authorized the deployment of ground combat troops to fight the Viet Cong in the Vietnamese countryside.

By the time the war did end, with the North Vietnamese invasion of the South in 1975, nearly 60,000 U.S. servicemen had lost their lives, along with nearly 250,000 South Vietnamese troops, 1.1 million Viet Cong and North Vietnamese fighters and more than two million civilians across the country. The question remains: How should we honor those who brought to light this "phantom" attack that led to such tragic destruction and losses? The following "tip" is adapted from #113 in *147 Practical Tips for Teaching Peace and Reconciliation*.

Peace and reconciliation often require new ideas and different thinking and, consequently, teaching can truly be transformative. One approach that can help people arrive at new insights is to guide an inductive analysis where data are grouped and regrouped, old ideas challenged and new concepts created. In *My Pilgrimage to Nonviolence,* Martin Luther King Jr. (2000) looked back over the conflicts in the first half of the twentieth century and, instead of seeing collapse and despair saw something emergent and hopeful. "We who live in the twentieth century are privileged to live in one of the most momentous periods of human history. It is an exciting age, filled with hope. It is an age in which a new social order is being born. We stand today between two worlds—the dying old and the emerging new. Now I am aware of the fact that there are those who would contend that we live in the most ghastly period of human history. They would argue that the rhythmic beat of the deep rumblings of discontent from Asia, the uprisings in Africa, the nationalistic longings of Egypt, the roaring cannons from Hungary, and the racial tensions of America are all indicative of the deep and tragic midnight which encompasses our civilization. They would argue that we are retrogressing instead of progressing. But far from representing retrogression and tragic meaninglessness, the present tensions represent the necessary pains that accompany the birth of anything new" (p. 178).

This inductive process for King began with a listing of the violence he was seeing both near and far. However, instead of accepting the despairing interpretations that he was hearing from others, he chose to organize this "data" differently and see something much more hopeful. Yes, there was a coming apart, but for King these events also meant a "birth" of freedom, a coming out for those seeking independence from the older colonial powers. Without trivializing the violence that accompanied these changes, King recognized these "pains" as necessary for the emergence of the new order.

In their book, Concepts and Choices for Teaching, *Timpson and Doe (2008) describe* the inductive process. Try a similar process for yourself or with others. Begin with a listing of conflicts that you can see—global, national, regional or local, personal or interpersonal. What would most people conclude? Now group these conflicts in ways that lead to a different conclusion. Move issues around until new groupings emerge. Try various labels. Step back and look for possible relationships. Hypothesize what may be the underlying concepts. For example, consider the "get tough" policies that have filled U.S. prisons at the turn of the twenty-first century. An analysis of offenses would show that many inmates are in prison because of drug offenses and addiction. Two fundamental questions emerge: What are the consequences, both positive and negative, if we de-criminalize addiction and use a therapeutic approach instead? How would cost be affected?

#94. Make connections

In August of 1492 Italian explorer Christopher Columbus set sail on a journey to find a western sea route to China, India, and the fabled treasures of Asia. A little more than two months later, the expedition sighted land, probably Watling Island in the Bahamas, and went ashore the same day, claiming it for Spain. Later that month, Columbus sighted Cuba, which he thought was mainland China, and in December the expedition landed on Hispaniola, which Columbus thought might be Japan. He established a small colony there with 39 of his men. The explorer returned to Spain with gold, spices, and "Indian" captives in March 1493 and was received with the highest honors by the Spanish court, inspiring other Europeans to follow his lead and journey to explore the Americas.

During his lifetime, Columbus led a total of four expeditions to the New World, discovering various Caribbean islands, the Gulf of Mexico, and the South and Central American mainland, but never accomplished his original goal—a western ocean route to the great cities of Asia. Columbus died in Spain in 1506 without realizing the great scope of what he did achieve: He had discovered for Europe the New World, whose riches over the next century would help make Spain the wealthiest and most powerful nation on earth. With a retelling of this history by Native Americans, however, we also remember Columbus for inspiring waves of other explorers as well as settlers who stole the wealth, land and lives of those who had been living in the Americas for centuries. The following "tip" is adapted from #63 in *147 Practical Tips for Using Experiential Learning*.

Most people will fragment or organize information into digestible pieces so that they can have better control or understanding (Bohm, 1980). Miller (1956) suggested that humans are limited in memory to seven plus or minus two (i.e., five to nine) units or chunks of information. In our need to fragment information—scholars will talk of "reductionism"—we can lose site of the whole, the "big picture." In *The Web of Inclusion*, Sally Helgesen (1995) speaks of a way of "conceptualizing our universe that emphasized the inescapable interdependence of all things, and thus affirms the value and importance of every fragment of the greater whole—the 'universal interwovenness' (p. 16)." In order to preserve the holistic quality of an experience, reflect on the following questions:

- When do you fragment knowledge about Columbus?
- What is the consequence of losing sight of the whole picture of the impact on the native populations?
- How can you design and facilitate a learning experience that sustains this "universal interwovenness", the full picture of the arrival of Europeans in the Americas?
- When we take the time to do this, we can help people see the interconnectedness of reality.

When you next make a presentation, ask yourself if you are doing enough to frame the big picture, the interconnectedness of concepts and meaning, what will inspire a deeper understanding.

#95. Create classroom community

Alex Haley, author of *Roots* and *The Autobiography of Malcolm X*, was born on August 11, 1921 in Ithaca, New York although he grew up in Henning, Tennessee, where his maternal grandparents lived and where he heard stories of his family history from his grandmother. At fifteen he graduated early from high school and then at eighteen enlisted in the Coast Guard. It was during those long stints at sea that he started writing to pass the time. In 1959 he began writing for magazines. He interviewed Malcolm X for *Playboy* magazine and turned this into his first book, *The Autobiography of Malcolm X*. Published shortly after Malcolm's assassination, this book sold 6 million copies in hardcover.

Haley's next novel, *Roots* (1976), was a fictionalized account of his own family's history, traced through seven generations. The novel was translated into 37 languages and won a special Pulitzer Prize. It later became the basis for a 1977 miniseries that became the most-watched broadcast in TV history to that time, drawing an unprecedented 100 million viewers over eight days. Haley inspired many Americans to look deeper through the human stories of slaves and the communities they were able to create. The following "tip" is adapted from #57 in *147 Practical Tips for Using Experiential Learning*.

> There are many reasons to put some effort and thought into creating a community that supports and inspires learning. You can help people overcome a sense of isolation, encourage them to engage more in the content and the activities, facilitate a deeper learning experience, hopefully increase everyone's intrinsic motivation to learn (i.e., without external rewards like points or grades), discourage drop outs, and promote a greater respect for the diversity of all learners (Lui, Magjuka, Bonk, & Lee, 2007).

> Creating a community can help people look to others to support their learning and capture the benefits of active and cooperative learning, some of the "synergy" that is available, i.e., where learning in the group is more than the sum of the parts. This will mean a shift away from a preoccupation with "pleasing the instructor" or "getting all their answers right." Trying new approaches and learning from mistakes will require some confidence and risk. When this occurs, when learning is more independent and interdependent, the facilitator can focus more on the quality of learning and trust that the group will rise to the challenge of supporting its individual members. The setting or classroom then represents a more holistic experience, mixing the learning of course content with personal and group development.

Identify instances when you felt that you had a sense of community. What aspects helped that community to develop? How could you inspire a greater sense of community in your classes, activities, or presentations?

#96. Find your own special place

In August of 2017, Grace Yenne visited her grandparent's homeland in Jaffa, Israel. In 1948 they had fled their home when armed Israeli forces took up the fight for an independent Jewish homeland, forcing some 500,000 Palestinians to flee as refugees. After landing in Lebanon, her grandparents eventually moved again to London where her grandad got work as an architect. The next move for them was to the U.S. For Grace in 2017, this trip to her ancestral home was very important, very moving. She remembered her grandparents talking about the beaches and the oranges, in particular, although her grandfather did not want to talk about the politics of the time. For Grace the visit to Jaffa was especially inspiring because her grandparents and parents had moved so much, had become part of the Palestinian diaspora. The following idea is adapted from "tip" #31 in *147 Practical Tips for Using Experiential Learning.*

> Lisa Pitot is an experienced Middle School science teacher who has also worked at the university. She writes: "In terms of place-based education, we have to ask what exactly is place? Place-based educators know that place is more than just a location, that place encompasses space and time. Individuals and people come to be defined by place as much as place comes to be defined by individuals and people (van Eijck & Roth, 2010). It is from ages 10-11 that we get our grounding. Taking the time to return to our roots can help us get re-grounded and re-inspired."

Respond to the following: Think about a special place when you were 'young.' Is it inside or outside? What stands out? What is inspiring? What do you see? Hear? Smell? After thinking about it for a while, draw a map of your special place. After completing your map, write down your observations. What emotions, if any, came up? Take time to share and discuss your map with others. Reflect on whether this exercise was easy or hard. Were your memories fact-based, more emotional, or both? Identify a special place in your life today. What connections are there with your special childhood place?

SEPTEMBER
Tips #97-108

In September of 1666 the great fire of London broke out, destroying over 13,000 houses. Over two hundred years later fire would sweep Chicago and destroy over 17,000 buildings and eventually inspired new housing and building codes that have greatly reduced these kinds of massive fire risks. In September of 1864 Atlanta would fall to the forces of Union General William Sherman, splitting the Confederacy and forecasting the ultimate defeat of the secessionist forces defending state's rights and slavery. In September of 1893 New Zealand became the first nation to grant women the right to vote, inspiring a long, slow challenge to patriarchal controls everywhere. In September of 1939 Hitler invaded Poland and galvanized the allies of the world to rise up over the next six years to defeat this racist, demonic and tragic drive for power, with the final surrender of Japan coming in September of 1945. In September of 1989 F. W. De Klerk became President of South Africa and helped usher in the reforms that would dismantle the racist system of apartheid controls, free Nelson Mandela from prison and, in collaboration with the African National Congress, inspire the nation's transformation to democracy.

#97. Read sacred texts

Mother Teresa, a Roman Catholic nun and missionary, has inspired so many with her selfless devotion to those in need. During her early years Teresa was herself moved by stories of the lives of missionaries and by age twelve she was convinced that she should commit herself to religious life. She was born in 1910 and died in September of 1997. After living in Macedonia for eighteen years she moved to Ireland and then to India, where she lived for most of her life.

In 1950 Teresa founded the Missionaries of Charity, a Roman Catholic religious congregation which had over 4,500 sisters and was active in 133 countries in 2012. The congregation manages a number of much needed operations—homes for people dying of HIV/AIDS, leprosy and tuberculosis; soup kitchens; dispensaries and mobile clinics; children's- and family-counselling programs; orphanages, and schools. Members profess four vows—to chastity, poverty, obedience, as well as free service to the poorest of the poor. Mother Teresa, who died in 1997, received a number of honors, including the 1979 Nobel Peace Prize. She was canonized (recognized by the church as a saint) in September of 2016. The following "tip" is adapted from #51 in *147 Practical Tips for Teaching Sustainability*.

> For clear communication, it is important to share a common language and to understand the underpinnings of what others value and believe. For example, the Bible has helped to shape thinking for many in the United States and elsewhere about the environment, the economy, and human relationships. Reading sacred texts can provide insight into these roots.

See what you can discover by searching for references to sustainability, peace and diversity within sacred texts. For example, if we recognize the "Triple Bottom Line" of sustainability—i.e., the interconnected health of the environment, society and the economy—we can see how Mother Teresa's dedication and service has inspired others.

#98. Understand the tipping point

The Great Galveston Hurricane was a Category 4 storm, with winds of up to 145 mph that made landfall on September 8, 1900, in Galveston, Texas. It killed over 6,000 people, making it the deadliest hurricane or natural disaster in U.S. history and inspiring new thinking about the future of development there. Because of contradictory forecasts, the people of Galveston felt no alarm until the official hurricane warning of September 7. The next morning, a storm surge of 15 feet washed over the long, flat island-city, which was only 8 feet above sea level, knocking buildings off their foundations and destroying over 3,600 homes. The disaster alarmed potential investors who turned to Houston instead. The Gulf of Mexico shoreline of Galveston Island was subsequently raised by 17 feet and a 10-mile seawall was erected.

On their website, the Union of Concerned Scientists assert that while hurricanes are a natural part of our climate system, recent research suggests that there has been an increase in intense hurricane activity particularly in the North Atlantic since the 1970s. In the future, there may not necessarily be more hurricanes, but there will likely be more intense hurricanes that carry higher wind speeds and more precipitation as a result of climate change. Sea level rise and a growing population along coastlines will certainly make the impact worse. Because of climate change, a storm system that used to occur once in every 100 years now repeats every 16 years. The following concept is adapted from "tip" #52 in *147 Practical Tips for Teaching Sustainability.*

> In *The Tipping Point,* Malcom Gladwell (2002) describes how decades, if not longer, were required to garner the critical mass of public support to achieve many of the United States' greatest successes. Review the history that led to these changes to understand how such milestones were often the culmination of decades of contributions by many people in the movement. Students and others will begin to understand that major shifts in societal behavior and values require some sparks—in the case of the Galveston area, a major natural disaster—to eventually ignite a mass of people to get involved and take action, to rethink development or do more to protect their existing communities. Eventually the desired changes become gradually accepted as the norm. Shifts in thinking impact policy and practice. Individuals can impact the tipping point of sustainability on a particular issue.

Reflect on various political changes from the past like women's suffrage and the civil rights movement to better understand what constitutes the "tipping point" when enough people are inspired to come together for a long enough time and exert enough pressure that a sustained change occurs in actions and beliefs.

#99. Identify new leaders

In early colonial New Zealand, as in other European societies, women were excluded from any involvement in politics. Public opinion began to change in the latter half of the nineteenth century, however, and inspired by the effort by activists over many years, in September of 1893, New Zealand became the first self-governing colony in the world in which all women had the right to vote in parliamentary elections. In the U.S. it would require another 27 years for the 19th Amendment to pass in 1920 and women would be allowed to vote. The following "tip" is adapted from #57 in *147 Practical Tips for Teaching Sustainability.*

> In *Enough: Staying Human in an Engineered Age,* Bill McKibben (2003) identifies Gandhi as someone who is widely revered for challenging the world to use nonviolent noncooperation as a mechanism for resistance to powerful oppressors. Yet Gandhi also represented much more. "It is no coincidence that Gandhi was also the most powerful twentieth-century spokesman for the proposition that less is more, that human satisfaction lies in respecting material limits, in opening yourself to the claims of others, in backing away from the hyper-individualism of the West" (p. 217). Are there any leaders who support sustainability, equity and social justice already in place in your community? How do we identify and unleash the leadership potential among students?

Given the changes needed for a more sustainable future that balances environmental, economic, and societal needs, we need to find leaders at every level of society and in every community, men and women, who will spearhead these changes and inspire others to follow their lead. Make a list of individuals who could lead this redirection. Identify leaders from the past who had the qualities needed today.

#100. Counter polarization

After 30 years of battling whites, the Apache warrior Geronimo finally surrendered in Arizona, on September 4, 1886. When he was a young man, Mexican soldiers had killed his wife and children during an attack on his village in Chihuahua, Mexico. Though Geronimo later remarried and fathered other children, the scars of that early tragedy inspired him as a warrior.

Operating in the border lands between the mountains of northern Mexico and the southwest of Arizona and New Mexico, Geronimo and his band of 50 Apache warriors were able to keep white settlers off Apache lands for decades. Geronimo armed his men with the best rifles he could get. He was a brilliant strategist who used the Apache knowledge of the land to his advantage. For years Geronimo and his men successfully evaded two of the U.S. Army's most talented Indian fighters. But by 1886, he had grown tired of fighting and further resistance seemed increasingly pointless: there were just too many whites and too few Apaches. On September 4, 1886, he turned himself over to the U.S. Army, becoming the last American Indian warrior in history to formally surrender to the United States.

After several years of imprisonment, Geronimo was given his freedom, and he moved to Oklahoma where he converted to Christianity and became a successful farmer. He even occasionally worked as a scout and adviser for the U.S. army. Transformed into a safe and romantic symbol of the already vanishing era of the Wild West, he became a popular celebrity at world's fairs and expositions and even rode in President Theodore Roosevelt's inaugural parade in 1905. He died at Fort Sill, Oklahoma, in 1909, still on the federal payroll as an army scout. The following idea is adapted from "tip" #46 in *147 Practical Tips for Teaching Diversity.*

> Learning requires that we be open and willing to move beyond defensiveness and rethink particular beliefs. William Perry (1999) notes that the hallmark of the highest stage of cognitive development is this ability to open up to other perspectives, accept the resulting ambiguities and better handle complexity.
>
> Roe Bubar and Irene Vernon (2003) offer this advice when sides are forming: "The class may devolve into standoffs between students of color versus whites, or women versus men, young versus old, and/or Native Americans versus others. If this type of polarization occurs, we reassert control over the class to ensure a classroom environment where everyone can speak and explore the issues at hand. With open discussions, students can reflect on their own biases, understandings, and histories as well as the biases, understandings, and histories of others" (p. 164). An overly simplistic approach sees Geronimo in dichotomous terms, as either a blameless victim of oppression by American and Mexican forces or as a marauding, dangerous renegade.

Reflect back on a discussion when everyone seemed to be polarized about a particular controversial issue, inspired or angered by one side or the other. Make some notes about what you might have done differently as discussion leader. For example, you could have shared your recognition of the arguments raised. You might also have shared how you have been able to rethink your ideas on a particular issue. You could also plan to do something proactive for an upcoming class or discussion, such as sharing your concern about polarization and discuss what ground rules everyone could follow.

#101. Prepare for sensitive topics

In September of 1986 Desmond Tutu was appointed the archbishop of Cape Town, two years after winning the Nobel Peace Prize for his role in helping to inspire the nonviolent opposition to apartheid in South Africa. As archbishop, he was the first black to head South Africa's Anglican Church and was later given the leadership of the Truth and Reconciliation Commission by Nelson Mandela, the newly elected President of this newly democratic nation, in an effort to help heal the wounds of that bitter history of racial oppression.

In 1948, South Africa's white minority government had imposed its policy of racial segregation and white supremacy known as apartheid–Afrikaans for "apartness." Eighty percent of the country's land was set aside for white use, and black Africans entering the white territory required special passes. Blacks, who had no representation in the government, were subjected to different labor laws and educational standards than whites and lived in extreme poverty while white South Africans prospered through their enforced privileges and state-sanctioned exploitation.

Organized anti-apartheid protests began in the 1950s, and in the 1960s Nelson Mandela and other anti-apartheid leaders were imprisoned. In the 1970s, a new phase of protest began, with black trade unions organizing strikes. After the Soweto uprising of June 1976, more than 500 black activists were killed by police. In the 1980s, protests continued, and the South African government resorted to brutal tactics, using the military and police to suppress and silence opposition to white rule. Thousands of blacks were tortured and killed.

Meanwhile, a black Anglican minister named Desmond Tutu was emerging as an important leader of the anti-apartheid movement. He advocated nonviolence and successfully pushed for international sanctions against South Africa. In 1984, he was awarded the Nobel Prize for Peace. The next year, he was installed as Johannesburg's first black Anglican bishop.

When Desmond Tutu was elected the archbishop of Cape Town, he became the spiritual leader of nearly two million Anglicans in South Africa and more than a million others in neighboring countries. In his new position, he continued his outspoken criticism of apartheid. Desmond Tutu retired as Anglican archbishop in 1996, two years after majority rule came to South Africa with the election of Nelson Mandela and the African National Congress. The following "tip" is adapted from #47 in *147 Practical Tips for Teaching Diversity.*

> In the aftermath of problems that surfaced in class around person-
> al commitments to addressing diversity, Timothy Davies (2003)
> describes how useful it was for him and his students to prepare
> for public discussions "by leading into them with the readings
> and reacting to the readings through an electronic private mail
> journal, which links the student and instructor. The students felt
> that, in this way, they could explore some of their thoughts and
> feelings in private before bringing them out to the cohort as a
> whole" (p. 51). Studying the anti-apartheid movement of South
> Africa and Bishop Tutu's role can inspire people everywhere to
> imagine how those same principles of nonviolent resistance could
> be applied to other problems and issues.

Have everyone write a few comments about times when they were hesitant to speak up in class. Ask them if they believe that shared readings and private reflections before a discussion occurs would have helped. Plan to prepare differently for the next time a sensitive topic is scheduled for discussion, perhaps asking everyone to share their concerns, questions and "hesitations" in advance of meeting again as a group. Ask in the name of Bishop Tutu what would inspire them to take action.

#102. Remember that emotions can also be constructive

In September of 1993 officials from Israel and the Palestine Liberation Organization exchanged letters of recognition. After decades of angry and at times violent exchanges, representatives of Israel and Palestine met at the White House to sign a framework for peace. The "Declaration of Principles" was the first agreement between the Israelis and Palestinians towards ending their conflict and sharing the holy land that they both claim as their homeland. In an area of the world considered by many to be locked into intractable conflict, these movements toward a peaceful co-existence provide inspiration for what may be possible.

Fighting between Jews and Arabs in Palestine dates back to the 1920s when both groups laid claim to the British-controlled territory. The Jews were recent emigrants from Europe and Russia who came as Zionists to what they believed to be their ancient and divinely ordained homeland to establish a Jewish national state. The native Arabs wanted to stop Jewish immigration and set up their own secular Palestinian state.

In May 1948, in the aftermath of the Holocaust and a world war that forced millions of Jews to flee their homelands and seek refuge, the State of Israel was proclaimed. Soon thereafter five Arab nations attacked in support of the Palestinian Arabs. The outnumbered Israelis fought off the Arab armies and seized substantial territory originally allocated to the Arabs in the 1947 United Nations partition of Palestine. In 1949, U.N.-brokered cease-fires left the State of Israel in permanent control of this conquered territory. The departure of hundreds of thousands of Palestinian Arabs from Israel during the war left the country with a substantial Jewish majority. Israel restricted the rights of the Arabs who remained. Most Palestinian Arabs who left Israeli territory retreated to the West Bank, then controlled by Transjordan, and others to the Gaza Strip, controlled by Egypt. Hundreds of thousands of exiled Palestinians moved permanently into refugee camps.

In 1964, the Palestinian Liberation Organization (PLO) was formed as a political organization for several Palestinian groups. The PLO called for the destruction of the State of Israel and the establishment of an independent Palestinian state. However, in the Six-Day War of 1967, Israel seized control of the West Bank, East Jerusalem, the Gaza Strip, the Sinai Peninsula, and the Golan Heights. Israel also annexed East Jerusalem and set up military administrations in the occupied territories. They let it be known that Gaza, the West Bank, the Golan Heights, and the Sinai might be returned in exchange for Arab recognition of the right of Israel to exist and guarantees against future attack. The Sinai was returned to Egypt in 1979 as part of an Israeli-Egyptian peace agreement, but the rest of the occupied territories remained under Israeli control. A faction of Israelis called for permanent annexation of these regions, and in the late 1970s nationalist Jewish settlers moved into the territories as a means of accomplishing this aim.

After the 1967 war, the PLO was recognized as the symbol of the Palestinian national movement, and PLO Chairman Yasser Arafat organized guerrilla attacks on Israel from the PLO's bases in Jordan and, after 1971, from Lebanon. The PLO also coordinated terrorist attacks against Israelis at home and abroad. The Palestinian guerrilla and terrorist activity provoked heavy reprisals from Israel's armed forces and intelligence services. By the late 1970s, Arafat had won international acceptance of the PLO as the legitimate representative of the Palestinian people.

Violence mounted in the 1980s, with Palestinians clashing with Jewish settlers in the occupied territories. In 1982, Israel invaded Lebanon to dislodge the PLO. In 1987, Palestinian residents of Gaza and the West Bank launched a series of violent demonstrations against Israeli authorities known as the *intifada*, or the "shaking off." Shortly after, Jordan's King Hussein renounced all administrative responsibility for the West Bank, thereby strengthening the PLO's influence there. As the intifada raged on, Yasser Arafat proclaimed an independent Palestinian state in the West Bank and Gaza Strip in November 1988. One month later, however, he returned to his dealings with the Israelis by agreeing to denounce terrorism, recognized the State of Israel's right to exist, and authorized the beginning of "land-for-peace" negotiations with Israel.

Initially, Israel refused to open direct talks with the PLO, but in 1991 Israeli diplomats met with a joint Jordanian-Palestinian delegation at the Madrid peace conference. In 1992, Labor Party leader Yitzhak Rabin became Israeli prime minister, and he vowed to move quickly on the peace process. He froze new Israeli settlements in the occupied territory and in January 1993 authorized secret negotiations between Israel and the PLO in Oslo, Norway. These talks resulted in several important agreements and led to the historic peace accord of September 13, 1993.

On the South Lawn of the White House that day, Israeli Foreign Minister Shimon Peres and PLO foreign policy official Mahmoud Abbas signed the Declaration of Principles on Interim Self-Government Arrangements. The accord called for the withdrawal of Israeli troops from the Gaza Strip and the West Bank town of Jericho and the establishment of a Palestinian government that would eventually be granted authority over much of the West Bank. President Bill Clinton presided over the ceremony, and more than 3,000 onlookers, including former presidents George Bush and Jimmy Carter, watched as Arafat and Rabin sealed the agreement with a handshake. The old bitter enemies had met for the first time at a White House reception that morning.

In his remarks, Rabin, a former top-ranking Israeli army general, told the crowd: "We the soldiers who have returned from the battle stained with blood; we who have seen our relatives and friends killed before our eyes; we who have fought against you, the Palestinians; we say to you today in a loud and clear voice: Enough of blood and tears. Enough!" And Arafat, the guerrilla leader who for decades was targeted for assassination by Israeli agents, declared that "the battle for peace is the most difficult battle of our lives. It deserves our utmost efforts because the land of peace yearns for a just and comprehensive peace."

Despite attempts by extremists on both sides to sabotage the peace process with violence, the Israelis completed their withdrawal from the Gaza Strip and Jericho in May 1994. In July, Arafat entered Jericho amid much Palestinian jubilation and set up his government–the Palestinian Authority. In October 1994, Arafat, Yitzhak Rabin, and Shimon Peres were jointly awarded the Nobel Peace Prize for their efforts at reconciliation.

In September 1995, Rabin, Arafat, and Peres signed a peace agreement providing for the expansion of Palestinian self-rule in the West Bank and for democratic elections to determine the leadership of the Palestinian Authority. Just over a month later, on November 4, 1995, Rabin was assassinated by a Jewish extremist at a peace rally in Tel Aviv. Peres became prime minister and pledged to continue the peace process. However, terrorist attacks by Palestinian extremists in early 1996 swayed Israeli public opinion, and in May Benjamin Netanyahu of the right-wing Likud Party was elected prime minister. Netanyahu insisted that Palestinian Authority Chairman Arafat meet his obligation to end terrorism by Palestinian extremists, but sporadic attacks continued and the peace process stalled.

In May 1999, Ehud Barak of the Labor Party defeated Netanyahu in national elections and pledged to take "bold steps" to forge a comprehensive peace in the Middle East. However, extended negotiations with the PLO ended in failure in July 2000, when Barak and Arafat failed to reach an agreement at a summit at Camp David, Maryland. In September 2000, the worst violence since the intifada broke out between Israelis and Palestinians after Likud leader Ariel Sharon visited the Temple Mount, the holiest Islamic site in Jerusalem. The tragedy of violence made work toward peace more urgent as well as more difficult.

Seeking a strong leader to suppress the bloodshed, Israelis elected Sharon prime minister in February 2001. Though Arafat pledged to join in America's "war on terror" after the attacks of September 11, 2001, he was not able to garner favor with U.S. President George W. Bush, who was strongly pro-Israel. In December 2001, after a series of Palestinian suicide attacks on Israel, Bush did nothing to stop Israel as it re-conquered areas of the West Bank and even steamrolled the Palestinian Authority's headquarters with tanks, effectively imprisoning Arafat within his compound.

After Israel dismissed a compromise offer put forth by the Arab League, Palestinian attacks increased, causing Israel to again turn to military intervention in the West Bank. Arafat finally was released from his compound in May 2002, after an agreement was reached which forced him to issue a statement in Arabic instructing his followers to halt attacks on Israel. It was ignored and the violence continued.

In a 2004 interview, George W. Bush rejected Arafat's status as a legitimate spokesperson for his people, ending hopes for a peace agreement while Arafat was still in power. In late October of that year, reports surfaced that Arafat was seriously ill. He was flown to Paris for treatment, and in early November fell into a coma. He was pronounced dead on November 11.

Mahmoud Abbas became the new chairman of the PLO and was elected president of the Palestinian Authority in January 2005. The next year, Hamas, seen by many observers as a terrorist organization, won control of the Palestinian legislative body, complicating any potential negotiations. Despite an Israeli withdrawal from the disputed Gaza territory, and the fact that both sides ostensibly are committed to a two-state solution, peace in the region remains elusive. The following idea is adapted from "tip" #48 in *147 Practical Tips for Teaching Diversity.*

> Strong emotions can be problematic in class polarizing discussions, stifling open exchanges, causing hurts and resentment, sparking angry rebuttals or withdrawal in response, sparking aggressiveness, and limiting honest reflection. However, tensions

can also be the catalysts for new and creative ideas, pushing people past old and familiar responses (Timpson & Doe, 2008). Kohlberg (1963), in particular, always argued for the benefits of dilemmas that could spark debates and disagreements, what he insisted could prompt higher order moral development.

Roe Bubar and Irene Vernon (2003) describe how they channel anger when it arises. "As teachers, if we can control the climate in class, anger can be an acceptable emotion. However, anger must be directed in healthy ways that contribute to deeper learning. We must help students direct their anger at the source of perceived problems, i.e., policy-makers and not at each other" (p. 163).

Jane Kneller (2003) observes that "rational discourse has been culturally defined as excluding emotion and feeling, just as objectivity or distance in an argument has come to be seen as excluding, or at least taking prominence over, care and sympathy. This is especially true in the academy" (p. 219). She believes, however, that "it is important to make the discussion process less painful by setting up an environment in which there is no disgrace in occasionally breaking down emotionally, 'rambling,' or simply losing the thread of a point a student is making. How the facilitator/ teacher responds is crucial in guiding the responses of the rest of the class" (pp. 220-221).

Discuss the issue of emotion before beginning a sensitive topic like peace in the Middle East. Come to some agreement about the ground rules everyone can agree to follow. Be sure to allow time for debriefing so that you can assess the impact of the agreement and make any necessary modifications for future discussions and debates. You can also question the agreement made after emotions may have flared, analyze the effect on climate and learning, and come to some consensus about what to do differently. These kinds of interactions can inspire the skills of citizenship that a vibrant democracy needs.

#103. Master the basics of making peace

In September of 1793 the American Revolution officially came to an end when representatives of the United States, Great Britain, Spain and France signed the Treaty of Paris. Britain formally recognized the independence of its thirteen former American colonies, and the boundaries of the new republic were agreed upon: Florida north to the Great Lakes and the Atlantic coast west to the Mississippi River.

The events leading up to the treaty stretched back to April 1775, on a common green in Lexington, Massachusetts, when American colonists answered King George III's refusal to grant them political and economic reform with armed revolution. On July 4, 1776, more than a year after the first volleys of the war were fired, the Second Continental Congress officially adopted the Declaration of Independence. Five difficult years later, in October 1781, British General Charles Lord Cornwallis surrendered to American and French forces at Yorktown, Virginia, bringing to an end the last major battle of the Revolution. During the talks U.S. Representative Benjamin Franklin demanded that Britain hand over Canada to the United States. This was not accepted but America did gain enough new territory south of the Canadian border to double its size. Despite five years of war and suffering, a new nation had been inspired. The following "tip" is adapted from #46 in *147 Practical Tips for Teaching Peace and Reconciliation.*

In *Concepts and Choices for Teaching,* Bill Timpson and Sue Doe (2008) make the case for mastery learning, especially when there are specific skills and information to be modeled, learned, practiced, assessed and refined and especially when the stakes are as high as a peace treaty between warring peoples. "*Mastery learning* is an instructional model promoted widely by John Carroll (1963, p. 64), Benjamin Bloom (1973), and others to ensure a foundation for learning and build student self-confidence by concentrating on concise segments of the curriculum and objective feedback.

"Founded on the principle that students should demonstrate competence at one level before moving on to the next, mastery learning rests on a foundation of faith in student ability to learn, indeed that nearly all will learn, *if* we provide sufficient time, adequate materials and appropriate instruction. When we organize instruction in this way, the consistent success which students experience can build confidence and enthusiasm for further learning. While much of Bloom's original work focused on students in inner city schools, the concepts that emerged are especially applicable whenever students need an academic foundation (e.g., for reading or math), a specific set of skills (e.g., laboratory equipment or computer) or wherever they enter with different backgrounds, aptitude, and motivation. Much good research supports mastery learning and many college and university instructors have adopted various aspects of this approach" (p. 175).

For anyone interested in peace and reconciliation studies, mastery represents a rich repository of research and practice for focusing on those essential skills of listening, empathic expressing, consensus building, negotiating, conflict management, etc. Seek out sources on mastery learning and think about the skills that you think are essential. What specific goals and objectives would you set, i.e., observable behaviors? Where and how could you see these skills modeled? Practiced? What assessments would be useful? Teachers at all levels do this routinely for the concepts that underlie all the academic subjects. When will we do the same for the study of peace and include these concepts in our educational systems?

For example, Stephanie King notes the role of language for defining peace and its varied components. "Recently, a local pastor preached a sermon about peace. Just as I was preparing to hear another message about the evils of war and another call for people to love thy enemy, the pastor redefined peace in a way that changed my perceptions. Using the Hebrew word *shalom*, which is often simply translated as *peace*, the pastor explained the fullness of the meaning of *shalom*. Shalom does not only mean freedom from war, conflict, and discord, rather, a hope for shalom embodies the hope for all good things that God intended for people.

"The pastor told us that Shalom is often used as a greeting or a way to wish someone well-being. A wish or prayer for shalom means that you are wishing a person completeness, soundness, good welfare, health, and prosperity. This is peace. If a shalom-like peace embraces all the good things God intends for humans, then peace is ensuring no one goes hungry, then peace is ensuring each child has the opportunity for an education, then peace is ensuring that everyone has access to good healthcare, then peace is ensuring each person has a place to lay their head at night, then peace is striving toward greater justice for all. So, how can I help ensure shalom for others in this world" (pp. 57-58)?

Stephanie then offers an idea any of us can master: "Next time you greet an old friend or a new acquaintance, a coworker or a stranger, greet them with Shalom or some other culture's word for peace. Wishing a person all the good things they could need is the first step in actively working toward peace for all people." Consider including the basic concepts that underlie peace — open and sensitive communication, teamwork and cooperation, mediation and negotiation, critical and creative thinking for nonviolent change — in your thinking about an upcoming class, meeting in the community or among co-workers. We have to wonder whether a commitment to these basic concepts could have inspired a different history between the colonists and their British overlords?

#104. Create learning communities for peace and reconciliation

Just after the end of the Irish War of Independence from British control (1919-1921) and the Civil War that followed, a general election allowed new members and an Executive Council of the Irish Free State to be seated on September 19th. Northern Ireland was sectioned off in 1921 and remained under British control. However, it would be another 75 years before the "Troubles" would largely end in the north and inspire the Good Friday Peace Agreement that was signed in 1998. The questions remain: Could a peace movement have taken hold much earlier and spared the lives lost and the damage done? The following "tip" is adapted from #47 in *147 Practical Tips for Teaching Peace and Reconciliation*.

In *The Keys to Effective Schools*, Judith Warren Little (2007) describes what schools can do to support ongoing improvement and high performance. Creating "professional learning communities" clearly help staff collaborate, support and assist each other. What has proven effective for schools can work in any organization that wants to develop a greater capacity to address conflict management and reconcile differences. "Overall, the prospects for school improvement grow as schools take deliberate steps to reduce the isolation of teachers and to build professional communication that is both intensive and extensive. Along the path from isolation to community are several possibilities worth cultivating: steady support for individual explorations, reason and opportunity for small collaborations, and a school-wide environment conducive to teacher learning" (p. 56).

Could history have been different if schools in Ireland had included peace education as part of their curricula and professional development? The U.S. funds four military academies but no peace academy at that same level of support. Military schools exist all over the world but very few schools have a clear commitment to peace as do Quaker and Mennonite institutions, for example, which are committed by faith to nonviolence.

We can also look to the nation of Costa Rica that abolished its military in 1948 and has prospered in a region that has been troubled by years of unrest, dictatorships and military take-overs. Inspired by this commitment the United Nations established the University for Peace (UPEACE) in the capital city of San Jose in 1980. Its stated mission is "to provide humanity with an international institution of higher education for peace with the aim of promoting among all human beings the spirit of understanding, tolerance and peaceful coexistence, to stimulate cooperation among peoples and to help lessen obstacles and threats to world peace and progress, in keeping with the noble aspirations proclaimed in the Charter of the United Nations."

Assess the commitment of your own organizations, groups, schools, nearby colleges and universities and networks to improve communication, cooperation and conflict resolution. How could people be better connected and their isolation reduced? How could individuals and small groups be better supported for exploring new possibilities? What would inspire a commitment to ongoing improvement?

#105.   Use consensus to fully explore alternatives

On September 11th of 2001 the Islamic terrorist group al-Qaeda orchestrated a series of suicide attacks in the United States by hijacking passenger airline jets and flying them into buildings at the World Trade Center in New York City and into the Pentagon in Arlington, Virginia although a fourth jet was aborted when passengers resisted and the plane crashed. The attacks killed 2,996 people, injured over 6,000 others, and caused at least $10 billion in infrastructure and property damage.

Enraged by these attacks, the United States responded by launching the War on Terror and invading Afghanistan to depose the Taliban, which had harbored al-Qaeda. The U.S. also invaded Iraq despite no known direct involvement in the September 11 attacks. The Iraq War was a military conflict that lasted seven years (2003 - 2011) and cost $1.06 trillion. The George W. Bush Administration tried to make a case to eliminate the threat from Iraq's Sunni leader, Saddam Hussein, after declaring that Iraq was developing weapons of mass destruction despite repeated reports from United Nations weapons inspectors to the contrary.

These military actions added more than $1 trillion to the U.S. debt. Between 2001 and 2014, the U.S. reported 2,350 military deaths and 20,092 injured in and around Afghanistan. In Iraq the U.S. has reported 4,424 deaths and 31,954 wounded. The wars in Iraq, Afghanistan, and Pakistan have taken a tremendous human toll on those countries. As of March 2015, approximately 210,000 civilians have died violent deaths as a result of the wars.

Although al-Qaeda's leader, Osama bin Laden, initially denied any involvement, in 2004 he claimed responsibility for the attacks. Al-Qaeda and bin Laden cited U.S. support of Israel, the presence of U.S. troops in Saudi Arabia, and sanctions against Iraq as motives. After evading capture for almost a decade, Osama bin Laden was located and killed by SEAL Team Six of the U.S. Navy in May 2011. The following "tip" is adapted from #51 in *147 Practical Tips for Teaching Peace and*

Reconciliation.

For teachers at all levels, consensus is a well-established mechanism for encouraging deeper listening and empathic understanding (Gordon, 1974). What works at the classroom level, however, also can have meaning for governments. While voting has long been considered essential to a democratic process, it is a commitment to consensus, where everyone agrees, that forces a group to take the time to understand the range of opinion among their members and explore alternative solutions.

For example, after the Japanese attacks on Pearl Harbor, the U.S. Congress was quick to unite in response to President Roosevelt's call to arms. After the September 11th attacks on the World Trade Center and the Pentagon in 2001, many in the U.S. were united in wanting to strike back. While the U.S. Congress was quick to endorse the Patriot Act, we later learned later that buried in the fine print were what many saw as dangerous infringements on the liberties of U.S. citizens. In 2003 we saw near consensus in Congress in support of President George W. Bush's call for an invasion of Iraq, using the fear of "weapons of mass destruction" being built up in that country. Later, those few dissenting votes took on greater significance when we learned that there were no weapons of mass destruction, when the war went badly and that the "intelligence" data had been "spun" by those leading the American charge to war. The power of consensus comes through its demand that the majority slows its rush to judgment and listens more deeply to the concerns of the minority.

Typically the consensus process begins with *problem definition* and then moves to *brainstorming* where judgment is withheld. Once a full range of ideas has surfaced, only then does the process move to an *exploration of the consequences* of various ideas and a *group decision*. However, the consensus process does not end here; it goes further and requires an *assessment* of the decision and, if needed, some *adjustments*. The inspiration for consensus comes from understanding these dynamics and this history, that a rush to seek revenge so often results in more bloodshed, destruction and tragedy. Eventually, all conflicts come to an end in some form of negotiated settlement. Why not sooner rather than later? Having leaders and citizens, teachers and students educated about consensus provides everyone with some inspiration for what the alternatives to war and violence can be.

Analyze your own experiences with voting and consensus, especially in the context of reaching across the differences that separate us. What has worked for each, what has not, and why? How important were the skills of deep or reflective listening? Empathy and understanding? Consensus?

#106. Trust your experiences

Jesse Owens was born on September 12, 1913 and later became an American athletic icon in track and field athlete winning four gold medals at the August 1936 Olympics in Berlin, inspiring millions at a time when the rising Nazi claims of Aryan racial supremacy threatened so many world-wide. Remarkably he had set three world records and tied another at the Big Ten Championships on May 23rd, 1935 in Ann Arbor, Michigan, all in less than an hour, an event that has been called the greatest 45 minutes in sports history. The following concept is adapted from "tip" #59 in *147 Practical Tips for Using Experiential Learning*.

Too often we become captive of the "stories" we tell ourselves, why we can't do this or why that is impossible, especially in the face of real threats. Noted Buddhist teacher and writer, Pema Chödrön (2001), encourages us to live fully, to "smile at fear," to go to "those places that scare us," to embrace life in all its rich tapestry, the tough and the easy, the tragic and the fun, all those facets that are essential to the very process of life itself, to the inevitability of death and our own mortality. Jesse Owens trusted his talents and training in the face of racist judgments at home and abroad.

Chödrön insists that "(our) greatest obstacles are also our greatest wisdom. In all the unwanted stuff there is something sharp and penetrating; there's great wisdom there. Suppose anger or rage is what we consider our greatest obstacle, or maybe it's addiction and craving. This breeds all kinds of conflict and tension and stress, but at the same time it has a penetrating quality that cuts through all the confusion and delusion. It's both things at once. When you realize that your greatest defilement is facing you and there seems no way to get out of it because it's so big, the instruction is, let go of the story line, let go of the conversation, and own your feeling completely. Let the words go and return to the essential quality of the underlying stuff" (p. 108). Jesse Owens let his accomplishments speak for themselves.

Reflect on those stories you tell yourself that get in the way of experiencing the richness that life has to offer, i.e., your anxieties, fears, or ambitions. Identify all those "lessons" that have made you cautious and self-conscious, eager to please your teachers, parents or bosses but increasingly unsure of your own abilities or what may be possible. How can you smile at those fears and let your talents inspire you instead?

#107. Use the language of encouragement

In September of 1620, the Mayflower sails from Plymouth, England, bound for the new world with 102 passengers inspired by a grand adventure and unique opportunity. The ship was headed for Virginia, where the colonists – half religious dissenters and half entrepreneurs – had been authorized to settle by the British crown. However, stormy weather and navigational errors forced the Mayflower off course, and on November 21 the "Pilgrims" reached Massachusetts, where they founded the first permanent European settlement in New England in late December.

Thirty-five of these Pilgrims were members of the radical English Separatist Church, who risked the Atlantic crossing to escape the jurisdiction of what they experienced as a corrupt Church of England. Ten years earlier, English persecution had led a group of Separatists to flee to Holland in search of religious freedom. However, many were dissatisfied with economic opportunities in the Netherlands, and under the direction of William Bradford they decided to immigrate to Virginia, where an English colony had been founded at Jamestown in 1607.

During their Atlantic crossing, the settlers formulated and signed the Mayflower Compact, an agreement that established constitutional law and the rule of the majority and became an important precursor to American democracy. On December 21 the Mayflower came to anchor in Plymouth harbor. Just after Christmas, the pilgrims began work on dwellings that would shelter them through their difficult first winter in America.

In the first year of settlement, half the colonists died of disease. In 1621, the health and economic condition of the colonists improved, and that autumn Governor William Bradford invited neighboring Indians to Plymouth to celebrate the bounty of that year's harvest season. Plymouth soon secured treaties with most local Indian tribes, and the economy steadily grew, and more colonists were attracted to the settlement. Just imagine the encouragement needed to inspire new settlers to risk the journey and the odds against surviving. The following idea is adapted from "tip" #61 in *147 Practical Tips for Using Experiential Learning*.

> "Whenever we make statements about attitudes, we are making predictions about future behavior of people based on our observations of past behavior" (Mager, 1997, p. 13). Encourage students, co-workers, friends and family even when they are struggling and you can help build the confidence that underlies the willingness to explore new ideas, to try different approaches, to learn from mistakes and to persevere. Alternatively, discouragement can lead to self-defeating or "avoidance behaviors" that for students are linked to lower academic accomplishment and feelings of low self-efficacy (Urdan, Ryan, Anderman, & Gheen, 2002, p. 71). According to Mager (1997), "No matter what we accomplish, or fail to accomplish, with our instruction, we should do no harm to student attitudes toward learning—and attitudes toward what we are teaching" (p. 14). Everyone who teaches, presents or leads can use more of the positive language of encouragement.

Reflect on those experiences you have had where the language of encouragement proved to be inspiring. When was it that you could have used more encouragement? Rethink an upcoming presentation and note places where you will be sure to add words of encouragement.

#108.   Develop self-leadership

Inspired by the defiance of segregationists in Arkansas, in September of 1957 President Dwight Eisenhower ordered the 101st Airborne Division of the United States Army to Little Rock and federalized the entire 10,000-member Arkansas National Guard to ensure that a group of nine African American students could enroll in Little Rock Central High School. Previously these courageous young people had been prevented from entering the racially segregated school by Orval Faubus, the Governor of Arkansas. Three years earlier the U.S. Supreme Court had issued its landmark decision in Brown versus Board of Education and declared that all laws establishing segregated schools would be unconstitutional. These experiences would help inspire the Civil Rights Movement that erupted some years later across the South and into the North. The following "tip" is adapted from #127 in *147 Practical Tips for Using Experiential Learning* to address the challenge of building a mass movement.

> When you facilitate learning, you are inherently a leader. How you choose to lead others can be a reflection of how you choose to lead yourself. Self-leadership represents the art and skill of knowing your origins, where you are now, and where want to go. Northouse (2010) outlines this form of critical self-assessment as part of the development of an authentic leadership style. You can ask yourself:
>
> • How have I developed my self-world view?
> • What hegemonic assumptions do I have?
>
> Be honest with where you are now. Ask yourself:
>
> • What areas of myself am I afraid to engage / change?
> • What areas of myself am I excited to change?
> • How do I see the various roles (facilitator, learner) in the environment?
> • What are my strengths and weaknesses in my ability to facilitate a learning experience?
> • Do I really believe in the methods that I use or have I just become accustomed to acilitating in a certain manner?

- Is my method fully connecting with the learner, exploring what is to be learned, and creating the highest potential for learning transfer?
- How is my self-world view coloring the design, facilitation, processing, and transfer of knowledge?

Be realistic of where you wish to go. Ask yourself:

- Have you set goals for your total development and not just your ability as a facilitator?
- Have you sought out mentors to help you along the path.?

Be ready to engage in critical self-reflection when you facilitate learning. Practitioners who are not willing to reflect critically on their own practices will face problems.

Always allow space and time for yourself as a facilitator of learning to critically reflect on your own practice. Identify areas of effectiveness as well as areas where you need to grow.

OCTOBER
Tips #109-120

Inspired by the grit of the earliest colonists at Plymouth as well as the graciousness of the neighboring native communities who helped set the stage for the Union that was to emerge, President Abraham Lincoln paused in October of 1863 during the brutal depths of the Civil War to proclaim the last Thursday in November as Thanksgiving Day. Given by the people of France in tribute to the promises of the American Revolution, the Statue of Liberty was dedicated in New York Harbor in October of 1886. Inspiring so many with his leadership of the Civil Rights Movement in the U.S., Martin Luther King, Jr. became the youngest person to receive the Nobel Peace Prize in October of 1964. If we look closely, even in the darkest times, we can find these shining moments.

#109. Think about your goals

In October of 1908 the Model T was introduced by Ford Motor Company. Because of its efficient assembly line production, this is generally regarded as the first really affordable car, an invention that inspired a revolution in travel and lifestyle. What no one could see at the time, however, was the subsequent fossil-fuel driven transformation that would later contribute to the pollution that is impacting the health of the planet as well as a series of military confrontations by different powers over the control of the world's oil reserves. The following "tip" is adapted from #60 in *147 Practical Tips for Teaching Sustainability.*

> As increases in population, industrial production, and waste take an increasing toll on people and the planet, we must find ways to change our course content and approaches to instruction as well as how we interact with the public as citizens in a democracy. Consider how you can incorporate sustainable practices into teaching about sustainability or your involvement with others. For example, on campus or at home, you can encourage others to practice recycling, reusing or refusing new purchases, turning off lights when the last person leaves a room or turning down the heat in colder months (environmental). As an instructor you can

consider the impact on budgets of what texts you require of your students—you may be able to put some on electronic reserve at your library's website. Be sure to be inclusive in your planning and, in class, push for including all classroom voices as much as possible (social). Of course, everyone can be reminded that cost issues underlie every action (economic).

Take time to reflect on your teaching practices, public involvements and talks, and other interactions in light of the environmental, economic, and social changes that have occurred in the past. Make a list of changes to implement in the design and delivery of your material as well as how you share your ideas and concerns with others. Connect specific and measurable goals whenever possible to your objectives. In the community or with friends and family you can inspire others to concrete action plans.

#110. Remember that there's more to education

On October 2, 1968, President Johnson signed the Act creating the Redwood National Park. When Euro-Americans first swept westward in the 1800s, they needed raw material for their homes and lives. Commercial logging followed the expansion of settlements as companies struggled to keep up with the enormous appetite of growth. Timber harvesting quickly became a leading industry in the west.

When gold was discovered in northwestern California in 1850, the rush was on. Thousands flooded in to search for riches and new lives. These people were also completely dependent upon lumber, and the redwoods conveniently provided the wood the people needed. The size of the huge trees made them prized timber, as redwood became known for its durability and workability. By 1853, nine sawmills were at work in the boom town of Eureka. Large-scale logging was soon underway and the once immense stands of redwoods began to disappear by the close of the 19th century.

At first, people used axes and saws to bring the trees down. But loggers quickly adopted improving technology to harvest more trees in less time. Transportation also advanced and locomotives replaced horses and oxen. The railroads soon became the fastest way to transport the logs to mills.

Land fraud was common, as acres of prime redwood forests were transferred from the public domain to private industry. Although some of the perpetrators were caught, many thousands of acres of land were lost in land swindles. By the 1910s, some concerned citizens began to clamor for the preservation of the dwindling stands of redwoods. The Save-the-Redwoods League was inspired and eventually the League succeeded in helping to establish the redwood preserves of various state parks. While the original redwood forest comprised nearly two million acres, about 750,000 acres of old growth redwoods remained when the National Park was created.

Nationally, the general public was overwhelmingly in favor of a Redwood National-al Park. To no one's surprise, the main opposition came from the forest products industry as well as from local authorities in the three northern California counties who feared for the loss of their traditional economy. The following "tip" is adapted from #61 in *147 Practical Tips for Teaching Sustainability*.

> In *Happiness and Education*, Stanford's Nel Noddings (2003) questions the traditional goals of education: "It is as though our society has simply decided that the purpose of schooling is economic—to improve the financial condition of individuals and to advance the prosperity of the nation. Hence, students should do well on standardized tests, get into good colleges, obtain well-paying jobs, and buy lots of things. Surely there is more to education than this" (p. 4). In a similar way, we could question the purpose of presentations that only offer basic information and ignore opportunities to challenge and inspire a larger vision, one that embraces all peoples and the health of the planet. Take some time to think about how your instruction, presentations, actions and interactions and can challenge others to be more than just consumers.

List the purposes of your own classes or presentations. Identify what is basic information and what goes beyond the basic and inspires consideration of bigger, life supporting issues.

#111. Explore multiple approaches to powerful ideas

In early October of 1914, the explorer Thor Heyerdahl was born in Norway and grew to study zoology, botany, and geography. He became notable for his *Kon-Tiki* expedition in 1947, when he embraced enormous risks to sail 5,000 miles across the Pacific Ocean. Inspired by questions about the early history of human contacts, he had wanted to demonstrate that ancient people could have made long sea voyages and established contacts between distant cultures. Old reports and drawings made by the Spanish Conquistadors of Inca rafts as well as native legends and archaeological evidence suggested contact between South America and Polynesia. Heyerdahl subsequently made other voyages designed to demonstrate this possibility of contact, notably the Ra II expedition of 1970, when he sailed from the west coast of Africa to Barbados in a papyrus reed boat. He said later that there were times in each of his raft voyages when he feared for his life. The following idea is adapted from "tip" #65 in *147 Practical Tips for Teaching Sustainability*.

> Some concepts are not always simple for people to define or easy for others to understand the first time around. Something like sustainability has many layers of complexity and may need to be rehashed numerous times and in different ways with varied examples. As with Hyerdahl, some questions may even require extended explorations in an effort to open up new understanding. For example, we can always ask what we can learn from the earliest inhabitants of this planet about living within the means of the environment. We can also ask what risks some of them must have taken to expand their own understanding of their worlds and what helped them survive and prosper? Hopefully, we all begin to notice that a variety of approaches to a powerful idea doesn't threaten its meaning; it actually can enhance the depth of our understanding.

Find areas of study that people feel that they "get" and challenge them with new ideas. Ask what explorations might help answer the questions that still linger and encourage conversations that bring out multiple viewpoints. Help people arrive at coherent, well thought-out conclusions, including agreements about the questions that still arise.

#112. Rethink stereotypes

In October of 1996 an eight-foot statue of a young Thurgood Marshall was dedicated adjacent to the Maryland State House near where he once argued the cases that led to the historic U.S. Supreme Court decision in Brown versus Board of Education that outlawed segregation in publicly supported education and inspired the Civil Rights Movement. When protests arose in 2017 about the many statues in the South for Confederate war heroes, one alternative that often arose involved the creation of statues that memorialize those who fought against slavery, racism, discrimination and prejudice. These statues can then inspire ongoing discussions about historical events and their current day implications.

Marshall was born on July 2, 1908, studied law at Howard University and eventually served as an Associate Justice of the Supreme Court of the United States from October 1967 until October 1991, the first African-American to do so. Born in Baltimore, Maryland, Marshall built a private legal practice before founding the NAACP Legal Defense and Educational Fund, for which he served as executive director. The following "tip" is adapted from #50 in *147 Practical Tips for Teaching Diversity.*

> Challenge people to research examples when longstanding stereotypes had to give way to new judgments, for example, when people were inspired by exceptional talents in African American athletes like Jesse Owens who set world records in track and won Olympic gold medals in the face of racist pronouncements in Germany by the Nazis. Or consider musicians who were blind, appreciate the achievements by athletes with various disabilities who were competing in the Special Olympics, and stretch to see the genius of someone like physicist Steven Hawking who continued to contribute to the advance of our scientific understanding of the physical universe despite his own worsening paralysis from ALS (Amyotrophic Lateral Sclerosis).

> As another example, consider the forty years of civil war in Burundi that followed independence in 1962, conflicts that were often attributed to longstanding African "tribalism" between the Tutsis (some 15% of the population) and the Hutus (approximately 80%

of the population). As an alternative interpretation we could also see this conflict as the legacy of colonial rule. In the mid-nineteenth century the Germans and later the Belgians used a classic strategy of "divide and conquer" to put the minority Tutsi in power and make them dependent on their colonial masters and their superior weaponry to stay in power. When the Arusha Peace and Reconciliation Agreement was signed in 2000, it was Nelson Mandela's genius that promoted power sharing between Tutsi and Hutu, offering a tangible way to overcome this historic tribal divide and the imposition of colonial controls. New thinking now sees the idea of "tribalism" or "colonialism" as stereotypes that overly simplify the interplay of complex, competing factors of gender, social class and political allegiance (Daley, 2007).

Ask your students, colleagues and friends to research other instances where we can see the need for rethinking historic stereotypes and inspiring alternative interpretations.

#113. Recognize that there is no spokesperson for an entire population in your class

In early October of 1981 Anwar Sadat, the President of Egypt, was assassinated during the annual victory parade held in Cairo to celebrate Operation Badr, during which the Egyptian Army had crossed the Suez Canal and taken back a small part of the Sinai Peninsula from Israel at the beginning of the Yom Kippur War. A fatwa approving the assassination had been obtained from Omar Abdel-Rahman, a cleric later convicted in the U.S. for his role in the 1993 World Trade Center bombing. The assassination was undertaken by members of the Egyptian Islamic Jihad.

Following the Camp David Accords that inspired the world to think that the intractable violence in the Middle East could be transformed, Sadat and Israeli Prime Minister Menachem Begin shared the 1978 Nobel Peace Prize. However, the world also quickly learned that no one person can be a spokesperson for an entire people, especially where there is such a diversity of opinion and belief as there is in Egypt. For example, Yasser Arafat, the leader of the Palestinian Liberation Organization, said "Let them sign what they like. False peace will not last."

Many of Egypt's Islamists felt betrayed and publicly called for the overthrow of the Egyptian president and the replacement of the nation's system of government with a government based on Islamic theocracy.

The last months of Sadat's presidency were marked by internal uprising. Following a failed military coup in June 1981, Sadat ordered a major crackdown that resulted in the arrest of numerous opposition figures. Though Sadat still maintained high levels of popularity in Egypt, it has been said that he was assassinated "at the peak" of his unpopularity. The following "tip" is adapted from #52 in *147 Practical Tips for Teaching Diversity.*

> It is quite common for minority individuals to feel pressured to speak for all of "their people." Remember that there is always greater diversity within any group than ever exists between or among groups. You can help students who feel as if they are suddenly in the spotlight by noting that no one can ever be expected to speak for an entire population. Perry's (1999) work on cognitive development shows the value of understanding the range of perspectives possible on a given topic and that it is the ability to handle this complexity and ambiguity that characterizes the highest level of cognitive development.

Try putting this issue of a "group spokesperson" on the table for discussion. Which generalizations are defensible, which are not, how can they be modified, and how should they be expressed? For example, broadly speaking, is there a cultural tradition and expectation among Jewish and Asian peoples, groups commonly labeled in U.S. school circles as "model minorities," that value study and academic achievement? Or does the variability within these groups make this kind of assertion too simplistic to be of value? What disclaimers are necessary when discussing "group characteristics"?

#114. Expose contradictions

On October 8, 1993 the General Assembly of the United Nations voted to lift its call for economic sanctions against South Africa and urged all countries to end any remaining restrictions. Although largely symbolic, the call for sanctions had discouraged banks and international financial institutions from dealing with South Africa. The sanctions also led many American states and cities, including New York, to penalize South Africa for its racial policy of apartheid. As an alternative to military actions against what was considered a very oppressive regime, these sanctions inspired the world to see the power of nonviolent alternatives for pressuring change. The following "tip" is adapted from #53 in *147 Practical Tips for Teaching Diversity.*

> Sometimes a desire to serve and help proves counterproductive to some degree, even oppressive. Rose Kreston (2003) often finds herself guiding students to face what may be problematic and stereotypical about their choice of a "helping career." However difficult the resulting re-evaluation, exposing these contradictions may be the best way for her to help students move toward a more functional belief system. "Their feelings of wanting to 'give to' and 'help' others may be the primary motivation for their career choice. It may be difficult to accept that one's kind-hearted efforts to help another who is less fortunate (less able) could be seen as oppressive. Understanding oppression based on kindness can create a great deal of dissonance, both intellectually and emotionally" (p. 174). When apartheid was the law in South Africa, white leaders often claimed that sanctions would hurt poor blacks more since they were the most vulnerable population. Prices would go up for everyone, they argued, but wealthy business owners would be far better prepared to survive this pressure.

Find examples of contradictions and dissonance in your field. Explore the various emotional dimensions involved. How could the dissonance be resolved in a constructive way?

#115. Examine values

Facing a threat of a German invasion in early October of 1938, the Munich Agreement was a settlement among the major powers of Europe permitting Nazi Germany's annexation of portions of Czechoslovakia along the country's borders mainly inhabited by German speakers, now referred to as "Sudetenland". Today, it is widely regarded as a failed act of appeasement toward Nazi Germany, a concession that many believe only whetted Hitler's appetite for seizing more land, power and control from others. Sudetenland was of immense strategic importance to Czechoslovakia, as most of its border defenses and banks were situated there, as well as heavy industrial districts. On 5 October, Edvard Beneš resigned as President of Czechoslovakia, realizing that the fall of Czechoslovakia was inevitable.

Only 20 years had passed since the end of World War I, the hoped for "war to end all wars." Who could blame European leaders for wanting to secure a peace, but at what price? Were there other alternatives? For example, could the international pressure that pushed the white South African government to dismantle oppressive system and embrace a transformation to democracy have worked with the policies of Germany? We know that Europeans, Americans and others continued to put profits ahead of humanity and conduct business with Nazi Germany as the horrors of Hitler's agenda unfolded. A commitment to nonviolence might have starved that beast before its cancerous feast overwhelmed so much of the world. The following concept is adapted from "tip" #129 in *147 Practical Tips for Teaching Peace and Reconciliation.*

> Examining our deeper cultural values sooner might have pushed more Americans to raise alarms about the growing atrocities in Hitler's Germany as well as the need for proactive actions and sanctions. For example, values underlie thinking and action yet are often considered off limits for direct instruction in the public classroom. The U.S. tradition that insists on a separation of church and state leaves most educators unsure about their role in addressing values. Anyone teaching can attempt to identify what underlies specific actions, but such an attempt can become speculative and a potential source of controversy.
>
> For example, the U.S. invasion of Iraq in 2003 could be seen as a reflection of an aggressive value of the Bush administration—using a pretext like the September 11th attacks to justify sending in the military and extending American control over the Middle East and its rich oil reserves. Alternatively, the Iraq invasion could also be seen as reflecting a value claimed within the Bush administration for defending America's national interests.

Note the focus on values in Martin Luther King's words below. "[In] all his speeches, King's voice was heard calling for what he described as 'a revolution in values' in the United States, a struggle to free ourselves from the 'triple evils of racism, extreme materialism, and militarism.' ...By the end of the fall (of 1967), King's voice...was setting forth a jarring theme, declaring, 'Something is wrong with capitalism as it now stands in the United States. We are not interested in being integrated into <u>this</u> value structure. Power must be relocated....We've got to make it known that until our problem is solved, America may have many, many days, but they will be full of trouble. There will be no rest; there will be no tranquility in this country, until the nation comes to terms with our problems'" (Harding, 2000, "We must keep going: Martin Luther King, Jr. and the future of America," *Peace is the Way*, p. 198-199).

Introducing a values framework can provide a useful mechanism for analyzing and discussing the range of values that might underline an issue and those involved. For example, at the lowest levels, we can choose our values freely and form alternatives after considering the consequences. At levels three and four, we can prize our values and affirm them publicly. At the highest levels, we act on our values, repeatedly and consistently. Facilitating this kind of analysis can allow individuals to come to their own conclusions and avoid any hint of proselytizing by instructors.

At the end of the day, however, we must also recognize the fundamental importance of tenure and academic freedom in our schools, colleges and universities, so that our democracy can have the free and open discussions, at least in these venues, it requires to remain healthy. The 2008 September-October issues of Academe, the Bulletin of the American Association of University Professors (AAUP), has an excellent range of articles on tenure in higher education although the principles are relevant at every level of education and in every context of organizational and democratic vitality.

Check with your audiences about the deeper values at play on a particular issue and whether actions are called for before events spiral into war.

#116. Take an international perspective

Mohandas Gandhi was born on October 2, 1869 and grew to inspire the world with peaceful strategies to challenge oppression and promote positive change. Employing nonviolent civil disobedience, Gandhi led India to independence from the British Empire and inspired movements for civil rights and freedom across the world. Born and raised in a Hindu merchant caste family in western India and trained in law in England, Gandhi first employed nonviolent civil disobedience in South Africa as the resident Indian community struggled for civil rights. After his return to India in 1915, he set about organizing peasants, farmers, and urban laborers to protest against excessive land-tax and discrimination. Assuming leadership of the Indian National Congress in 1921, Gandhi inspired nationwide campaigns for various social causes and for achieving self-rule.

Gandhi famously led Indians in challenging the British-imposed salt tax with a march in 1930 and later in calling for the British to leave India altogether. He was imprisoned for many years and on many occasions in both South Africa and India. He lived modestly in a self-sufficient residential community and wore the traditional Indian home spun cloth, following a simple vegetarian diet and undertaking long fasts as a means of both self-purification and political protest. The following concept is adapted from "tip" #103 in *147 Practical Tips for Teaching Peace and Reconciliation.*

> The path to peace and reconciliation can be blurred by the blinders of local context. Contrasting what we can see around us with what happens overseas can offer striking new insights. In *Long Shadows* (Giffey, 2006), Israeli veteran Esty Dinur contrasts her experience in the military with what she now sees in the U.S. "I am willing to allow that some people, possibly like (former Israeli military commander and politician Ariel) Sharon . . . really think that militarism is good, that the iron fist is good, and that the Palestinians are really bad. . . When it comes to the American govern-

ment, to American presidents, the situation is different. Nobody ever tried to invade the U.S. directly. . . To me, having studied history and looked at patterns, to me it's clear that we're talking, more than anything, about economics. We're talking about making money off of other lands. We're talking empire. Even though it looks different from the empires of the nineteenth century, that is what we're looking at" (p. 246).

With the perspective of having lived in Israel before relocating to the U.S., Esty Dinur can see the differences between these two countries quite clearly. In Israel, militarism becomes more understandable because it has been surrounded by hostile nations and factions. But what could explain the extraordinary military preparedness in the U.S. which is protected by oceans to the east and west and has friendly neighbors to the north and the south? Dinur concludes that it must be something else, "economics" and "empire."

When you make comparisons between countries on issues of peace and reconciliation, what do you notice? What questions arise for you? What tragedies could have been avoided. When did "worst case thinking lead to those avoidable tragedies?

#117. Hear and respect other voices

In early October of 1990, shortly after the destruction of the Berlin Wall, East and West Germany came together on what is known as "Unity Day" inspiring many world-wide that old and bitter disputes could be addressed in peaceful ways. Since 1945, when Soviet forces occupied eastern Germany, and the United States and other Allied forces occupied the western half of the nation at the close of World War II, divided Germany had come to serve as one of the most enduring symbols of the Cold War.

Some of the most dramatic episodes of the Cold War took place there. The Soviet Union blocked all travel into and out of West Berlin from June 1948 until May 1949 and supported the construction of the Berlin Wall in 1961 that attempted to stem the flow of those fleeing to the West. With the gradual waning of Soviet power in the late 1980s, the Communist Party in East Germany began to lose its grip on power. Tens of thousands of East Germans began to flee the nation, and by late 1989 the Berlin Wall started to come down. Shortly thereafter, talks between East and West German officials, joined by officials from the United States, Great Britain, France, and the USSR, began to explore the possibility of reunification. Two months following reunification in October 1990, all-German elections took place; Helmut Kohl became the first chancellor of the reunified Germany. Although this action came more than a year before the dissolution of the Soviet Union, for many observers the reunification of Germany effectively marked the end of the Cold War. In hindsight, how do we recognize all those who contributed to this move toward peace and reconciliation? The following "tip" is adapted from #117 in *147 Practical Tips for Teaching Peace and Reconciliation*.

In *Long Shadows* (Giffey, 2006), Vietnam veteran Joel Garb describes how he changed while serving in the military during wartime, how he benefitted from seeking different opinions. "I decided to join the Army even though by that time I was relatively certain that the war was wrong. And yet there was so much official propaganda that I felt like I should go see for myself. Not having much common sense, I didn't realize that you can't see a lot from the perspective of a soldier in a war. You can't see a lot about the causes and reasons for a war when you're in a war. And yet I was fortunate enough to actually meet a Vietnamese man, a colonel, who had been involved in Vietnam's politics since he completed high school and joined the Viet Minh in 1944 or 1945. And so I learned a lot about Vietnam, and the things that he told me reinforced what I already thought, that it was wrong to be there and that we were acting criminally, that our country was acting criminally, and that our soldiers were acting criminally" (p. 182).

Early on Garb realized that he needed to look beyond what he was being told by official Army sources and learn for himself. For example, he was always deeply troubled by the common reference to the Vietnamese people as "gooks." He now appreciates the perspectives of his new allies that much more. "And I think

that's one thing that distinguishes people that are in Veterans for
Peace is that we do have a sense that we're the same as others. We
do not appreciate, what's the word, this dehumanization of the
so-called enemy or the people that are different from us" (p. 184).

*Evaluate your own perspectives about the wars and "enemies" you have heard about in
your lifetime? What has changed? Why? What prejudices have you held against people
who are different? Who are your role models for seeing people without prejudice?*

#118. Nurture discovery

On October 4, 1957 the Soviet Union launched the unmanned satellite Sputnik I
and sent shock waves across the U.S., inspiring new thinking about science and
mathematics education, in particular. Suddenly the federal government wanted
to see a rethinking of school curricula and a shift from traditional instructional
approaches that may have cost the U.S. its presumed lead in technology. New
funding was provided for what became discovery learning and the "new math."
Many in the U.S. also feared that the Soviets might have gained the upper hand in
the arms race and would attract the allegiance of nations in the developing world.
Democrats scorched the Republican administration of Dwight D. Eisenhower for
allowing the United States to fall so far behind the communists. Eisenhower responded by speeding up the U.S. space program, which resulted in the launching of the satellite *Explorer I* on January 31, 1958. The "space race" had begun.
The following "tip" is adapted from #64 in *147 Practical Tips for Using Experiential
Learning*.

> "Discovery learning is designed to engage students as active par-
> ticipants in the pursuit of knowledge, allowing them to confront
> a puzzle, a problem, or a challenge, and to follow their own lead
> towards a solution. It has much in common with higher educa-
> tion's research mission. Instead of asking students to demonstrate
> their mastery of existing facts and theories, we ask them to turn
> their attention, creativity, and intelligence toward problems and
> issues that have no known immediate answer or solution. It is in
> this cauldron of possibilities that students can best begin to think
> critically and independently" (Timpson, 2002, p. 86).

Reflect on your experiences with traditional presentations and approaches. Contrast these with experiences when you were inspired to discover connections that made sense and increased your understanding. Rethink an upcoming event and identify places where you could emphasize what you hope everyone will learn at a deeper level.

#119. Make use of Transactional Analysis (TA)

Credited with leading an effort to design and build the world's first liquid-fueled rocket, Robert Goddard—an American engineer, professor, physicist, and inventor—was born in October of 1882. First launched in 1926, his rocket ushered in an era of space flight and innovation. Between 1926 and 1941, Goddard and his team launched 34 rockets. Although his work in the field was clearly cutting edge, Goddard received very little public support for his research and development efforts. The press sometimes ridiculed his ideas. Accordingly, he became protective of his privacy and his work. Years after his death, at the dawn of the Space Age, he came to be recognized as one of the founding fathers of modern rocketry, someone who would inspire future generations. The following "tip" is adapted from #67 in *147 Practical Tips for Using Experiential Learning.*

> In the *Games People Play,* the classic adaptation of Freudian psychoanalytic theory, Eric Berne (1964) describes three "ego states" that have proven both useful and easily accessible for audiences of all ages to better understand communication and enhance self-awareness, essential components for making the most of experiential learning. In place of the "Superego" where Freud saw our conscience, Berne uses "Parent." Where Freud had our rational selves in the "ego," Berne used "Adult." Where Freud used "Id" to describe our emotional selves, Berne used the "Child." After a morning in the cold, wind and rain on a university ropes course, Bill Timpson's first year Honors students were able to use the language of Transactional Analysis to help talk about "what they should do" (Parent), problem solve various obstacles (Adult), and overcome the potentially paralyzing effects of their fears (Child). For Robert Goddard, the challenge would be in using his "Parent" to remain clear about the bigger picture, his "Child" to navigate

the painful criticisms, and the "Adult" to reason his way and his work forward.

Use the TA model to plan for experiential learning about a topic that is difficult, in unchartered waters perhaps, and then process what happens. List the insights and inspirations you have for future presentations.

#120. Know that learning maybe better served by dialogue

In October of 1927 audiences were inspired by the very first "talkie" film, The Jazz Singer, quickly ending the silent film era. Featuring six songs performed by Al Jolson, the film depicts the fictional story of Jakie Rabinowitz, a young man who defies the traditions of his devout Jewish family. After singing popular tunes in a beer garden he is punished by his father, prompting Jakie to run away from home. Some years later, now calling himself Jack Robin, he has become a talented jazz singer and attempts to build a career as an entertainer but his professional ambitions ultimately come into conflict with the demands of his home and heritage.

To effect the breakthrough, the 89-minute Warner Brothers feature presentation relied on the projectionist to manually sync each of the 15 film reels to its own phonograph record containing dialogue and music. Budgeted at the then-gargantuan sum of $422,000 (about $5.3 million in today's cash), The Jazz Singer represented a major gamble for studio boss Harry Warner, who pawned his wife's jewelry and moved the family into a small apartment to finance the film. Debating the merits of silent and sound films quickly lost out to the dialogue that helped point the way forward. Advances in film and television technology continue to revolutionize what is possible in the classroom and in the community. The following "tip" is adapted from #72 in *147 Practical Tips for Using Experiential Learning*.

> Debate is a common mode of discourse in academic settings. The experiential classroom, however, can be better served through the techniques of dialogue. In her book, *From Debate to Dialogue: Using the Understanding Process to Transform Our Conversations*, Deborah Flick (1998) discusses the primary differences between a culture of debate and a culture of dialogue. In dialogue, one listens for

understanding rather than listening for errors in logic and the emphasis is on understanding the other rather than being right or wrong. According to Flick, during the dialogue process "the need to agree with each other becomes less important" and that from a place of understanding each other, new possibilities and ways of thinking may emerge (p. 44). During the processing of experiential activities, it will be important to help people learn and incorporate the dialogue process to avoid devolving into debate. Flick recommends using sentence starters such as, "Help me understand," "Say more about that," "Tell me more," as ways to facilitate the dialogue process.

When facilitating experiential learning and the follow-up processing discussions, you can begin to inspire a culture of understanding and creative exploration with your participants by modeling the dialogue process using the words, "Tell me more."

NOVEMBER
Tips #121-132

James Naismith, the inventor of the game of basketball, was born in November of 1861. Who could have predicted that this sport would grow into being one of the most popular in the world and unite all nations in friendly competition every four years at the Olympics? Fast forward to the Winter Games in PyeongChang in 2018 when North and South Korean athletes joined together in hockey at a time when headlines had been blaring about the threat of nuclear war between the U.S. and North Korea? Having inspired millions of Americans to rally out of the depths of the Great Depression and then join the Allies in defeating the horrors of Fascism in the Second World War, Franklin D. Roosevelt was elected to an unprecedented fourth term as U.S. President on November 7, 1944. In November of 1967 Carl Stokes became the first African American to be elected mayor of Cleveland, Ohio. In 1989, the East German government resigned after pro-democracy protests ushered in its collapse and the Berlin Wall was opened. In November of that next year Mary Robinson became Ireland's first female president. In 1993 South Africa adopted a new constitution after more than 300 years of white rule and inspired the world with a peaceful transformation to democracy.

#121. Take that leap of faith

In November of 1860, Abraham Lincoln's election as the 16th president of the United States over a deeply divided Democratic Party inspired those who were opposed to the spread of slavery and the threatened secession of the Southern states. Although he was the first Republican to win the presidency, Lincoln received only 40 percent of the popular vote, handily defeating the three other candidates: Southern Democrat John C. Breckinridge, Constitutional Union candidate John Bell, and Northern Democrat Stephen Douglas, a U.S. senator for Illinois.

Lincoln first gained national stature during his campaign against Stephen Douglas of Illinois for a U.S. Senate seat in 1858. The senatorial campaign featured a remarkable series of public encounters on the slavery issue, known as the Lincoln-Douglas debates, in which Lincoln argued against the spread of slavery, while Douglas maintained that each territory should have the right to decide whether it would become free or slave. Lincoln lost the Senate race, but his campaign brought national attention to the young Republican Party. In 1860, Lincoln won the party's presidential nomination.

In this election, Lincoln again faced Douglas, who represented the Northern faction of a heavily divided Democratic Party, as well as Breckinridge and Bell. The announcement of Lincoln's victory signaled the secession of the Southern states, which had been publicly threatening secession if the Republicans gained the White House.

By the time of Lincoln's inauguration on March 4, 1861, seven states had seceded, and the Confederate States of America had been formally established, with Jefferson Davis as its elected president. One month later, the American Civil War began when Confederate forces under General P.G.T. Beauregard opened fire on Union-held Fort Sumter in South Carolina. In 1863, as the tide turned against the Confederacy, Lincoln emancipated the slaves and in 1864 he won reelection. In April 1865, he was assassinated by Confederate sympathizer John Wilkes Booth at Ford's Theatre in Washington, D.C. The attack came only five days after the American Civil War effectively ended with the surrender of Confederate General Robert E. Lee at Appomattox. The following "tip" is adapted from #78 in *147 Practical Tips for Teaching Sustainability*.

> One instructor has regularly used a Challenge Ropes Course. The infamous "leap of faith" really gets everyone's heart pounding. He writes, "Roped in, students climb a thirty-foot telephone pole, find a way to balance themselves on the top and, when their knees stop knocking, leap toward a trapeze hanging some eight feet or so away. Many grab for their own safety ropes as soon as they jump. Others are too timid in their jump to come very close. Some get a finger or two on the trapeze but not enough to hold on. And a few are able to grab, hold, and swing. Whatever happens, everyone cheers. When we debrief this activity, the connections they find to meeting the challenges in their own lives or about finding more sustainable solutions are direct and useful. I asked: What fears do you face and how are you able to climb past them? What supports do you have in place? What were you able to learn from

each attempt?" With or without a ropes experience, ask students and other audiences to evaluate their fears and challenges regarding learning, teaching, and living sustainability.

With over 620,000 American soldiers killed during the Civil War, almost as many as the number of U.S. casualties in all other wars combined, how do you think that Abraham Lincoln would have explained his commitment to the union using that triple bottom line logic of sustainability, i.e., preserving the interconnected health of the environment, society and the economy?

Moving toward a more sustainable future can happen if enough people begin moving in the right direction. Inspire people you know and with whom you work to take that first step in reducing waste, conserving energy, standing up for fairness, challenging greed, and promoting community.

#122. Focus the group

In November of 1885, the Canadian Pacific Railroad was completed, uniting various smaller lines across Canada. Despite the logistical difficulties posed by areas such as the bogs region of northwestern Ontario and the high rugged mountains of British Columbia, the railway was completed six years ahead of schedule. The transcontinental railway was instrumental in populating the vast western lands of Canada, providing supplies and commerce to new settlers. Many of western Canada's great cities and towns grew up around Canadian Pacific Railway stations. The construction of a transcontinental railroad inspired a stronger connection of British Columbia and the Northwest Territories to the Dominion of Canada they had recently joined, and acted as a bulwark against potential incursions by the United States. The question people often face is how to build bridges and inspire connections across distances and differences and in the face of external threats? The following "tip" is adapted from #80 in *147 Practical Tips for Teaching Sustainability*.

Getting groups to work well can be a challenge, especially when complex issues like sustainability demand informed and coordinated action. Know that your use of various experiential activities can be helpful in raising awareness about teamwork.

Have students pair up and face each other in one long line with index fingers held out at chest height, fingernails pointing out. Place a "helium stick," a lightweight collapsible tent pole, on top of their fingers. As a group, have them get the pole to the ground. The only rule is that everyone must keep contact with the pole at all times. "Very quickly," said one instructor, "that pole began to rise. We talked through what was happening and tried to find a strategy we all could agree on but that pole quickly rose again. It was very frustrating. Then a student who was majoring in music, very involved with jazz, and disciplined to listen closely to his fellow musicians in rehearsal and performance, suggested that we close our eyes. That did it. We all seemed better able to block out the distractions and focus more intently. Slowly, we got control and the pole began to go down. What a useful lesson in the demands of effective teamwork."

Try this activity with your own group or class. Everyone will quickly see the need for finding a coordinated focus. We can only marvel at what inspired the teamwork that was needed for Canadians to conceive of their transcontinental railroad and then successfully complete it.

#123. Focus on investigations

In November 1938, in an event that would foreshadow the Holocaust, German Nazis launched a campaign of terror against Jewish people and their homes and businesses in Germany and Austria. The violence, which continued through November 10 and was later dubbed "Kristallnacht," or "Night of Broken Glass," after the countless smashed windows of Jewish-owned establishments, left approximately 100 Jews dead, 7,500 Jewish businesses damaged and hundreds of synagogues, homes, schools and graveyards vandalized. An estimated 30,000 Jewish men were arrested, many of whom were then sent to concentration camps for several months; they were released when they promised to leave Germany. Kristallnacht represented a dramatic escalation of the campaign started by Adolf Hitler in 1933 when he became chancellor to purge Germany of its Jewish population.

The Nazis used the murder of a low-level German diplomat in Paris by a 17-year-old Polish Jew as an excuse to carry out the Kristallnacht attacks. On November 7, 1938, Ernst vom Rath was shot outside the German embassy by Herschel Grynszpan, who wanted revenge for his parents' sudden deportation from Germany to Poland, along with tens of thousands of other Polish Jews. Following vom Rath's death, Nazi propaganda minister Joseph Goebbels ordered German storm troopers to carry out violent riots disguised as "spontaneous demonstrations" against Jewish citizens. Local police and fire departments were told not to interfere. In the face of all the devastation, some Jews, including entire families, committed suicide.

In the aftermath of Kristallnacht, the Nazis blamed the Jews and fined them 1 billion marks (or $400 million in 1938 dollars) for vom Rath's death. As repayment, the government seized Jewish property and kept insurance money owed to Jewish people. In its quest to create a master Aryan race, the Nazi government enacted further discriminatory policies that essentially excluded Jews from all aspects of public life.

Over 100,000 Jews fled Germany for other countries after Kristallnacht. The international community was outraged by the violent events of November 9 and 10. Some countries were inspired to break off diplomatic relations in protest, but the Nazis suffered no serious consequences, leading them to believe they could get away with the mass murder that was the Holocaust, in which an estimated 6 million European Jews died. We have to ask what would have happened if more countries would have broken with Germany once this savagery was reported. And what is happening now around each of us, both of large and small scale, where history will record silence, where sustainability, for example, was sacrificed? The following idea is adapted from "tip" #81 in *147 Practical Tips for Teaching Sustainability.*

> John Dewey (1938) firmly believed that students should explore new concepts through self-directed studies. You could ask students or other audiences to generate a list of potential investigations that would get them into the field to think about the interrelationships of the three dimensions of sustainability: the environment, the economy, and society. For example, you could

ask what research might have shed some light on possible actions by the international community once the threats, abuses and tragedies that were emerging in Hitler's Germany were clear? Using history as a reference, were there any lessons to be learned from the American Revolution about resisting tyrannical leaders? Were there useful lessons from the American Civil War about the willingness of people in the North to fight against the continued expansion of slavery and support the Union?

While Dewey would applaud these efforts, he would urge us to go further and encourage students to direct their own investigations rather than treating field experiences as rote laboratory exercises. Tim Pearson has his elementary school classes energized with meaningful student-generated investigations that tie into sustainability. He asked: "How does fertilizer runoff from the municipal golf course or farms affect the health of local streams, rivers, and lakes? What happens to the population of prairie dogs when a new development begins and people want manicured lawns" (p. 94)?

Identify possible issues for investigation in your classroom, on your campus or in your community. For example, is the landscaping sustainable? What plants could be removed or introduced to lower water, fertilizer, and pesticide usage? How could Dewey's ideas help inspire a community?

#124. Understand privilege

In November 1848, the first term of classes for the new Boston Female Medical College began with twelve students from across New England, New York and Ohio. In 1856, the college changed its name to the New England Female Medical College (NEFMC) and ranks as the oldest medical school in the United States exclusively for women. After only 26 years of existence, the New England Female Medical College merged with Boston University School of Medicine in 1874.

Prior to 1847 when Elizabeth Blackwell was inspired as the first woman to enroll in a United States medical school when she entered the Geneva Medical College, many women had served as family physicians, but they were denied attendance at medical lectures and examinations. Blackwell set a new standard for young women everywhere, helping them gain entrance into the medical world by claiming that women had something unique to offer medicine that men could not. Basic graduation requirements consisted of previous medical study, two years of attendance at NEFMC, a final thesis, and passing a final exam.

The Female Education Society opened in Boston in 1848, and was created exclusively for the medical education of women. Its members sought to establish a medical school in Boston complete with its own teaching hospital that would teach women midwifery and nursing so they could treat women and children. The willingness to challenge male privilege would grow slowly in various pockets of enlightened thinking and eventually prevail. The following "tip" is adapted from #54 in *147 Practical Tips for Teaching Diversity.*

> Help students and others discuss the privileges enjoyed by various groups of people. You could start with "white privilege" — "those unspoken, unwritten rules of conduct by which Whites are treated by others," usually including the "freedom to select any place to live, to shop without being followed, to write checks without showing identification, to secure bank loans with no collateral, and to be offered employment on the basis of one's family or friends rather than one's resume" (Paccione, 2003, p. 151). In addition to the impact of racist prejudices, privilege comes in many other forms as well, including gender, social class, sexual orientation, religious prejudices, and disabilities.

Allow people to explore the various implications for privilege, i.e., historical, economic, educational, social, even personal and emotional. You could also explore the implications of "social class privilege" or "majority privilege." Ask what could inspire change.

#125. Speak the truth and name the oppression

On November 11, 1962, the United Nations General Assembly adopted a resolution condemning South Africa's racist apartheid policies and calling on all its members to end economic and military relations with the country. In effect from 1948 to 1993, apartheid, which comes from the Afrikaans word for "apartness," was government-sanctioned racial segregation and political and economic discrimination against South Africa's non-white majority. Among many injustices, blacks were forced to live in segregated areas and couldn't enter whites-only neighborhoods unless they had a special pass. Although whites represented only a small fraction of the population, they held the vast majority of the country's land and wealth.

Following the 1960 massacre of unarmed demonstrators at Sharpeville near Johannesburg, South Africa, in which 69 blacks were killed and over 180 were injured, the international movement to end apartheid grew rapidly. However, some in the international community argued that sanctions would disproportionately harm the Black majority while others noted how South Africa had been a vocal opponent of communism in a part of the world where Cold War competition was putting nations in one camp or the other. Nonetheless, opposition to apartheid within the U.N. grew, and in 1973 a U.N. resolution labeled apartheid a "crime against humanity." In 1974, South Africa was suspended from the General Assembly.

After decades of strikes, sanctions and increasingly violent demonstrations, many apartheid laws were repealed over the next 30 years. Finally, in 1991, under President F.W. de Klerk, the South African government repealed all remaining apartheid laws and committed to writing a new constitution. In 1993, a multi-racial, multi-party transitional government was approved and, the next year, South Africa held its first fully free elections. Political activist Nelson Mandela, who spent 27 years in prison along with other anti-apartheid leaders after being convicted of treason, became South Africa's new president.

In 1996, the South African Truth and Reconciliation Commission (TRC), established by the new government, began an investigation into the violence and human rights violations that took place under the apartheid system between 1960 and 1994. The commission's objective was not to punish people but to inspire South Africans to heal by dealing with its past in an open manner. People who committed crimes were allowed to confess and apply for amnesty.

Headed by 1984 Nobel Peace Prize winner Archbishop Desmond Tutu, the TRC listened to testimony from over 20,000 witnesses from all sides of the issue—victims and their families as well as perpetrators of violence. It released its report in

1998 and condemned all major political organizations—the apartheid government in addition to anti-apartheid forces such as the African National Congress—for contributing to the violence. Based on the TRC's recommendations, the government began making reparation payments of approximately $4,000 (U.S.) to individual victims of violence in 2003. The following "tip" is adapted from #56 in *147 Practical Tips for Teaching Diversity*.

> Although challenging, it is important to help students and others learn how to face injustice, past and present, how to understand pain and suffering, what our ethical responsibilities are, and how healing can happen. The language and the concepts we use can have a powerful effect on learning, organizing what we read and hear into categories, while inspiring others to action as well. For example, in an argument for curriculum reform that supports sustainable peace and development at the University of Ngozi in Burundi, a church leader uses language in a new and provocative way when he calls for a "war against war" (Timpson, Ndura & Bangayimbaga, 2015).

> As another example, Roe Bubar and Irene Vernon (2003) describe what they face when addressing the history of law and policies for Native Americans in the United States. "We focus on how Indian nations in this country never have been afforded the ability to assert their sovereignty in its fullest extent within the confines of the judicial system. ... In the face of this kind of (in)justice, it becomes a real challenge for us to get students to learn this history and to then empower them to think about the law in a more ethical and equitable manner" (p. 156). For instance, should we call Christopher Columbus an "explorer" or label him an "emissary" for European imperialists greedy for the resources of the new world or, given the resulting deaths of millions of Native peoples, judge him guilty of "war crimes" and "genocide"?

> Here is a third example. Rose Kreston (2003) teaches about the terrible history that disabled people have suffered. "Society's response to disability (as deviant) has ranged from such atrocities as infanticide and the holocaust (i.e., first groups for the Nazi gas

chambers) to relatively benign habits of designing facilities with
only one accessible restroom per floor or protesting group homes
in neighborhoods. As a result, people with disabilities have experienced systematic oppression, discrimination, isolation, and
devaluation from those who are non-disabled" (p. 171).

*Help students and others identify problems in your area of study, what "truths" need to be
explored and what "oppressions" need to be identified. Use time in a debriefing session to
assess the impact of this kind of discussion. Just how inspiring is it to publicly state what
only a few radical types dare to say?*

#126. Have courage

In early November of 1962, during the Cuban Missile Crisis, U.S. President John
F. Kennedy announced on television that "the Soviet bases in Cuba are being dismantled, their missiles and related equipment being crated, and the fixed installations at these sites are being destroyed." Earlier, on October 22 Kennedy had
notified Americans about the presence of the missiles, explained his decision to
enact a naval blockade around Cuba and made it clear the U.S. was prepared to
use military force if necessary to neutralize this perceived threat to national security. Following this news, many people feared the world was on the brink of nuclear
war. However, disaster was avoided when the U.S. agreed to Soviet leader Nikita
Khrushchev's offer to remove the Cuban missiles in exchange for the U.S. promising not to invade Cuba. Kennedy also secretly agreed to remove U.S. missiles
from Turkey.

For American officials, the urgency of the situation had stemmed from the fact that
the nuclear-armed Cuban missiles were being installed so close to the U.S. mainland–just 90 miles south of Florida. From that launch point, they were capable of
quickly reaching targets in the eastern U.S. The Soviets had long felt uneasy about
the number of nuclear weapons that were targeted at them from sites in Western
Europe and Turkey, and they saw the deployment of missiles in Cuba as a way to
level the playing field.

Another key factor in the Soviet missile scheme was the hostile relationship between the U.S. and Cuba. The Kennedy administration had already launched one attack on the island–the failed Bay of Pigs invasion in 1961–and Castro and Khrushchev saw the missiles as a means of deterring further U.S. aggression. Perhaps it was this miscalculation that inspired Kennedy to negotiate both publicly and privately.

Despite the enormous tension, Soviet and American leaders found a way out of the impasse. During the crisis, the Americans and Soviets had exchanged letters and other communications, and on October 26, Khrushchev sent a message to Kennedy in which he offered to remove the Cuban missiles in exchange for a promise by U.S. leaders not to invade Cuba. The following day, the Soviet leader sent a letter proposing that the USSR would dismantle its missiles in Cuba if the Americans removed their missile installations in Turkey.

Officially, the Kennedy administration decided to accept the terms of the first message and ignore the second Khrushchev letter entirely. Privately, however, American officials also agreed to withdraw their nation's missiles from Turkey. U.S. Attorney General Robert Kennedy personally delivered the message to the Soviet ambassador in Washington, and on October 28, the crisis drew to a close. The following "tip" is adapted from #57 in *147 Practical Tips for Teaching Diversity*.

> Teaching about diversity requires a certain sophistication in our approaches as well as strong character traits. As Timpson, Canetto, Borrayo, and Yang (2003, p. 288) conclude in *Teaching Diversity*: "This is admittedly complex terrain to navigate and requires understanding, skill, clarity, and courage on everyone's part."

Model for others a process in which you explore your own prejudices publically and then open up to new thinking. Reflect back on challenging experiences you have had around issues of diversity, such as angry outbursts or tearful responses. Assess your courage in handling what occurred. Make plans on how best to inspire better responses to those same topics in the future.

#127. Study and re-create the symbols of peace

In November 1969, independent investigative journalist Seymour Hersh, after ex-tensive interviews with Second Lieutenant William Calley, broke the My Lai Mas-sacre story on the Associated Press wire service. The massacre included the killing of between 347 and 504 unarmed Vietnamese civilians in South Vietnam on March 16, 1968. It was committed by U.S. Army soldiers from (Charley) Company C of the 23rd Infantry Division. Victims included men, women, children, and infants. Some of the women were gang-raped and their bodies mutilated. Twenty-six sol-diers were charged with criminal offenses, but only platoon leader Calley was con-victed. Found guilty of killing 22 villagers, he was originally given a life sentence, but served only three and a half years under house arrest.

Remembering these horrors can inspire renewed commitments to peace. Here are the details: On the Saturday morning of the massacre, some 100 soldiers from Charlie Company led by Captain Ernest Medina, following a short artillery and helicopter gunship barrage, landed in helicopters at Son My, a patchwork of set-tlements, rice paddies, irrigation ditches, dikes, and dirt roads, connecting an as-sortment of hamlets and sub-hamlets. Though the GIs were not fired upon after landing, they still suspected there were Vietcong guerrillas hiding underground or in the huts. Confirming their suspicions, the gunships engaged several armed enemy in the vicinity of My Lai; later, one weapon was retrieved from the site.

On approach, platoons fired at people they saw in the rice fields and in the brush. The villagers, who were getting ready for a market day, at first did not panic or run away, and they were herded into the hamlet's commons. Harry Stanley, a machine gunner from Charlie Company, said during the U.S. Army Criminal Investiga-tion Division's (CID) inquiry that the killings started without warning. He first observed a member of 1st Platoon strike a Vietnamese man with a bayonet. Then, the same trooper pushed another villager into a well and threw a grenade in the well. Next, he saw fifteen or twenty people, mainly women and children, kneeling around a temple with burning incense. They were praying and crying. They were all killed by shots in the head.

A large group of approximately 70–80 villagers was rounded up and led to an irrigation ditch to the east of the settlement. All detainees were pushed into the ditch and then killed after repeated orders issued by Lieutenant Calley, who was also shooting. Private Paul Meadlo testified that he expended several M16 magazines. He recollected that women were allegedly saying "No VC" and were trying to shield their children. He remembered that he was shooting into women with babies in their hands since he was convinced at that time that they were all booby-trapped with grenades and were poised to attack. On another occasion during the security sweep of My Lai, Meadlo again fired into civilians side-by-side with Lieutenant Calley.

Private Dennis Konti, a witness for the prosecution, told about one especially gruesome episode during the shooting: "A lot of women had thrown themselves on top of the children to protect them, and the children were alive at first. Then, the children who were old enough to walk got up and Calley began to shoot the children". Other 1st Platoon members testified that many of the deaths of individual Vietnamese men, women and children occurred inside My Lai during the security sweep. Livestock were shot as well.

Inspired by the reporting of Hersh and others, the incident prompted global outrage when it became public knowledge. Learning about the My Lai massacre helped to increase domestic opposition to the U.S. involvement in the Vietnam War when the scope of killing and cover-up attempts were exposed. Initially, three U.S. servicemen who had tried to halt the massacre and rescue the hiding civilians were shunned, and even denounced as traitors by several U.S. Congressmen, including Mendel Rivers, Chairman of the House Armed Services Committee. Only after thirty years were they recognized and decorated, one posthumously, by the U.S. Army for shielding non-combatants from harm in a war zone. My Lai was one of the largest single massacres of civilians by U.S. forces in the 20th century. The following "tip" is adapted from #57 in *147 Practical Tips for Teaching Peace and Reconciliation*.

> Dean Nelson is a combat veteran who now refers to himself as a "peacenik." He writes: "Although different peace symbols are used throughout the world, the meanings are typically the same, that is, the absence of war, strife and suffering, a nicer and gentler world free from fear. Several symbols seem to have near universal appeal, e.g., the white dove with an olive branch. Others may be associated more with a particular culture; e.g., the peace crane.

Helping people learn more about the origins of these symbols can lead to valuable discoveries and rich discussions" (pp. 66-67). The Buddhist practice of *Tonglen* guides us in breathing in the horrors of events like the My Lai Massacre and breathing out positive thoughts of healing and peace.

In remembering the horrors of the atom bomb that the U.S. dropped on Hiroshima, Nelson found that the origin of the white dove as a symbol of peace has its roots in the Bible and the story of Noah's Ark. The olive branch in its bill signaled the end of the flood and God's forgiveness. The peace crane has its origins in post-World War Two Japan and the story of Sadako Sasaki and the thousand paper cranes. The following description can be found on the web site for the Children's Peace Monument in Hiroshima's Peace Memorial Park:

Visitors to Peace Memorial Park see brightly colored paper cranes everywhere. These paper cranes come originally from the ancient Japanese tradition of origami or paper folding, but today they are known as a symbol of peace. They are folded as a wish for peace in many countries around the world. This connection between paper cranes and peace can be traced back to a young girl named Sadako Sasaki, who died of leukemia ten years after the atomic bombing.

Sadako was two years old when she was exposed to the A-bomb. She had no apparent injuries and grew into a strong and healthy girl. However, nine years later in the Fall when she was in the sixth grade of elementary school (1954), she suddenly developed signs of an illness. In February the following year she was diagnosed with leukemia and was admitted to the Hiroshima Red Cross Hospital. Believing that folding paper cranes would help her recover, she kept folding them to the end, but on October 25, 1955, after an eight-month struggle with the disease, she passed away.

Sadako's death triggered a campaign to build a monument to pray for world peace and the peaceful repose of the many children killed by the atomic bomb. The Children's Peace Monument that stands in Peace Park was built with funds donated from all over Japan. Later, this story spread to the world, and now, approximately 10 million cranes are offered each year before the Children's Peace Monument. (See City of Hiroshima (n.d.). Paper cranes and the Children's Peace Monument. Retrieved from http://www.city.hiroshima.lg.jp/shimin/heiwa/crane.html)

Try your hand at folding a peace crane. Inspire others to get involved whenever there is a tragedy to be remembered and a call for healing and peace is needed. Breathe in these difficult memories—including what we know of war-time horrors like at My Lai during the Vietnam War or the bombing of Hiroshima during World War Two—and then write wishes for peace in the paper squares. You can easily find directions by searching various web sites. You can display your cranes locally or, if you want, send them to Hiroshima's Peace Memorial Park by using the directions they provide on their website.

#128. Keep the faith about peace and reconciliation

In November of 1936, Italian Dictator and Prime Minister Benito Mussolini declared that all other European countries would from then on rotate on the Rome–Berlin axis, thus creating the term "Axis". What became the Rome–Berlin–Tokyo Axis had their brief and bloody run to power as they eventually inspired the Allied forces to join together once World War II exploded. In the darkest hours, it has always been important for people to keep their faith in the potential for peace and reconciliation.

This "Axis" had grown out of the diplomatic efforts in Germany, Italy, and Japan to secure their specific expansionist interests in the mid-1930s. The "Rome–Berlin Axis" became a military alliance in 1939 under the so-called "Pact of Steel", with the Tripartite Pact of 1940 leading to the integration of the military aims of Germany, Italy and Japan. Using intimidation, power and brutality to achieve demented aims, some leaders have exacted great damage.

At its zenith during World War II, the Axis presided over territories that occupied large parts of Europe, North Africa, and East Asia. There were no three-way summit meetings and cooperation and coordination was minimal. The war ended in

1945 with the defeat of the Axis powers and the dissolution of their alliance. As in the case of the Allies, membership of the Axis was fluid, with some nations switching sides or changing their degree of military involvement over the course of the war. The following "tip" is adapted from #58 in *147 Practical Tips for Teaching Peace and Reconciliation*.

When the attacks of September 11th, 2001 occurred in the U.S., Bill Timpson was scheduled to meet his large lecture class for first-year students later that morning. He had often used music as a way to transition into a particular topic. For example, he had used Bob Marley's reggae classic *One Love* as a general and optimistic introduction to his course, *College Learning for a Sustainable Future*. On this particular day Timpson found himself wanting to say something about hope and faith in the darkest hours. He quickly went to the soulful *a cappella* by a wonderfully original African-American and politically aware group called *Sweet Honey in the Rock*. Their song, *I Remember, I Believe* (Bernice Johnson Reagon, 1995), chronicles a faith that helped them and so many others through the hardest of times.

> *I don't know how my mother walked her trouble down*
> *I don't know how my father stood his ground*
> *I don't know how my people survived slavery*
> *I do remember, that's why I believe*
>
> *I don't know why the rivers overflow their banks*
> *I don't know why the snow falls and covers the ground*
> *I don't know why the hurricane sweeps thru the land now and then*
> *Standing in the rain, I believe*
>
> *I don't know why the angels woke me up this morning soon*
> *I don't know why the blood still runs through my veins*
> *I don't know how I rate to run another day*
> *I am here still running, I believe*
>
> *My God calls to me in the morning dew*
> *The power of the universe knows my name*

> *Gave me a song to sing and sent me on my way*
> *I raise my voice for justice, I believe*

In the midst of conflict, what music inspires your hopes? When you need to reconcile differences, what sustains your faith? What "angels" help you wake up to meet another day?

#129. Imagine possibilities and act

In November of 1862, Richard Gatling patented his rapid-fire machine-gun which used rotating barrels around a central mechanism to load, fire and extract cartridges. This weapon became the forerunner of the modern machine gun and was first used by Union forces in the American Civil War. The Gatling gun was also used to expand European colonial empires by defeating indigenous warriors mounting massed attacks. Gatling had written that he created this weapon to reduce the need for large armies and lessen the number of deaths by combat and disease, thereby showing how futile war was. Throughout history technological inventions have been adapted by military forces and used for both conquest and defense. Enforcing international agreements about limiting the spread of nuclear weapons or banning the use of chemical weapons, for example, continue to inspire and challenge leaders across the globe. The following idea is adapted from "tip" #64 in *147 Practical Tips for Teaching Peace and Reconciliation.*

Violence can destroy possibilities and cripple the spirit. Yet, somehow, people do survive, finding hope and inspiration in different places, their creativity rekindled. Andrea Taylor has learned many lessons from a childhood that left her too often traumatized. In particular, she has found so many new and positive experiences through an exploration of creative outlets. "I like to remember the line from George Elliot, 'It is never too late to be what you might have been.' As an injured or neglected person progresses through Maslow's (1959) hierarchy of human needs, something begins to happen, unexpected things, wonderful things. Von Oech (1986) talks about the four roles involved in the creative process—explorer, artist, judge, and warrior—and it is at the point of Maslow's highest stage of "self-actualization" that they can spontaneously appear. How can any of us as individuals help curb the deadly potential of old and new weaponry? The mass shootings in the U.S. are painful reminders to act and teach others that peace is possible.

"For me, it was the artist. I began to imagine possibilities and to act on them. I had not sensed any creativity in me during my turbulent childhood, into adolescence, or well in to my adult life. Then one day it happened. I began to paint—simple, focused watercolor. This demonstration of deep heart-healing has brought about a wonderful new dimension to my life. I have met new friends. I have ventured out into new territory—hanging my paintings in public places, selling them to people across the country! As a teacher, I believe that what I do must reach further than the thing just done. It is my hope that I can reach those students who need my help to become who 'they might have been'" (p. 75)!

By yourself or with others, explore these questions: When has creative exploration inspired you to move past old hurts and see new possibilities? When have you helped others take those first steps? How can we bring new thinking to the ongoing advances of and danger of new weaponry?

#130. Build confidence in knowing, thinking, and acting

Marie Curie was born on November 7th, 1867 in Warsaw, Poland and later became a naturalized-French physicist and chemist who conducted pioneering research on radioactivity. Over the years her accomplishments were inspirational for so many. She was the first woman to win a Nobel Prize, the first person and only woman to win twice, the only person to win a Nobel Prize in two different sciences, and was part of the Curie family legacy of five Nobel Prizes.

Curie was born in Warsaw and began her practical scientific training there. In 1891 at the age of 24, she followed her older sister to study in Paris, where she earned her higher degrees and conducted her subsequent scientific work. She shared the 1903 Nobel Prize in Physics with her husband Pierre Curie and with physicist

Henri Becquerel. In 1911 she won the Nobel Prize in Chemistry.

Her achievements included the development of the theory of radioactivity (a term that she coined), techniques for isolating radioactive isotopes, and the discovery of two elements, polonium and radium. Under her direction, the world's first studies into the treatment of neoplasms were conducted using radioactive isotopes. She founded the Curie Institutes in Paris and in Warsaw, which remain major centers of medical research today. During World War I, she developed mobile radiography units to provide X-ray services to field hospitals. Marie Curie died in 1934, aged 66, at a sanatorium in France from exposure to radiation during the course of her scientific research—a life of exploration and discovery that enriched our understanding of the physical universe. The following "tip" is adapted from #80 in *147 Practical Tips for Using Experiential Learning*.

> In *Teaching Community,* bell hooks (2003, *Teaching Community: A pedagogy of hope*) offers her insights into the problems of modern day classrooms. "In our nation, most colleges and universities are organized around the principles of dominant culture. This organizational model reinforces hierarchies of power and control. It encourages students to be fear-based, that is, to fear teachers and seek to please them. Concurrently, students are encouraged to doubt themselves, their capacities to know, to think, and to act. Learned helplessness is necessary for the maintenance of dominator culture" (p. 130). Curie's life can stand as a testimonial to thinking independently, taking the actions needed to shed light on some of the enduring mysteries of the universe, and contributing to our general knowledge of the world and its components.

List ways in which experiential learning, exploration and the pursuit of new knowledge could inspire confidence in knowing, thinking, and acting. Offer examples from your own life. Plan a presentation that attempts to build greater confidence in exploration and discovery.

#131. Be elegant in your responses and become comfortable in your discomfort

In November 1895, physicist Wilhelm Conrad Rontgen became the first person to observe X-rays, a significant scientific advancement that would inspire other discoveries and applications, ultimately benefiting a variety of fields, most of all medicine, by making the invisible visible. Rontgen's discovery occurred accidentally in his German lab, where he was testing whether cathode rays could pass through glass when he noticed a glow coming from a nearby chemically coated screen. He dubbed the rays that caused this glow X-rays because of their unknown nature.

X-rays are electromagnetic energy waves that act similarly to light rays, but at wavelengths approximately 1,000 times shorter than those of light. Rontgen holed up in his lab and conducted a series of experiments to better understand his discovery. He learned that X-rays penetrate human flesh but not higher-density substances such as bone or lead and that they can be photographed.

Rontgen's discovery was labeled a medical miracle and X-rays soon became an important diagnostic tool in medicine, allowing doctors to see inside the human body for the first time without surgery. In 1897, X-rays were first used on a military battlefield, during the Balkan War, to find bullets and broken bones inside patients.

Scientists were quick to realize the benefits of X-rays, but slower to comprehend the harmful effects of radiation. Initially, it was believed X-rays passed through flesh as harmlessly as light. However, within several years, researchers began to report cases of burns and skin damage after exposure to X-rays, and in 1904, Thomas Edison's assistant, Clarence Dally, who had worked extensively with X-rays, died of skin cancer.

Dally's death caused some scientists to begin taking the risks of radiation more seriously, but they still weren't fully understood. During the 1930s, 40s and 50s, in fact, many American shoe stores featured shoe-fitting fluoroscopes that used to X-rays to enable customers to see the bones in their feet; it wasn't until the 1950s that this practice was determined to be risky business. Wilhelm Rontgen received numerous accolades for his work, including the first Nobel Prize in physics in 1901, yet he remained modest and never tried to patent his discovery. Today,

X-ray technology is widely used in medicine, material analysis and devices such as airport security scanners. Rontgen wore his humility with elegance while others would have to stay open to their discomfort in later applications once the dangers of x-rays was proven to be real. The following "tip" is adapted from #81 in *147 Practical Tips for Using Experiential Learning*.

> Getting out of the routine of the presentations that you make to incorporate experiential learning can raise new worries: What distractions will surface? How can control be maintained in the face of so much that is unpredictable? What about all those potential liability issues out of doors? What if…? What about…? In the Shambhala tradition of Buddhism, *elegance* has a very special and important meaning. According to Chogyam Trungpa, "Elegance means appreciating things as they are. There is a sense of delight and of fearlessness. You are not fearful of dark corners. If there are any dark or mysterious corners, black and confusing, you override them" (Gimian, 2008, *The Pocket Chogyam Trungpa*, p. 80).

> In *Leadership and the New Science*, Meg Wheatley (2001), makes a case for disequilibrium in groups and organizations, what Piaget (1952, 1970) and others have described as essential for an individual's growth and development. "The things we fear most in organizations—disruptions, confusion, chaos—need not be interpreted as signs that are about to be destroyed. Instead, these conditions are necessary to awaken creativity" (p. 21).

Reevaluate an experience you have had that seemed disorienting at the time, even disturbing. In hindsight, what insights emerged for you? How important was that "disequilibrium"? List the ways in which you can become more "comfortable" with the kinds of discomfort that can lead to developmental shifts for individuals and groups, to new discoveries. When you consider some experiential activity, try reframing any worries you have within the context of the "elegance" with which you could face anything new and different, as challenges that can delight and inspire you, and fears that you can override. At the same time, be alert to any discomforts about the applications of your discovery.

#132. Embrace change

In mid-November 1869, the Suez Canal was officially opened, connecting the Mediterranean and Red Seas. The canal took more than fifteen years to plan and build, and its construction was repeatedly hindered by political disputes, labor shortages and even a deadly cholera outbreak. When finally completed, the 101-mile-long waterway inspired a permanent transformation of international shipping by allowing vessels to skip the long and treacherous transit around the southern tip of Africa. Although numerous technical, political, and financial problems had been overcome, the final cost was more than double the original estimate. Change is often more complicated than what we plan.

When it opened, the Suez Canal was only 25 feet deep, 72 feet wide at the bottom, and 200 to 300 feet wide at the surface. Consequently, fewer than 500 ships navigated it in its first full year of operation. Major improvements began in 1876, however, and the canal soon grew into one of the world's most heavily traveled shipping lanes. In 1875, Great Britain became the largest shareholder in the Suez Canal Company when it bought up the stock of the new Ottoman governor of Egypt. Seven years later, in 1882, Britain invaded Egypt, beginning a long occupation of that country. The Anglo-Egyptian treaty of 1936 made Egypt virtually independent, but Britain reserved rights for the protection of the canal.

After World War II, Egypt pressed for evacuation of British troops from the Suez Canal Zone, and in July 1956 Egyptian President Gamal Abdel Nasser nationalized the canal, hoping to charge tolls that would pay for construction of a massive dam on the Nile River. In response, Israel invaded in late October, and British and French troops landed in early November, occupying the canal-zone. Under pressure from the United Nations, Britain and France withdrew in December, and Israeli forces departed in March 1957. That month, Egypt took control of the canal and reopened it to commercial shipping.

Ten years later, Egypt shut down the canal again following the Six Day War and Israel's occupation of the Sinai Peninsula.

For the next eight years, the Suez Canal, which separates the Sinai from the rest of Egypt, existed as the front line between the Egyptian and Israeli armies. In 1975,

Egyptian President Anwar el-Sadat reopened the Suez Canal as a gesture of peace after talks with Israel. Today, an average of 50 ships navigate the canal daily, carrying more than 300 million tons of goods a year. The following "tip" is adapted from #82 in *147 Practical Tips for Using Experiential Learning*.

> Change can be very challenging, both emotionally and intellectually. Scholars like Howard Gardner (1999) and Dan Goleman (2002) want us to pay greater attention to the emotional requirements in experiential learning through a change process. Feelings arise and often require attention and skill to navigate. The good news is that these "skills" are learnable and teachable.

> In *Primal Leadership*, Goleman, Boyatzis and McKee (2004) make the case for emotional intelligence in leadership. "Whatever a leader's repertoire of styles today, it can grow wider tomorrow. The key lies in strengthening the underlying emotional intelligence abilities that drive a given style. Leadership is learnable… The process is not easy. It takes time and, most of all, commitment. But the benefits that flow from leadership with a well-developed emotional intelligence, both for the individual and the organization, make it not only worthwhile but invigorating" (p. 88).

Identify experiences when you were inspired to change. When was it that you feared change. In your experience, when has leadership reflected a "well-developed emotional intelligence." List the key players and what their skills were. If you can, contrast what was required for a major project like a Suez Canal and something much smaller.

DECEMBER
Tips #133-144

In December of 1865 the 13th Amendment to the U.S. Constitution was ratified abolishing slavery and ending a horrific period of brutal exploitation of human labor for private profit. Almost a hundred years later the hysteria of the Red Scare mushroomed and the recklessness of Senator Joe McCarthy eventually inspired a censure from his colleagues in 1954. In the next year the AFL-CIO was founded when two separate labor organizations, the American Federation of Labor and the Congress of Industrial Organizations, joined together following 20 years of rivalry and became the leading advocate for trade unions in the U.S. In December of 1987 the world breathed a bit more easily when President Ronald Reagan and Soviet Russia's General Secretary Mikhail Gorbachev signed the INF (Intermediate Nuclear Forces)Treaty eliminating all intermediate-range and shorter-range nuclear missiles. As the month ends with the celebration of Christmas, people everywhere are inspired once again to join in to sing about the birth of the "king of peace."

#133. Develop trust

In December of 1773, a group of Massachusetts colonists disguised as Mohawk Indians boarded three British tea ships and dumped 342 chests of tea into Boston Harbor. The midnight raid, popularly known as the "Boston Tea Party," was inspired by the British Parliament's Tea Act of 1773, a bill designed to save the faltering East India Company by greatly lowering its tea tax and granting it a virtual monopoly on the American tea trade. The low tax allowed the East India Company to undercut even tea smuggled into America by Dutch traders, and many colonists viewed the act as another example of taxation tyranny.

When three tea ships arrived in Boston Harbor, the colonists demanded that the tea be returned to England. After Massachusetts Governor Thomas Hutchinson refused, Patriot leader Samuel Adams organized the "tea party" with about 60 trusted members of the Sons of Liberty, his underground resistance group. The British tea dumped in Boston Harbor on the night of December 16 was valued at some $18,000. Great courage was needed by these rebels to challenge the authority of England over its colonies.

Parliament, outraged by the blatant destruction of British property, enacted the Coercive Acts, also known as the Intolerable Acts, in 1774. The Coercive Acts closed Boston to merchant shipping, established formal British military rule in Massachusetts, made British officials immune to criminal prosecution in America, and required colonists to quarter British troops. The colonists subsequently called the first Continental Congress to consider a united American resistance to the British. The following concept is adapted from "tip" #83 in *147 Practical Tips for Using Experiential Learning*.

>Christine Aguilar and Nereida Perdigon spent time together in a graduate seminar that incorporated experiential learning in a mountain retreat setting into its capstone content on educational leadership, renewal, and change. They expressed the following: "We know that there are some 1,400 students and scholars from 85 countries at our university who are engaged in academic work and research both on and off campus. We also know that these people could, under the right circumstances, contribute more to the creative synergy that is possible with this degree of diversity. When planning experiential learning, however, we must consider how those beliefs might impact someone's ability to participate or learn in ways that instructors may not have envisioned." In Michael Fullan's (2005) *Leadership and Sustainability*, Aguilar and Perdigon found this reference relevant: "High-trust cultures make the extraordinary possible, energizing people and giving them the wherewithal to be successful under enormously demanding conditions and the confidence that staying the course will pay off" (p. 73).

Identify those times and places when you felt that your organizational culture made the "extraordinary possible," inspiring you and others even under "enormously demanding conditions." What could you do to build more of a "high-trust culture" in your organization?

#134. Be aware of complexity and ambiguity

Margaret Mead was born in Philadelphia, Pennsylvania, on December 16, 1901. She grew up in a free-thinking intellectual home. Her father was a professor at the Wharton School of Finance and Commerce and the founder of the University of Pennsylvania's evening school. Her mother was a sociologist and an early supporter of women's rights. Margaret's grandmother was a child psychologist and played an active role in the lives of Margaret, her three sisters and her brother. It was her grandmother who inspired Margaret to watch the behavior of the younger children to figure out the reasons behind their actions. Eventually Mead became a dominant force in developing the field of culture and personality.

Mead thrived on change outside of her religious beliefs. In 1919 Mead transferred from DePauw University, in Indiana, to Barnard College, in New York City, where she majored in psychology. Her senior year anthropology course with Franz Boas was the most powerful event in her life, since it was then that she decided to become an anthropologist. She graduated from Barnard in 1923 and entered the anthropology department of Columbia University.

Mead drew heavily on psychology, especially learning theory and psychoanalysis. In return she contributed significantly to the development of psychoanalytic theory by emphasizing the importance of culture in personality development. She served on many national and international committees for mental health and was instrumental in introducing the study of culture into training programs for physicians and social workers.

Her theoretical position is based on the assumption that an individual matures within a cultural context which includes an ideological system (ideas), the expectations of others, and techniques of socialization (methods of fitting in with one's social environment) which affect not only outward responses but also the inner mental structure.

Mead was criticized by certain other social scientists for neglecting quantitative (measuring) methods and for what has been called "anecdotal" handling of data, i.e., relying on short stories of interesting incidents for proof. She was also accused of applying concepts of individual psychology to the analysis of social process while ignoring historical and economic factors.

There is no question that Mead was one of the leading American intellectuals of the twentieth century. Through her best-selling books, her public lectures, and her well-read column in Redbook magazine, Mead popularized anthropology in the United States. She was also an inspirational role model for American women, encouraging them to pursue professional careers previously closed to women while at the same time championing their roles as mothers. The following "tip" is adapted from #85 in *147 Practical Tips for Using Experiential Learning.*

> According to Perry (1981, 1999), we move beyond dichotomous, right-wrong, yes-no thinking as we mature intellectually, we learn to hear and understand other perspectives, and how to handle complexity and ambiguity. In his seminal model of moral development, Lawrence Kohlberg (1963) sees humans moving beyond strict obedience to develop ethical principles that can guide their thinking. The Buddhist leader, Chogyam Trungpa , once wrote: "When we talk of emptiness, it means the absence of solidity, the absence of fixed notions which cannot be changed" (Gimian, 2008, *The Pocket Chogyam Trungpa,* p. 69). In our research on learning, we have come to see how the higher levels of cognitive and moral development reflect a similar openness to other views, to ideas that are different or new. Experiential learning can offer those different and new perspectives. Margaret Mead's groundbreaking work traversed various fields and made inspired new connections and ideas.

Review a recent troubling experience and concentrate on avoiding an oversimplification of the issues. Practice embracing the richness of the inherent complexities and ambiguities to see where these could lead.

#135. Build on experience

The Voyage of the Beagle was written by Charles Darwin as a chronicle of his explorations and experiences as an unpaid naturalist on a ship that sailed from England in December of 1831. This expedition—originally planned to last two years, it lasted almost five—was funded by the British government to survey the coastline and chart the harbors of South America in order to make better maps and help protect British interests in the Americas. Darwin was charged with making scientific observations.

Eventually he would bring back specimens of more than 1,500 different species, hundreds of which had never been seen before in Europe. The book proved inspiring both as a travel memoir and as a detailed scientific field journal that demonstrated Darwin's keen powers of observation. It was written at a time when Western Europeans were exploring and charting the world usually for their colonial self-interest.

Darwin's notes made during the voyage include comments hinting at his changing views on the nature of species and their changes over time. On his return, he wrote his book based on these notes at a time when he was first developing his theories of evolution. By the 1870s—forty years after the original voyage—the scientific community and much of the general public had accepted evolution as a fact. Darwin's scientific discovery inspired what some refer to as the unifying theory of the life sciences, explaining the diversity of life. By the time of his death, Darwin was described as one of the most influential figures in human history. His experiences and careful observations led him to the ideas that challenged conventional wisdom and prompted new thinking, ideas that are still debated in some communities to this day. The following "tip" is adapted from #91 in *147 Practical Tips for Teaching Sustainability.*

> Like Darwin you can consider new ideas through connections with everyday experiences. Be alert to the experiences of your audiences. Start personal and up-close. What do people share in common? A cell phone? Car? Bicycle? Credit card? Put these items in the center of a discussion and ask exhaustive questions as to their resource use and waste streams, pricing and access, social assets, and shadow effects. Are such items contributing to a healthier world, greater prosperity for all, and stronger community? Could they better designed or need it be replaced to meet these goals?

During the session debrief, refer back to the story of Darwin, his experiences, observations and theorizing. How could your discussion of common experiences lead to new insights into old explanations?

#136. Balance openness and safety

In December of 1955, in Montgomery, Alabama, Rosa Parks, then 42 years old, refused to obey a bus driver's order to give up her seat in the "colored section" to a white passenger, after the whites-only section was filled. Parks was, at that time and from then on, an activist in the Civil Rights Movement, whose actions inspired millions including the United States Congress who later honored her with the titles of "the first lady of civil rights" and "the mother of the freedom movement".

Parks was not the first person to resist bus segregation. Others had taken similar steps as early as 1942. However, NAACP—National Association for the Advancement of Colored People—organizers believed that Parks was the best candidate for seeing through a court challenge after her arrest for civil disobedience.

Parks' act of defiance and the Montgomery bus boycott became inspirational symbols for the modern Civil Rights Movement. She became an international icon of resistance to racial segregation. She organized and collaborated with civil rights leaders, including Martin Luther King, Jr., a new minister in town in 1955 who was gaining national prominence for his efforts in the civil rights movement.

At the time, Parks was secretary of the Montgomery chapter of the NAACP. She had recently attended the Highlander Folk School, a Tennessee center for training activists for workers' rights and racial equality. She acted as a private citizen "tired of giving in". Although widely honored in later years, she also suffered for her act; she was fired from her job as a seamstress in a local department store, and received death threats for years afterwards.

Shortly after the boycott, she moved to Detroit, where she briefly found similar work. From 1965 to 1988 she served as secretary and receptionist to John Conyers, an African-American US Representative. She was also active in the Black Power movement and the support of political prisoners in the US.

After retirement, Parks wrote her autobiography and continued to insist that the struggle for justice was not over and there was more work to be done. In her final years, she suffered from dementia. Parks received national recognition, including the NAACP's 1979 Spingarn Medal, the Presidential Medal of Freedom, the Congressional Gold Medal, and a posthumous statue in the United States Capitol's National Statuary Hall. Upon her death in 2005, she was the first woman and third non-US government official to lie in honor in the Capitol Rotunda. California and Missouri commemorate Rosa Parks Day on her birthday February 4, while Ohio and Oregon commemorate the occasion on the anniversary of the day she was arrested, December 1. Becoming a public figure in challenging the status quo meant that Parks was both celebrated and subjected to threats. The following "tip" is adapted from #58 in *147 Practical Tips for Teaching Diversity*.

> The complexities inherent in teaching diversity require a certain degree of instructional sophistication. Specifically, the value of free and open interactions needs to be balanced against the requirements for psychological safety. A positive classroom climate enables students to discuss and challenge ideas without fear of personal attack by other students or retaliation by an instructor when the grades are given. When students and instructors come together to explore an issue, probing the underlying arguments, everyone should have the opportunity to speak and differences should be accepted.
>
> Timpson, Canetto, Borrayo, and Yang (2003) note: "Creating an open and safe classroom involves a complicated and sometimes contradictory set of actions .... Openness may mean allowing a spontaneous flow of contributions; safety, however, may involve managing the traffic of contributions so that there is a diversity of speakers who won't fear retaliation" (pp. 277-278). This balance of openness and safety refers to both the intellectual and emotional domains as well as a commitment to honest, sensitive exchanges.

As part of a discussion about ground rules in a class or meeting, encourage your students or other audience members to help you define what "openness" and "safety" mean for them and their learning. How does the Rosa Parks story inspire their thinking?

#137. Teach from the heart

In 1990 there was a "battle" at Wounded Knee on the Pine Ridge Lakota Reservation, an event in the series of encounters known as the "Indian Wars" that were not officially deemed ended until 1924. On December 29, in the bitter cold of a South Dakota winter, members of this same U.S. 7th Cavalry had surrounded an encampment of Lakota families—warriors, women, children and elders. When the soldiers attempted to disarm the Lakota, a fight broke out although it remains unclear what actually started the shooting.

By the time the "battle" was over, more than 150 men, women and children of the Lakota had been killed and 51 were wounded. Some estimates place the number closer to 300. For the U.S. cavalry, 25 died and another 39 were wounded, six of whom died later. The staggering difference in losses along with the deaths of so many women, children and the elderly inspired some residents on the Pine Ridge Reservation to change the language on the signage there, substituting the word "Massacre" where it once read "The Battle of Wounded Knee." In 1990, both houses of the U.S. Congress were inspired to pass a resolution on the historical centennial formally expressing "deep regret" for the massacre. The following idea is adapted from "tip" #80 in *147 Practical Tips for Teaching Diversity*.

> Roe Bubar and Irene Vernon (2003) describe how they make better connections between head and heart in their teaching. "As Native women, we agree that much of our teaching is from the heart, a process whereby both teachers and students learn together. .... We try to overturn what we term 'academic distance.' ...When teachers are content to simply lecture, there is no acknowledgement that the students and their interactions with one another merit any academic value" (p. 160).

Find ways to connect with students and others more deeply to events and issues. Allow those moments and opportunities some space in your teaching or presenting and allow yourself some time to follow your instincts, to grab onto those "teachable moments." Use debrief time to assess impact and weigh this against a preoccupation with content coverage or information giving. Less (coverage) may be more (or deeper and engaged learning)!

#138. Encourage participation

In December 1865, the 13th Amendment to the U.S. Constitution, officially ending the institution of slavery, was ratified. "Neither slavery nor involuntary servitude, except as a punishment for crime whereof the party shall have been duly convicted, shall exist within the United States, or any place subject to their jurisdiction." With these words, the single greatest change inspired by the Civil War was officially noted in the Constitution.

The ratification came eight months after the end of the war, but it represented the culmination of the struggle against slavery. When the war began, some in the North were against fighting what they saw as a crusade to end slavery. Although many northern Democrats and conservative Republicans were opposed to slavery's expansion, they were ambivalent about outlawing the institution entirely.

The war's escalation after the First Battle of Bull Run, Virginia, in July 1861 inspired many to rethink the role that slavery played in creating the conflict. By 1862, Lincoln realized that it was wrong to wage such a bloody war without plans to eliminate slavery altogether. In September 1862, following the Union victory at the Battle of Antietam in Maryland, Lincoln issued the Emancipation Proclamation, declaring that all slaves in the territory still in rebellion on January 1, 1863, would be declared forever free. The move was largely symbolic, as it only freed slaves in areas outside of Union control, but it changed the conflict from a war for the reunification of the states to a war whose objectives included the elimination of slavery.

Lincoln came to believe that a constitutional amendment was necessary to ensure the end of slavery. In 1864, Congress debated several proposals. Some insisted on including provisions to prevent discrimination against blacks, but the Senate Judiciary Committee provided the eventual language. It borrowed from the Northwest Ordinance of 1787, when slavery was banned from the area north of the Ohio River. The Senate passed the amendment in April 1864.

A Republican victory in the 1864 presidential election would guarantee the success of the amendment. The Republican platform called for the "utter and complete destruction" of slavery, while the Democrats favored restoration of states' rights, which would include at least the possibility for the states to maintain slavery. Lincoln's overwhelming victory set in motion the events leading to ratification of the amendment. The House passed the measure in January 1865 and it was sent to the states for ratification. When Georgia ratified it on December 6, 1865, the institution of slavery officially ceased to exist in the United States. Lincoln and his allies knew that they needed the widest possible participation to end the slavery discussion forever in the U.S. The following "tip" is adapted from #59 in *147 Practical Tips for Teaching Diversity*.

> Citing *Women's Ways of Knowing: The Development of Self, Voice, and Mind* (Belenky, Clinchy, Goldberger, and Tarule, 1986), William Timpson et al. (2003) contends that "it becomes important for instructors to encourage participation in classroom discussions because it is in this way that students, and females, in particular, 'find their voices' and mature intellectually. Early on in this process, acceptance of contributions without harsh judgment can be important for learning and development" (p. 17).

> As Nathalie Kees (2003) notes, you can use gestures and eye contact to encourage participation from your students: "I tell students that I won't always be looking at them when they speak so that I can observe other students' reactions to what they are saying, draw other students into the conversation through eye contact, and encourage them to speak to each other rather than just to, or through, me as the instructor. If students continue to respond only to me, I will redirect them to the rest of the group through hand gestures and verbal cues" (pp. 58-59).

> When navigating complex and sensitive issues, however, remember that students learn best when they can feel safe to participate fully and learn from their explorations and mistakes. Knowing the classroom norms and expectations needed for respectful interactions helps to set that foundation; every student should feel included, supported, and validated as well as encouraged and hopefully inspired to rethink beliefs, opinions and interpretations based on new information.

Try polling to assess reactions generally—"How many of you agree with that last point?

How many disagree? How many are unsure?" Then, you might call on specific individuals to elaborate. A free writing opportunity can give everyone, especially those who may be more introverted, the opportunity to participate. Reflect on what inspires others to speak out against injustice.

#139. Cultivate a sense of universal responsibility for building peace

In mid-December of 1991, leaders of North and South Korea were inspired to sign a treaty of reconciliation and nonaggression, renouncing armed force against each other and saying that they would formally bring the Korean War to an end 38 years after the fighting ceased. The agreement would also re-establish some measure of regular communication between the two countries, including telephone lines, mail, some economic exchanges and the reunion of some families who had been separated since war broke out in 1950. It would also commit the countries to rebuilding railway and road links across the heavily guarded border, known as the Demilitarized Zone (DMZ), which has been the symbol of the armed division of the country for almost four decades. Despite the headlines when North Korea fires off missiles or the U.S. and South Korean military forces conduct war exercises, the hopes and efforts for reunification and peace continue.

Officials on both sides described the accord as the first step toward what they termed the inevitable reunification of the Koreas. In the accord, the two sides agreed to reject all acts of terrorism or any efforts to overthrow the government of the other. They stopped short, however, of calling the agreement a peace treaty, saying that the armistice agreement signed in 1953 between the American-led United Nations forces and the army of North Korean President Kim Il Sung would remain in effect until it can be transformed into a formal peace.

For the United States, which lost 54,000 men and suffered 103,000 casualties before signing the truce with North Korea on July 27, 1953, the new reconciliation and non-aggression pact raised a host of new questions. The most critical is whether the new North-South relationship would undercut the rationale for keeping 40,000 American troops stationed in South Korea, formally serving under the United Nations Command that directed combat operations during the war. In recent years, the United States has slowly been turning command of those forces over to South

Koreans, but soon after the signing American troop reductions were halted until North Korea agreed to allow international inspection of its nuclear complexes and dismantled a fuel reprocessing plant that could produce weapons-grade plutonium.

The Korean War began with an invasion of the South by North Korean forces on June 25, 1950 and lasted until an armistice was signed on July 27, 1953. This war was a legacy of World War Two and the growing divisions of the Cold War that pitted countries like North Korea and its Soviet and Chinese Communist allies against countries like South Korea and its support from the United States and the United Nations once the North invaded.

According to the U.S. Department of Defense, South Korea reported some 373,599 civilian and 137,899 military deaths. Although reports will vary, most Western sources estimate that the Chinese People's Volunteer Army (PVA) suffered some 400,000 killed and 486,000 wounded, while the Korean People's Army suffered some 215,000 killed and 303,000 wounded.

In direct response to this war, the Graduate Institute for Peace Studies (GIP) was founded in 1984 by Dr. Young Seek Choue Who had fled the north before the war with deeds to the family fortunes. Despite the devastation of that conflict, the deaths and destruction on such a small peninsula—or rather, inspired by that suffering and wanting to invest in the search and study of alternatives—Choue partnered with Kyung Hee University to design and build a branch campus that would be dedicated to peace studies. Taught in English, students could enroll from anywhere in the world and, if admitted, expect a full scholarship for the two-year program of study. In 1993 UNESCO awarded the Graduate Institute of Peace Studies the "Prize for Peace Education" and Kyung Hee became the first university in the world to receive this prize. The question remains: How do we inspire others to take responsibility for building peace? The following "tip" is adapted from #43 in *147 Practical Tips for Teaching Peace and Reconciliation.*

> The Dalai Lama (1999) writes about a peace building ethic, universal responsibility: "To develop a sense of universal responsibility—of the universal dimension of our every act and of the equal right of all others to happiness and not to suffer—is to develop an attitude of mind where when we see an opportunity to benefit

others, we will take it in preference to merely looking after our narrow interests" (p. 162-163).

Other-centeredness rather than self-centeredness emerges as a powerful force when cultivating the peace building self. Peace builders are those who actively seek out opportunities to benefit others—sometimes at the expense of self-interest or self-aggrandizement. Sometimes other-centered action results in mutually beneficial outcomes for all people or parties involved.

Create action inventories of recent acts under the following three categories: self-interested acts, other-centered acts, and mutually beneficial acts. Invite individuals into small groups to talk about their action inventories. Ask the groups to pick one from each category (self, other, and mutually beneficial acts) and create a role play that exemplifies those scenarios. Ask them to perform these skits for other groups. Then have those in the audience reflect on the actions and outcomes within the skit and respond to the following questions:

- *Who benefited from the actions?*
- *Who did not?*
- *How was power wielded?*
- *Were positive or negative emotions present?*
- *Were positive or negative outcomes present?*
- *How might the scenario be changed for the better of all?*
- *What actions help to build peace? Which do not?*

As a debriefing exercise, ask the acting groups which scenarios felt right or better and why?

#140. Restore hope and instill motivation

On December 7, 1941, the U.S. naval base at Pearl Harbor near Honolulu, Hawaii, was the target for a devastating surprise attack by Japanese forces. Just before 8 a.m. on that Sunday morning, hundreds of Japanese fighter planes descended on the base, where they managed to destroy or damage nearly 20 American naval vessels, including eight enormous battleships, and over 300 airplanes. More than 2,400 Americans died in the attack, including civilians, and another 1,000 people were wounded. This assault inspired President Franklin D. Roosevelt to ask Congress on the next day to declare war on Japan.

The attack on Pearl Harbor was a surprise, but Japan and the United States had been edging toward war for decades. The United States was particularly unhappy with Japan's increasingly belligerent attitude toward China. The Japanese government believed that the only way to solve its economic and demographic problems was to expand into its neighbor's territory and take over its import market. To this end, Japan declared war on China in 1937, resulting in the Nanking Massacre and other atrocities.

American officials responded to this aggression with a battery of economic sanctions and trade embargoes. They reasoned that without access to money and goods, and especially essential supplies like oil, Japan would have to rein in its expansionism. Instead, the sanctions made the Japanese more determined to stand their ground. During months of negotiations between Tokyo and Washington, D.C., neither side would budge. It seemed that war was all but inevitable.

In all, the Japanese attack on Pearl Harbor failed to cripple the Pacific Fleet. By the 1940s, battleships were no longer the most important naval vessel: Aircraft carriers were, and as it happened, all of the Pacific Fleet's carriers were away from the base on December 7. Moreover, the Pearl Harbor assault had left the base's most vital onshore facilities—oil storage depots, repair shops, shipyards and submarine docks—intact. As a result, the U.S. Navy was able to rebound relatively quickly from the attack.

On December 8, Congress approved Roosevelt's declaration of war on Japan. Three days later, Japan's allies Germany and Italy declared war against the United States. Roosevelt's speech embodied the motivation needed to respond. The hope for a better world would have to come later. The following "tip" is adapted from #65 in *147 Practical Tips for Teaching Peace and Reconciliation*.

> Conflicts can traumatize the strongest of spirits. Yet, somehow people can also learn the lessons that help define their character. Nations and communities can rally as can individuals. Andrea Taylor learned about hope and motivation by surviving through some very tough circumstances. She vividly remembers the time

when she was stopped short by something she had seen in a novel by Marilyn French: " 'You don't have to shoot a woman to kill her; all you have to do—is marry her.' When I read this line many years ago, I dropped my head into my hands and wept—right there in front of everyone. That is what it felt like to me. After an emotionally blighted childhood, I found myself pregnant at sixteen, then married, and later abandoned with three little ones to raise on my own. For many, that might be the end, but not for me.

"With a deep desire for something more, I pressed through the natural tendencies to give up and just let life happen. I passed the test and received a GED, relocated to a college town and found a job on campus. After 17 years of working and going to school, I earned a BA in English with teaching credentials. Within a few months of graduating from college, I remarried and relocated to the Seattle area with a new and blended family. Within two years I was working with street kids in Seattle's inner city in a junior and senior high school that I founded. The kids in our school desperately needed that deep desire that I had felt many years ago. It became our stated mission *to restore hope* to their hearts and *instill motivation* to their minds so that they, too, could press through and find another kind of life. The school is now in its 19th year" (pp. 75-76).

Make a list of those experiences that have helped restore your hope. Who has helped motivate you to "press through" tough times and leave something of lasting value? Pose these questions for others to consider.

#141. Promote restorative justice and violence reduction

In December 2016, prosecution began for two retired British soldiers who are accused of the killing of an Irish Republican Army commander in Belfast, Northern Ireland, in 1972, during the "Troubles," the twenty-five year period that preceded the 1998 signing of the Peace Agreement. In what many considered to have been an intractable conflict dating back to British colonization of Ireland in the 1600's, this trial appears to demonstrate a good faith in a commitment to peace building on the part of the former British overlords.

The IRA commander, Joe McCann, was walking on Joy Street near the city center on April 15, 1972, when a patrol ordered him to stop. He ran, and the soldiers opened fire, fatally injuring him. McCann, 24 at the time, had four children and was a well-regarded leader in the Official Irish Republican Army, an outlawed paramilitary Marxist group that sought Northern Ireland's independence from Britain and union with the Republic of Ireland. A year earlier, he and his unit took over a local bakery and defended it from 600 British soldiers who were seeking to arrest paramilitary suspects there.

After McCann's death, boys threw rocks and paving stones at British troops in retaliation. The next month, the Official I.R.A. declared a cease-fire, but another faction of the Republican movement, the Provisional I.R.A., continued a deadly campaign of resistance for more than two decades, until the 1998 Good Friday Agreement largely brought about an end to the Troubles. An investigation by the Royal Ulster Constabulary, the police force for Northern Ireland at the time that historically had been allied with the British military and political ruling authorities, declined to prosecute anyone for McCann's death in 1972. Perhaps a commitment to the principles of restorative justice will help inspire the healing of more of the wounds from this long and bitter struggle. The following "tip" is adapted from #68 in *147 Practical Tips for Teaching Peace and Reconciliation*.

> Many of us talk about peace education and restorative justice, but not everyone practices it daily as Wendy Cohen does. The life of Wendy Cohen's daughter Lacy was taken in a violent murder in 2003 when Lacy was 21 and working toward her teaching license at the University of Northern Colorado. Since that time, Wendy has spent her energy and resources forging an incredible journey of restorative justice and violence reduction in honor of the life of her daughter.
>
> One of Wendy's first acts of restorative justice was when she asked the court to consider life imprisonment for her daughter's killer instead of the death penalty. As they left court that day, Wendy reached out to the mother of Lacy's killer and hugged her, real-

izing that both mothers had lost a child. Wendy and James Clausen, the brother of Lacy's killer, have spent the past several years speaking together publicly about the experiences and losses of the family of the victim and the perpetrator. No one is left unaffected by acts of violence, or by their presentations.

Wendy has also created 2 Hearts: The Lacy Jo Miller Foundation and a school called 2Hearts Academy. The students in her school are often referred from the juvenile justice system or have not been successful in the public schools for a variety of reasons. The curriculum for the school has been developed out of Wendy's 20 plus years as a teacher of high-risk children. It focuses on violence reduction and restorative justice through providing knowledge and information, expanding students' choices, improving self-esteem and decision making skills, and providing service to the school and community. Creating a safe and nurturing environment where students feel respected and welcomed is at the foundation of the school's success.

Have participants read some of the other offerings at the www.2Hearts4Lacy.org website. Follow up with a discussion related to the following questions. How would you have reacted if you were Wendy? How would you have reacted if you were the brother, sister, mother, or father of Lacy's killer? What role can community service play in violence reduction and restorative justice? How do the peace-building lessons from the long and bitter struggles in Northern Ireland help inspire others?

#142. Conduct an ecological footprint audit

In December 1942, Enrico Fermi, the Italian-born Nobel Prize-winning physicist, directed and controlled the first nuclear chain reaction in his laboratory at the University of Chicago, inspiring the advent of a nuclear age with immense potential as an energy source and as well as fearsome implications as weapons. Once the experiment had proven successful, a coded message was transmitted to President Roosevelt: "The Italian navigator has landed in the new world." Along with environmental impacts, an ecological footprint audit would have highlighted the potential societal and economic impacts that a full definition of sustainability demands.

Fermi remained skeptical about his discovery, despite the enthusiasm of his fellow physicists. He became a believer in 1938, when he was awarded the Nobel Prize in physics for "his identification of new radioactive elements." Although travel was restricted for men whose work was deemed vital to national security, Fermi was given permission to leave Italy and go to Sweden to receive his prize. He and his wife, Laura, who was Jewish, never returned because both feared and despised Mussolini's fascist regime.

Fermi immigrated to New York City and Columbia University, specifically, where he recreated many of his experiments with Niels Bohr, the Danish-born physicist, who suggested the possibility of a nuclear chain reaction. Fermi and others saw the possible military applications of such an explosive power, and quickly composed a letter warning President Roosevelt of the perils of a German atomic bomb. The letter was signed and delivered to the president by Albert Einstein on October 11, 1939. The Manhattan Project, the American program to create its own atomic bomb, was the result.

It fell to Fermi to produce the first nuclear chain reaction, without which such a bomb was impossible. He created a jury-rigged laboratory with the necessary equipment, which he called an "atomic pile," in a squash court at the University of Chicago. With colleagues and other physicists looking on, Fermi produced the first self-sustaining nuclear chain reaction and the "new world" of nuclear power was born. The following "tip" is adapted from #93 in *147 Practical Tips for Teaching Sustainability*.

> In *Sustainability on Campus: Stories and Strategies for Change*, Barlett and Chase (2004) offer a number of case studies that describe how infusing sustainability into courses and curriculum can lead to a dialogue about sustainability issues that extends to community, region, and beyond. One experiential learning course entitled "Greening the Campus" led to remarkable responses, often unanticipated, from a diverse set of university leaders, faculty, and students. These responses ultimately set the stage for a broader

institutional commitment to sustainability issues. Identify those who could conduct a similar audit in your school, college, university, organization, or community.

Daniel Birmingham teaches classes in STEM education at Colorado State University and has worked with middle school students to conduct sustainability audits of their local school. As one youth argued, "Our district was in trouble. We saw this as a way to make a difference." The local district had a large budget deficit that was leading to talk of closing schools and laying off teachers. These young people decided to act by auditing their school through an examination of behavioral and technological implications of various school activities. The youth eventually proposed changes, calculated the amount of money and pounds of CO_2 that would be saved if these changes were implemented, and delivered these recommendations to school leaders and teachers. Based on this presentation, the school was inspired to alter behaviors and shared their actions with other schools in the district.

Use your school, campus or organization as a laboratory. We can learn much about our surroundings from a sustainability audit that, in turn, could inspire constructive changes. Use different calculators, share the results and consider the implications if the numbers differ.

#143. Focus on metacognition

In December 1967, a 53-year-old man received the first human heart transplant in Cape Town, South Africa. The donor was a 25-year old woman who had been fatally injured in a car accident. Surgeon Christiaan Barnard, who trained at the University of Cape Town and in the United States, performed the revolutionary medical operation. The technique Barnard employed had been initially developed by a group of American researchers in the 1950s. After the surgery, the patient was given drugs to suppress his immune system and keep his body from rejecting the heart. These drugs also left him susceptible to sickness, however, and 18 days later he died from double pneumonia. Despite the setback, his new heart had functioned normally until his death and this partial success inspired others to further develop this technique further.

In the 1970s, the development of better anti-rejection drugs made transplantation more viable. Dr. Barnard continued to perform heart transplant operations, and by the late 1970s many of his patients were living up to five years with their new hearts. Successful heart transplant surgery continues to be performed today, but finding appropriate donors is extremely difficult. New medical procedures like this require the broader perspective that a metacognitive perspective can offer where those involved can routinely reflect on their own thinking. The following "tip" is adapted from #89 in *147 Practical Tips for Using Experiential Learning*.

> Experiential learning draws on many aspects of effective instruction including metacognition, for at its core, we are asking people to step back from some activity and make sense of their reactions, thoughts and feelings. The focus shifts away from acquired or memorized knowledge. In *Metateaching and the Instructional Map*, William Timpson (1999) describes the basics of inquiry or discovery learning. "One of the more challenging approaches to teaching, discovery learning or inquiry, attempts to foster critical and creative thinking, to help students better understand their own thinking processes (metacognition), and to give students experiences with problem solving in which answers may be complex and in which different perspectives and approaches are possible" (p. 94). In order to inspire others, surgeons who attempt new approaches must be able to reflect on their thinking and recalibrate their actions as they proceed.

Reflect on what you have been able to discover from your more memorable learning experiences. List the ways in which you can emphasize discovery in an upcoming program or presentation. What role does metacognition play?

#144. Be honest

Born on December 8, 1765, Eli Whitney patented the cotton gin and inspired a transformation in the production of cotton by greatly speeding up the process of removing seeds from cotton fiber. Growing up on a farm, Whitney was inspired by the challenges that emerged and proved to be a talented mechanic and inventor. Among the objects he designed and built as a youth were a nail forge and a violin.

By the mid-19th century, cotton had become America's leading export and Whitney's invention offered Southern planters a justification to maintain and expand slavery even as a growing number of Americans supported its abolition. In 1794 he received a patent for his invention and later formed a cotton gin manufacturing company. With his partner he planned to build cotton gins and install them on plantations throughout the South, taking as payment a portion of all the cotton produced by each plantation.

While farmers were delighted with the idea of a machine that could boost cotton production so dramatically, they had no intention of sharing a significant percentage of their profits. Instead, the design for the cotton gin was pirated and plantation owners constructed their own machines—many of them an improvement over Whitney's original model. Because it depends on the interconnected health of the environment, society and the economy, sustainability demands honesty from all of us for its applications. The following "tip" is adapted from #104 in *147 Practical Tips for Using Experiential Learning*.

> There are so many ways to express your beliefs and desires. When it comes to addressing sustainability, nothing comes across cleaner and more sincerely than a basic honesty. Share inspirational success stories, the places where the challenges seemed to be too great for you, or the paths your organization decided not to go down. This honesty makes for a tangible connection and encourages buy-in. Engage in meaningful conversations and share ideas with those in attendance while recognizing that there really are no "experts." There are many and different ways forward. Sustainability is an ongoing process and we are all in it together. Sharing our experiences is part of this process.

TIPS FOR ANYTIME OF YEAR
Tips #145-148

#145. Sustainability: share what has touched you

Earth Day is an annual event celebrated on April 22. Worldwide, various events are held to inspire support for environmental protection and health. First celebrated in 1970, Earth Day events in more than 193 countries are now coordinated globally by the Earth Day Network. On Earth Day 2016, the landmark Paris Agreement was signed by the United States, China, and some 120 other countries. This signing satisfied a key requirement for the climate protection treaty adopted by consensus of the 195 nations present at the 2015 United Nations Climate Change Conference in Paris.

In 1969 at a UNESCO Conference in San Francisco, peace activist John McConnell proposed a day to honor the Earth and the concept of peace. A month later a separate Earth Day was founded by United States Senator Gaylord Nelson as an environmental teach-in first held on April 22, 1970. While this particular Earth Day was focused on the United States, an organization launched to take it international in 1990 when organized events were created in 141 nations. The following idea is adapted from "tip" #105 in *147 Practical Tips for Teaching Sustainability*.

> Alie Sweany recalls what inspired her to embrace sustainability: "One great example in my life was an Environmental Ethics class I took at Colorado State University back in the late '90s. The class was taught by a now world renowned philosopher of environmental ethics, Holmes Rolston. This class was so life-altering that today, seven years later, I think of the lessons I learned there. The main idea I took is that humans are not separate from other life forms; in fact, we are not superior to an ant, a piece of moss, or a bird. This lesson seems so simple, yet for me it was so profound. This changed my perspective about life, directing many of my lifestyle and career decisions to this day" (p. 112).

Look back at your own life and find a time when a book, a class, a workshop, or maybe a statement about sustainability inspired you. How did your feelings, beliefs, or ideals change? Rediscover those moments and dive deeper. Reread a book that sparked your interest or hunt down that teacher, professor, or person for some follow-up conversations.

#146. Diversity: practice democracy and promote citizenship

Cesar Chavez was born on March 31, 1927 and grew to become an American and civil rights activist who helped inspire the creation of the United Farm Workers (UFW) union. His skills and nonviolent tactics made the farm workers' struggle successful in gaining nationwide support. By the late 1970s, his tactics had forced growers to recognize the UFW as the bargaining agent for 50,000 field workers in California and Florida.

After his death in 1993, Chavez became a major historical icon for the Latino community, with many schools, streets, and parks being named after him. He also became an icon for organized labor and progressive politics generally, symbolizing support for workers and for Hispanic empowerment based on grass roots organizing. He is also famous for popularizing the slogan "Sí, se puede" (Spanish for "Yes, one can" or, roughly, "Yes, it can be done"), which was adopted as the 2008 campaign slogan of Barack Obama. His birthday has become a state holiday in California, Colorado, and Texas. Among many other honors he would receive, he was awarded the Presidential Medal of Freedom in 1994. The following concept is adapted from "tip" #64 in *147 Practical Tips for Teaching Diversity*.

> Every instructor and every presenter at every level can better model in the classroom, lecture hall, or community space, what is needed from citizens in a democracy—acceptance, tolerance, sensitive communication, listening, understanding, a commitment to civility, an ethical framework, critical thinking, skills for teamwork and cooperation. For example, we know that we can get better and more creative decisions when we can handle the diversity of opinions and attitudes expressed, within classrooms and far beyond (Timpson & Doe, 2008).

> Roe Bubar and Irene Vernon (2003) connect active learning, stu-

dent empowerment, and a larger sense of democratic citizenship within a course on Native American laws and treaties: "Empowerment comes in a variety of ways. We think it is imperative for students to recognize their rights, how precarious those rights may be, and how easily they can be taken away. Another way to build student empowerment is to encourage them to speak out at public meetings and represent themselves and others effectively" (p. 165).

Take opportunities to emphasize listening as a skill for learning and living in a democracy. Show your students how accepting responsibility for a group project, for example, can help inspire others and counter the divisive competition that characterizes too many classrooms and organizational cultures. Instead, you can point to various challenges in group work — finding agreements across differences, negotiating constructive ways forward — and reinforce important components of citizenship. You could also consider using a service learning type of assignment where those attending tie their learning to an assignment in the field or larger community.

#147. Be mindful about action

Thich Nhat Hanh is a Vietnamese Buddhist monk who was born on October 11, 1926 and grew to inspire many world-wide with his prolific writings and teachings on meditation and peace. He has lived in the Plum Village meditation center in southwest France and travelled internationally to give retreats and talks. He coined the term "Engaged Buddhism" in his book *Vietnam: Lotus in a Sea of Fire* (1967). After a long term of exile, he was given permission to make his first return trip to Vietnam in 2005. Nhat Hanh has published more than 100 books, including more than 40 in English. He is active in promoting nonviolent solutions to conflict and, for example, refrains from eating animal products as a means of nonviolence towards non-human animals. The following "tip" is adapted from #135 in *147 Practical Tips for Teaching Peace and Reconciliation*.

From role plays to simulations to meditations, there are many activities and exercises that can deepen and extend learning about peace and reconciliation. In *Curriculum Planning*, Kenneth Henson (2006) describes a useful hierarchy for the potential role of activity.

- At level 1 is *perception* where "phenomena act as guides to motor activity. The individual must first become aware of a stimulus, pick up on cues for action, and then act upon these cues."
- At level 2, *set* refers to an "individual's readiness to act."
- At level 3, a *guided response* may be needed in the beginning when students must use complex skills.
- At level 4, *mechanism* means that we can perform an act "somewhat automatically without having to pause to think through each separate step."
- At level 5, *complex overt responses* involve "more complicated tasks."
- At level 6, *adaptation* requires individuals to "adjust performance as different situations dictate."
- And at level 7, *organization* means that someone can "create new movement patterns to fit the particular situation" (pp. 198-199).

As instructors or group leaders, we can use these levels to think through our goals and objectives, when and how we want people to practice the skills of peace-keeping, peace-making and peace-building. For example, consider the writings on mindfulness by noted Vietnamese Buddhist monk, Thich Nhat Hahn (1991), "I think the most important precept of all is to live in awareness, to know what is going on—not only here but there. For instance, when we eat a piece of bread, we may choose to be aware of how our farmers grow the wheat. It seems that chemical poisons are used a bit too much. And while we eat the bread, we are somehow co-responsible for the destruction of our ecology. When we eat a piece of meat, we may become aware that eating meat is not a good way to reconcile oneself with millions of children in the world. Forty thousand children die each day in the Third World for lack of food. And in order to produce meat, you have to feed the cow or the chicken with a lot of cereal...What we are, what we do every day, has much to do with world peace. If we are aware of our lifestyle, our way of consuming and looking at things, then we know how to make peace right at the present moment. If we are very aware, we will do something to change the course of things" (p. 156).

How do you perceive food differently after reading this passage? Are you ready to respond (i.e., set)? Does this passage provide enough of a guided response for you? If not, what more will you need? Does the concept of mechanism mean that you are so automatic in your eating habits that this kind of mindfulness would take some effort to develop? What complex overt responses would increase your mindfulness about food? What adaptations would allow you to take this mindfulness about food to every meal and snack? What organization would you need in your life to have this mindfulness about food ever present?

REFERENCES

Allport, G. (1954). *The Nature of prejudice.* Cambridge, MA: Addison-Wesley.

Arum, R. and Roksa, J. (2011). *Academically adrift: Limited learning on college campuses.* Chicago, IL: University of Chicago Press.

Barlow, M. and Clarke, T. (2005). *Blue gold: The fight to stop corporate theft of the world's water.* New York, NY: The New Press.

Barlett, P., and Chase, G. (2004). *Sustainability on campus: Stories and strategies for change.* Cambridge, MA: MIT Press.

Bennett, M. (1979). Overcoming the golden rule: Sympathy and empathy. In D. Nimmo (Ed.), *Communication Yearbook* 3 (pp. 407-422). Beverly Hills, CA: Sage.

Bloom, B. (1973). *Every kid can: Learning for mastery.* Washington, DC: College University Press.

Bohm, D. (1980). *Wholeness and the implicate order.* New York, NY: Routledge.

Booth Sweeny, L. & Meadows, D. (2010). *The systems thinking playbook: Exercises to stretch and build learning and systems thinking capabilities.* White River Junction, VT: Chelsea Green Publishing.

Boulding, E. (2000). *Cultures of peace: The hidden side of history.* New York, NY: Syracuse University Press.

Boulding, E. (1990). *Building a global civic culture: Education for an interdependent world.* Syracuse, NY: Syracuse University Press.

Brantmeier, E. (2008). Building empathy for intercultural peace: Teacher involvement in peace curricula development at a U.S. Midwestern High School. In J. Lin, E. Brantmeier, and C. Bruhn (Eds.). *Transforming education for peace.* Greenwich, CT: Information Age Publishing.

Brown, T. (1999). Adventure risk management. In J. Miles, and S, Priest (Eds.). *Adventure programming,* (pp. 273-283). State College, PA: Venture Publishing, Inc.

Bruner, J. (1975). The ontogenesis of speech acts. *Journal of Child Language, 2,* 1-40.

Bubar, R. and Vernon, I. (2003). A Native perspective on teaching law and U.S. policy: The inclusion of federal Indian law and policy in a college curriculum. In

W. Timpson, S. Canetto, E. Borrayo, and R. Yang (Eds.), *Teaching diversity* (pp. 153-168). Madison, WI: Atwood Publishing.

Bullard, R. (2005). Race and poverty are out of the closet. *Sierra*, November/December 2005, 28–29.

Carroll, J. (1963). A model of school learning. *Teachers College Record*, 64, 723-733.

Chödrön, P. (2001). *The places that scare you*. Boston, MA: Shambhala.

Collins, J. (2001). *Good to great*. New York, NY: HarperCollins.

Covey, S. (2004). *The 7 habits of highly effective people: powerful lessons in personal change*. New York, NY: Free Press.

Csikszenthmihalyi, M. (1990). *Flow*. New York, NY: HarperCollins.

Daley, P. (2007). *Gender and genocide in Burundi*. Bloomington, IN: Indiana University Press.

Davies, T. (2003). Experiencing Diversity in Distance Learning. In W. Timpson, S. Canetto, E. Borrayo, and R. Yang (Eds.), *Teaching diversity* (pp. 43-54). Madison, WI: Atwood Publishing.

Dewey, J. (1938). *Experience & education*. New York, NY: Touchstone.

Dinur, E. (2006). In D. Giffey (Ed.), *Long shadows* (p. 246). Madison, WI: Atwood Publishing.

Ewen, S. (1986). *All-consuming images*. New York, NY: Basic Books.

Freire, P. (1970). *Pedagogy of the oppressed*. New York, NY: Seabury.

Garb, J. (2006). In D. Giffey (Ed.), *Long shadows* (p. 182). Madison, WI: Atwood Publishing.

Gardner, H. (1999). *Intelligence reframed: Multiple intelligences for the 21st century*. New York, NY: Basic Books.

Giffey, D. (Ed.). (2006). *Long shadows: Veterans' paths to peace*. Madison, WI: Atwood Publishing.

Gladwell, M. (2002). *The tipping point*. Boston, MA: Back Bay Books.

Gordon, T. (1974). *Teacher effectiveness training*. New York: Peter H. Whyden.

Hanh, Thich Nhat (1991) *Peace in every step*. New York, NY: Bantam.

Haley, A. (1964). *The autobiography of Malcolm X*. New York, NY: Random House.

Haley, A. (1976). *Roots*. New York, NY: Doubleday.

Helgesen, S. (1995). *The web of inclusion*. New York, NY: Doubleday.

Henson, Kenneth. 2006. *Curriculum planning*. Long Grove, IL: Waveland.

Kees, N. (2003) , In Timpson, W., Canetto. S., Borrayo, E., and Yang, R. K. (Eds.). *Teaching diversity: Challenges and complexities, identities and integrity*. Madison, WI: Atwood Publishing.

Kimbrough, R. (2006). In D. Giffey (Ed.), *Long shadows* (pp. 46, 47, 49). Madison, WI: Atwood Publishing.

King, M. (2000). My pilgrimage to nonviolence. In W. Wink (Ed.), *Peace is the way* (pp. 64-71). New York, NY: Maryknoll.

Kliese, D. (2006). In D. Giffey (Ed.), *Long shadows* (pp. 251-262). Madison, WI: Atwood Publishing.

Kneller, J. (2003). Recalling the canon. In W. Timpson, S. Canetto, E. Borrayo, and R. Yang, R. (Eds.). *Teaching diversity* (pp. 217-226). Madison, WI: Atwood Publishing.

Kohlberg, L. (1963). The development of children's orientation toward moral order: Sequence in the development of moral thought. *Vita Humana*, 6, 11-33.

Kolb, D. (1984). *Experiential learning: Experience as the source of learning and development*. Indianapolis, IN: FT Press/Pearson.

Kreston, R. (2003). In Timpson, W., Canetto. S., Borrayo, E., and Yang, R. K. (Eds.). *Teaching diversity: Challenges and complexities, identities and integrity*. Madison, WI: Atwood Publishing.

Kuhn, T. (1970). *The structure of scientific revolutions*. Chicago, IL: University of Chicago Press.

Lama, D. (1999). *Ethics for a new millennium*. New York, NY: Riverhead/Penguin.
Lama, D. and Tutu, D. (2016). *The book of joy*. New York, NY: Penguin.

Land, G., and Jarman, B. (1992). Future pull: The power of vision and purpose. *The Futurist, Vol. 26* (4 July/August).

Lin, J. (2006). *Love, peace, and wisdom in education. Vision for education in the 21st century.* Lanham, MD: Rowman and Littlefield.

Little, J. (2007). Professional communication and collaboration. In W. Hawley (Ed.), *The keys to effective schools* (pp. 51-65). Thousand Oaks, CA: Corwin.

Lui, X., Magjuka, R., Bonk, C., and Lee, S. (2007). Does a sense of community matter? An examination of participants' perceptions of building learning communities in online courses. *The Quarterly Review of Distance Education, 8*(1), 9-24.

Louv, R. (2008). *Last child in the woods.* Chapel Hill, NC: Algonquin.

Lyons, O. (1996). Ethics and spiritual values and the promotion of environmentally sustainable development: "50 years of the World Bank, over 50 tribes devastated." *Akwesasne Notes New Series, 2*(1), 88-93. Retrieved from https://ratical.org/co-globalize/OrenLyons.html

Mager, R. (1997). *How to turn learners on...without turning them off: Ways to ignite interest in learning.* Atlanta, GA: The Center for Effective Performance, Inc.

McGinty, J (2013). In Timpson, W., Foley, J., Kees, N., and Waite, A. *147 practical tips for using experiential learning.* Madison, WI: Atwood Publishing.

McGlynn, C. (2009). In Timpson, W., Brantmeier, E., Kees, N., Cavanagh, T., McGlynn, C., and Ndura-Ouédraogo, E. *147 practical tips for teaching peace and reconciliation.* Madison, WI: Atwood Publishing.

McKibben, W. (2003). *Enough.* New York, NY: Henry Holt.

Miller, G. (1956). The magical number seven, plus or minus two: Some limits on our capacities for processing information. *Psychological Review, 63,* 81-97.

Morales, A., Sheafor, B., and Scott, M. (2012). *Social work: A profession of many faces* (12th ed.). London, UK: Pearson.

Nelson, D. (2009). In Timpson, W., Brantmeier, E., Kees, N., Cavanagh, T., McGlynn, C., and Ndura-Ouédraogo, E. *147 practical tips for teaching peace and reconciliation.* Madison, WI: Atwood Publishing.

Noddings, N. (2003). *Happiness and education.* New York, NY: Cambridge University Press.

Northern Ireland Council for Integrated Education. (2014). *ABC: Promoting an anti-bias approach to education in Northern Ireland* [PDF document]. Retrieved from http://www.nicie.org/wp-content/uploads/2018/01/ABC-Promoting-an-Anti-Bias-Approach-to-Education-in-Northern-Ireland-2014.pdf

Northouse, P. (2010). *Leadership theory and practice.* (5th ed.). Thousand Oaks, CA: Sage.

Paccione, A. (2003) E Pluribus Unum: Teaching diversity in rural Colorado, In Timpson, W., Canetto. S., Borrayo, E., and Yang, R. K. (Eds.). *Teaching diversity: Challenges and complexities, identities and integrity.* Madison, WI: Atwood Publishing.

Palmer. P. (1998). *The courage to teach: Exploring the inner landscape of a teacher's life.* San Francisco, CA: Jossey-Bass.

The Parents Circle – Families Forum. (n.d.). About us. Retrieved from http://theparentscircle.org/en/about_eng/

Pausch, R. (2008). *The last lecture.* New York, NY: Hyperion.

Perry, W. (1981). Cognitive and ethical growth: The making of meaning. In W. Arthur Chickering (Ed.), *The modern American college: Responding to the new realities of diverse students and a changing society* (pp. 76-116). San Francisco: Jossey-Bass.

Perry, W. (1999). *Forms of intellectual and ethical development in the college years: A scheme.* San Francisco, CA: Jossey-Bass.

Piaget, J. (1952). *The origins of intelligence in children.* (M. Cook, trans.) New York: International University Press.

Piaget, J. (1970). *The science of education and the psychology of the child.* New York: Orion.

Pitot, L. (2013). In Timpson, W., Foley, J., Kees, N., and Waite, A. *147 practical tips for using experiential learning.* Madison, WI: Atwood Publishing.

Poncelow, C. (2009). In Timpson, W., Brantmeier, E., Kees, N., Cavanagh, T., McGlynn, C., and Ndura-Ouédraogo, E. *147 practical tips for teaching peace and reconciliation.* Madison, WI: Atwood Publishing.

Reardon, B. (2009). Welcome to utopia: Reflections on realities and possibilities. *Global Campaign for Peace Education.* Retrieved from http://www.peace-ed-campaign.org/welcome-to-utopia-reflections-on-realities-and-possibilities/.

Reardon, B. (1999). *Peace education: A review and projection* (No. 17). Malmo, Sweden: Malmo University School of Education.

Robinson, K. (2006, February). *Do schools kill creativity?* [Video file]. Retrieved from https://www.ted.com/talks/ken_robinson_says_schools_kill_creativity?language=en

Roehlkepartain, E, Naftali, E., and Musegades, L. (1989). *Growing up generous*. Herndon, VA: Alban Institute.

Salomon, G. (2007). Challenging questions facing education in regions of conflict. A keynote address to Education for Peace International Conference, Vancouver, BC 14-16 November 2007.

Simpson, E. (1972). *The classification of educational objectives in the psychomotor domain: The psychomotor domain, Vol. 3.* Washington, DC: Gryphon House.

Thoreau, H. (2017). *Walden.* Nashville, TN: American Renaissance.

Timpson, W. (1999). *Metateaching and the instructional map.* Madison, WI: Atwood Publishing.

Timpson, W. (2002). *Teaching and learning peace.* Madison, WI: Atwood Publishing.

Timpson, W., Brantmeier, E., Kees, N., Cavanagh, T., McGlynn, C., and Ndura-Ouédraogo, E. (2009). *147 practical tips for teaching peace and reconciliation.* Madison, WI: Atwood Publishing.

Timpson, W., and Broadbent, F. (Eds.). (1995). *Action learning: Experience and promise.* Brisbane, Australia: University of Queensland/The Tertiary Education Institute.

Timpson, W., and Burgoyne, S. (2002). *Teaching and performing: Ideas for energizing your classes* (2nd ed.). Madison, WI: Atwood Publishing.

Timpson, W., Canetto. S., Borrayo, E., and Yang, R. K. (Eds.). (2003). *Teaching diversity: Challenges and complexities, identities and integrity.* Madison, WI: Atwood Publishing.

Timpson, W., and Doe, S. (2008). *Concepts and choices for teaching: Meeting the challenges in higher education* (2nd ed.). Madison, WI: Atwood Publishing.

Timpson, W., Dunbar, B., Kimmel, G., Bruyere, B., Newman, P., Mizia, H., Birmingham, D., and Harmon, R. (2017). *147 practical tips for teaching sustainability: Connecting the environment, the economy and society* (2nd ed.). Madison, WI: Atwood Publishing.

Timpson, W., Foley, J., Kees, N., and Waite, A. (2013). *147 practical tips for using experiential learning.* Madison, WI: Atwood Publishing.

Timpson, W., and Holman, D. (Eds.). (2012). *Case studies of classrooms and communication: Integrating diversity, sustainability, peace and reconciliation.* Madison, WI: Atwood Publishing.

Timpson, W., and Holman, D. (Eds.). (2014). *Controversial case studies for teaching on sustainability, conflict, and diversity.* Madison, WI: Atwood Publishing.

Timpson, W, Ndura-Ouédraogo, E., and Bangayimbaga, A. (2015). *Conflict, reconciliation, and peace education: Moving Burundi toward a sustainable future.* New York, NY: Routledge.

Timpson, W., Yang, Y., Borrayo, E., Canetto, S., Gonzalez-Voller, J., and Scott, M. (2019). *147 practical tips for teaching diversity.* 2nd ed. Madison, WI: Atwood Publishing.

Tochterman, S. (2003). Majority as minority: Transferring lessons learned from teaching k-12 inner-city students to the university. In W. Timpson, S. Canetto, E. Borrayo and R. Yang (Eds.). *Teaching diversity* (pp. 133-144). Madison, WI: Atwood Publishing.

Tuckman, B. (1965). Developmental sequence in small groups. *Psychological Bulletin* 63(6), 384-399.

Tutu, D. (1997). *No future without forgiveness.* New York, NY: Doubleday.

Urdan, T., Ryan, A., Anderman, E., and Gheen, M. (2002). Goals, goal structures, and avoidance behaviors. In C. Midgley (Ed.), *Goals, goal structures, and patterns of adaptive learning (pp. 55-83).* Mahwah, NJ: Lawrence Erlbaum Associates Publishers.

van Eijck, M., and Roth, W. (2010). Towards a chronotopic theory of "place" in place-based education. *Cultural Studies of Science Education,* 5(4), 869–898.

Wade, C., and Tavris, C. (2017). *Psychology,* 12th Edition, Boston, MA: Pearson.

Wheatley, M. (2001). *Leadership and the New Science: Discovering order in a chaotic world.* (rev. ed.) San Francisco: Berrett-Koehler.

Williams, W. (2006). In D. Giffey (Ed.). *Long shadows. Veterans' paths to peace* (pp. 67-83). Madison, WI: Atwood Publishing.

York, S. and Zimmerman, M. A. (Producers). (2000). *A Force More Powerful.* Washington DC: WETA. (http://www.aforcemorepowerful.org/index.php)

www.ingramcontent.com/pod-product-compliance
Lightning Source LLC
Chambersburg PA
CBHW020250030426
42336CB00010B/697